POSITIONS AND POLARITIES IN CONTEMPORARY SYSTEMIC PRACTICE

Systemic Thinking and Practice Series

edited by Charlotte Burck and Gwyn Daniel
published and distributed by Karnac

This influential series was co-founded in 1989 by series editors David Campbell and Ros Draper to promote innovative applications of systemic theory to psychotherapy, teaching, supervision, and organizational consultation. In 2011, Charlotte Burck and Gwyn Daniel became series editors, and aim to present new theoretical developments and pioneering practice, to make links with other theoretical approaches, and to promote the relevance of systemic theory to contemporary social and psychological questions.

Other titles in the series include

Jones, E., & Asen, E. *Systemic Couple Therapy and Depression*

Asen, A., & McHugh, B. (Eds.) *Multiple Family Therapy: The Marlborough Model and Its Wider Applications*

Krause, I.-B. *Culture and System in Family Therapy*

Mason, B., & Sawyerr, A. (Eds.) *Exploring the Unsaid: Creativity, Risks, and Dilemmas in Working Cross-Culturally*

Campbell, D., & Mason, B. (Eds.) *Perspectives on Supervision*

Johnsen, A., & Wie Tortsteinsson, V. *Self in Relationships: Perspectives on Family Therapy from Developmental Psychology*

Smith, G. *Systemic Approaches to Training in Child Protection*

Seikkula, J., & Arnkil, T. E. *Dialogical Meetings in Social Networks*

Baum, S., & Lynggaard, H. (Eds.) *Intellectual Disabilities: A Systemic Approach*

Anderson, M., & Jensen, P. *Innovations in the Reflecting Process*

Wilson, J. *The Performance of Practice: Enhancing the Repertoire of Therapy with Children and Families*

Bertrando, P. *The Dialogical Therapist: Dialogue in Systemic Pratice*

Flaskas, C., & Pocock, D. *Systems and Psychoanalysis: Contemporary Integrations in Family Therapy*

Groen, M., & van Lawick, J. *Intimate Warfare: Regarding the Fragility of Family Relations*

Fredman, G., Anderson, E., & Stott, J. (Eds.) *Being with Older People: A Systemic Approach*

Burck, C., & Daniel, G. *Mirrors and Reflections: Processes of Systemic Supervision*

Singh, R., & Dutta, S. *Race and Culture: Tools, Techniques and Trainings: A Manual for Professionals*

Seidenfaden, K., & Draiby, P. *The Vibrant Relationship: A Handbook for Couples and Therapists*

Seidenfaden, K., Draiby, P., Søborg Christensen, S., & Heigaard, V. *The Vibrant Family: A Handbook for Parents and Professionals*

Krause, I.-B. (Ed.) *Culture and Reflexivity in Systemic Psychotherapy: Mutual Perspectives*

For a full listing, see our website: www.karnacbooks.com

POSITIONS AND POLARITIES IN CONTEMPORARY SYSTEMIC PRACTICE

The Legacy of David Campbell

Edited by

*Charlotte Burck, Sara Barratt,
and Ellie Kavner*

KARNAC

First published in 2013 by
Karnac Books Ltd
118 Finchley Road, London NW3 5HT

British Library Cataloguing in Publication Data

A C.I.P. for this book is available from the British Library

ISBN 978 1 78049 087 8

Edited, designed and produced by The Studio Publishing Services Ltd
www.publishingservicesuk.co.uk
e-mail: studio@publishingservicesuk.co.uk

Printed in Great Britain

www.karnacbooks.com

CONTENTS

ACKNOWLEDGEMENT

We thank the Association for Family Therapy's *David Campbell Fund for Creative Initiatives* for its financial support to enable the interviews with David Campbell to be transcribed.

Angela Abela is the Director of the Centre for Family Studies at the University of Malta, where she is course director of the Professional Master in Clinical, Counselling and Educational Psychology. She was also course proposer for the first Master in Family Therapy and Systemic Consultation. Angela is a registered clinical psychologist and a UKCP registered family therapist and supervisor. She supervises professionals working in public social agencies in the area of children and families. On an international level, she has worked extensively as an expert of the Council of Europe in the area of parenting children at risk of social exclusion. She holds a PhD from the Tavistock Clinic and the University of London and a Masters degree in Clinical Psychology from the Université de La Sorbonne Paris V. She is an associate editor on *Clinical Child Psychology and Psychiatry* and an international advisory editor of *Contemporary Family Therapy*.

Sara Barratt is a consultant systemic psychotherapist and team leader of the Fostering, Adoption and Kinship Care Team at the Tavistock and Portman NHS Trust, where she also teaches on the Masters Training and the Systemic Supervision course. In her independent practice, she consults to systemic psychotherapists, local authority social work teams, and works with individuals, couples, and families in general practice.

Charlotte Burck is a consultant systemic psychotherapist, trainer, and researcher at the Tavistock & Portman NHS Trust, where she runs the family therapy supervision course and is co-organising tutor of the Doctoral research programme. She worked closely with David Campbell for many years. Her publications include *Multilingual Living. Explorations of Language and Subjectivity*, and *Gender and Family Therapy* (with Gwyn Daniel). She co-edited *Mirrors and Reflections. Processes of Systemic Supervision* (with Gwyn Daniel) and *Gender, Power and Relationships* (with Bebe Speed), and is currently the co-editor (with Gwyn Daniel) of the Karnac Systemic Theory and Practice series. Her interests, among others, lie in supervision and consultation, systemic research, and in developing and researching clinical work with families where parents have high conflict or have experienced domestic violence. cburck@tavi-port.nhs.uk

Gwyn Daniel is a systemic psychotherapist, supervisor, and trainer at the Tavistock Clinic, London and in private practice in Oxford. She is co-editor (with Charlotte Burck) of the Systemic Theory and Practice series for Karnac Books. She is co-author of *Growing Up in Stepfamilies* (Oxford University Press), *Gender and Family Therapy* (Karnac) and co-editor of *Mirrors and Reflections: Processes of Systemic Supervision* (Karnac). Her other published work embraces many aspects of systemic psychotherapy with children and parents, as well as issues in systemic supervision and training. She teaches widely, both within the UK and internationally.

Roberta Zahra de Domenico is a pioneering team member of the first family therapy service developed in Malta, as well as being among the first set of tutors on the training courses in family therapy and systemic practice held in Malta in conjunction with the Tavistock Clinic, London. She is a warranted psychologist, having studied clinical psychology at Masters level at the University of Malta. After years of study with the Tavistock Clinic, London, she was accredited as a family therapist by AFT in 2004. She has extensive experience working with families in a variety of settings. She is currently working in private practice, as well as lecturing on systemic theory at both undergraduate and postgraduate levels at the University of Malta. Her current research interests include systemic supervision, as well as working with families of incarcerated persons.

Glenda Fredman is a clinical psychologist and systemic psychotherapist. She works with children, adults, and older people, their families, and staff teams in hospitals and community settings. She is currently Consultant Clinical Psychologist in Systemic Psychotherapy with University College London Hospital and Camden and Islington Mental Health Foundation Trust, and freelance trainer and consultant. Glenda is author of *Death Talk: Conversations with Children and Families* (Karnac); *Transforming Emotion: Conversations in Counselling and Psychotherapy* (Whurr/Wiley); and co-editor of *Being with Older People: A Systemic Approach* (Karnac).

Stephen Frosh is Pro-Vice-Master and Professor in the Department of Psychosocial Studies at Birkbeck College, University of London. He is the author of many books and papers on psychosocial studies and on psychoanalysis, including *Psychoanalysis Outside the Clinic* (Palgrave, 2010); *Hate and the Jewish Science: Anti-Semitism, Nazism and Psychoanalysis* (Palgrave, 2005); *For and Against Psychoanalysis* (Routledge, 2006); *After Words* (Palgrave, 2002); and *The Politics of Psychoanalysis* (Palgrave, 1999). His most recent books are *Feelings* (Routledge, 2011), and *A Brief Introduction to Psychoanalytic Theory* (Palgrave, 2012). Stephen was a colleague of David Campbell's at the Tavistock Clinic throughout the 1990s and continued to see him regularly for management consultation until David's illness took hold.

Marianne Grønbæk is an organisational consultant with a background in systemic family therapy and management. Since 1997, she has been the manager of MG-UDVIKLING, a successful consulting firm based in Denmark offering consultation, supervision, and training to managers and employees in private and public organisations in Denmark, the UK, and Scandinavia. She is a practice-centred consultant, and her particular interest is in working with organisations to create models of organisation and communication that lead to better practice. Her work is inspired by systemic thinking, appreciative inquiry, positioning theory, and semantic polarities. Her publications include *The Dream. From Thought to Action; Taking Positions in the*

Organisation (with David Campbell); and *The Growth Model: The Road to Good Conversation* (with Pors); and *The Growth Model: Dialogue-based Leadership and Management* (with Pors and David Campbell).

Ivan B. Inger, PhD, is a clinical psychologist in independent practice, Clinical Professor of Child and Adolescent Psychiatry, Oregon Health Sciences University, Consulting Psychologist to St Vincent Hospital Eating Disorders Clinic (in Family Therapy) and former Co-director, Family Studies Institute, Portland Oregon. He has authored and co-authored books and articles in the family therapy field, and has conducted workshops and seminars in the USA and abroad.

Jeri Inger, MS, LMFT, is a family therapist and counsellor in independent practice, Consulting Family Therapist to St Vincent Hospital Eating Disorders Clinic, and former Co-director, Family Studies Institute, Portland, Oregon. She has authored and co-authored books and articles in the family therapy field, and has conducted workshops and seminars in the USA and abroad.

Ellie Kavner is a consultant family therapist in the Children & Families Department of the Tavistock & Portman NHS Trust and is Trust-Wide Head of Discipline, with both a clinical and training responsibility, including professional training in the Masters in Systemic Psychotherapy and courses for organisations in leadership and management. She holds special clinical and training interests in familial violence and early years.

Caroline Lindsey is a child and adolescent psychiatrist and systemic family and EMDR therapist. Until her retirement, she worked at the Tavistock Clinic, and is now in private practice. She is a systemic supervisor and trainer. During the course of her career, she was the Chair of the Tavistock Child and Family Department and chaired the Faculty of Child and Adolescent Psychiatry at the Royal College of Psychiatrists; she also led the CAMHS module of the Childrens' National Service Framework for the Department of Health. Her clinical interests include abuse and trauma, work with children in the care system, or who are fostered or adopted. She co-edited *Creating New Families: Therapeutic Approaches to Fostering, Adoption and Kinship Care*.

Barry Mason is a freelance systemic psychotherapist, supervisor, and consultant working in the private, public, and voluntary sectors. He is also Chair of the training programme in the supervision of family and systemic psychotherapy at the Institute of Family Therapy, London, and contributes to numerous courses in the UK and overseas.

Marie Murray is a clinical psychologist, author, broadcaster and *Irish Times* health columnist. She directed The Student Counselling Services in University College Dublin, prior to which she was Director of Psychology at St Vincent's Psychiatric Hospital Dublin, member of the Mater Family Therapy Training faculty and the Academic Advisory Board of CTYI at Dublin City University. She has lectured in Europe and Asia and is a member of The Irish Medical Council. marie.murray@ucd.ie

Rob Senior is a consultant child and adolescent psychiatrist and systemic psychotherapist at the Tavistock and Portman NHS Foundation Trust. He is the Medical Director of the Trust and a Senior Research Fellow at the Institute of Child Health. He is involved in research and clinical work as well as teaching and training.

Patrick Sweeney is a Catholic priest and a systemic psychotherapist, living and working in Dublin, where he is currently part of a team there offering support and care to clergy and church workers. His particular responsibilities include one-to-one support, facilitation of, and consultation to, teams and groups, and personal and professional development. He has been involved in the family therapy training programmes at the Clanwilliam Institute, and Mater Hospital in Dublin, and is a co-founder of the Ireland–Romania family therapy training programme, which created training for family therapists and systemic practitioners in Cluj Napoca, Romania. He has worked in church and family therapy contexts in several European and African countries.

Yoko Totsuka is a family therapist at Newham Child and Family Consultation Service and Marlborough Family Service. She completed her doctoral thesis at Tavistock, titled "Young people's perspectives on family life: experience of parental mental illness and admission to psychiatric hospital". She is an approved supervisor registered with the Association for Family Therapy.

Valeria Ugazio is Director of the European Institute of Systemic-relational Therapies, Milan, Italy. She is also Professor of Clinical Psychology and Coordinator of the Doctorate in Clinical Psychology, University of Bergamo. E-mail: valeriaugazio@eist.it and valeria.ugazio@unibg.it

Ruth L. Formosa Ventura is one of the pioneering team members who founded family therapy/systemic practice in Malta in 1995. She is an accredited family therapist and systemic practitioner. She worked within The Family Therapy Service unit for the national social welfare organisation in Malta for fourteen years. She was the co-ordinator of the unit from 2004 until 2007, and the co-ordinating tutor for the Diploma in Systemic Theory from 2006 till 2009. At the end of 2009, she moved to Switzerland, and is currently working in private practice. She is a registered psychologist with the Swiss Federation for Psychology/Psychotherapy (FSP), and a recognised systemic practitioner with "Systemis" association. Her present interests are cultural sensitive therapy and migration issues, couple therapy and attachment theory, as well as narrative and postmodern practices. She is actively involved in working collaboratively with other professionals, of foreign and Swiss nationalities, as she seeks to nourish her curiosity around Swiss culture and its practices.

Jenny Zammit started her professional life teaching chemistry, and read theology and counselling at the University of Durham. She furthered her studies in family therapy and systemic supervision and is UKCP registered in these areas. She is the counsellor in a post-secondary institution and a visiting lecturer at University of Malta. She is a founder member of the Hospice Movement (Malta) and contributes to training and supervision. She is also a founder member of the associations for counselling and family therapy in Malta. She is interested in staff support and the maintenance of their sanity. She has recently read for a Masters in Historical Mediterranean Studies in an effort to maintain her sanity and be on the receiving end of teaching. She is a keen musician, traveller, reader, and hiker.

SERIES EDITORS' FOREWORD

Some of our reasons for being delighted that this book has been written are obvious: the chance to honour our friend, colleague, and series co-founder, David Campbell, and also to disseminate the innovative thinking and practice contained within its chapters. Perhaps less obviously, but equally crucially, it is an opportunity to celebrate the idea of mutual influence in the evolution of ideas, itself so crucial to David's philosophy and, as the volume's editors have commented, so deeply embedded within systemic thinking itself. While everyone who contributes to the world of ideas could (or should) surely say, in Isaac Newton's phrase "If I have seen a little further it is by standing on the shoulders of Giants", in practice, the acknowledgement of intellectual forebears is a tricky and contested business, often related to the staking out of claims to innovation and the "ring-fencing" of ideas.

It is a feature of the generosity of spirit evoked in the *Festschrift* that not only does the voice of the person honoured infuse the event and, consequently, the contents of this book, but also the ideas of other theoreticians emerge in new forms, as mediated through this voice and further elaborated through the voices of others.

In the systemic field where virtually all its theoreticians have been clinicians, unlike that of psychoanalysis, our theoretical gurus have mostly come from outside the world of therapeutic practice: Gregory Bateson, Umberto Maturana, Michel Foucault, Rom Harré, and Mikael Bakhtin, to name a few, were certainly not clinicians and their ideas have, therefore, required some translation to be relevant to therapeutic practice.

David Campbell was one such translator, first in relation to the Milan group's development of Gregory Bateson's ideas, and then of the positioning theories of Rom Harré and the dialogism of Mikael Bakhtin. David Campbell happily acknowledged that his field of vision was only possible from the vantage point of these giants' shoulders; the staking out of intellectual territory as his own was not for him. In a way that is consistent with our theory, "decentring" individual writers by placing them in the context of other ideas and influences was a key value for David and is embodied in this work, where the editors have demonstrated their commitment to the spirit of dialogism and, as they have argued, to the fertile and creative edge "in the spaces between ideas".

As well as honouring David Campbell, the volume exemplifies many of the key aims of the Systemic Theory and Practice series, covering as it does theory and practice, teaching research, consultation, and supervision, as well as new and creative applications to the world beyond therapy.

We are sure that this volume will have much to offer to a wide readership of psychotherapists and others interested in multiple ways of applying systemic ideas.

Gwyn Daniel and Charlotte Burck

Introduction

Charlotte Burck, Sara Barratt, and Ellie Kavner

This book honours the contributions which David Campbell, one of the UK's most respected family therapists, made to his colleagues, his students, and the field of systemic psychotherapy and consultation. David Campbell was well known for his own publications (see Bibliography), as well as his ability to enable others to translate their ideas and practice into writing. With his colleague, Ros Draper, he founded this Karnac Systemic Thinking and Practice Series, which has brought out fifty books over the last twenty years. He became one of the main proponents of the Milan approach in the UK, with Ros Draper, in the 1980s (Campbell & Draper, 1985; Campbell, Draper, & Crutchley, 1990; Campbell, Draper, & Huffington, 1991; Campbell, Reder, & Pollard, 1983), and was centrally involved in the systemic trainings at the Tavistock Clinic. David Campbell was invested equally in working with families and in consulting to organisations, and has described the movement between relating more closely in working with families and being more distant in organisations as working well for him. He made good use of his position as an American in Britain, choosing to "do" power in a way that fitted with his view of himself as an observer, on the margins, who developed ways of influencing which were indirect, though no less powerful for that.

David Campbell's striking ability to articulate very complex ideas in simple and engaging ways helped many others to connect to the ideas which underlie systemic family therapy and systemic consultation. He was especially adept at drawing on theoretical sources from fields outside psychotherapy to synthesise and make use of these ideas in practice. His more recent work (Campbell & Grønbæk, 2006) elaborated positioning theory, developed by Rom Harré (Davies & Harré, 1990, Harré & van Langenhove, 1999), which he made engagingly accessible to family therapists and the organisations to which he consulted. Throughout David Campbell's working life, he valued his relationship with the ideas of other writers, and cherished the creative potential of constructing ideas with others, including his colleagues, trainees, and the organisations and families with whom he worked.

A Festschrift was planned to mark David Campbell's retirement from the Tavistock Clinic, where he had spent almost his entire professional career. However, David was diagnosed with pancreatic cancer and his increasing ill health lent an urgency to the task of convening a Festschrift, which was held on 1 May 2009, when he was already very ill. That event, attended by systemic professionals from around the world, was infused with an emotional and vibrant timbre, as the presenters who honoured his work also conveyed their profound feeling for him as a man and for his impending loss. Many of the chapters in this volume are based on presentations delivered at that Festschrift, which has posed a challenge in transforming those addresses into written versions for this book. Here, Marie Murray gives an account of what the Festschrift encompasses and the challenges it holds for the writer:

> Speakers at a Festschrift for a systemic thinker inevitably address the issue of 'self' in their presentations particularly because that 'self' has usually been influenced significantly by the person being honoured. 'Our sense of who we are depends upon what meaning others make of us and how they convey that meaning back to us' (Campbell, 2000, p. 16). The Festschrift 'contains' emotion: contains (in the sense of keeping in check) and contains (in the sense of including) the emotions and feelings they evoke. Readers of Festschrift books receive a 'second text'. In this process, the dialogic polyphony is silenced, segmented into chapters, contributions are sequential and the vivacity of the event must find new vitality and give new life to the person it honours by continuing his work through their written words in book form. This is a formidable task.

However, there is a different kind of dialogic polyphony at work here. What these individual authors convey are the ways in which they connect with another's ideas and go on to interweave, elaborate, and expand these in their own ways, styles, and contexts. The writers in this volume present their perspectives of their interactions with David Campbell and how they continue to interact with his ideas in their present contexts. For some individuals, particular phrases continue to resonate and contribute to their internal as well as external dialogues. It was Bakhtin (1981) who identified how we selectively assimilate and appropriate the words of others in our "ideological becoming".

> The word in language is always half someone else's. It becomes 'one's own' only when the speaker populates it with his own intention, his own accent, when he appropriates the word, adapting it to his own semantic and expressive intention. (Bakhtin, 1981, pp. 293–294)

It is the multi-voiced nature of language which many of the authors convey; that the words carrying the intentions of a previous speaker, David Campbell, and in their previous contexts are now infused with their own intentions in other contexts. In his absence, David Campbell is present in these chapters as a powerful memory, as person, as writer, as clinician, as supervisor, and as consultant. What is always surprising is that the interaction with one person's ideas can unfold and lead to such different developments of thinking and practice, demonstrating the "unfinalizability" of ideas and persons (Bakhtin, 1984).

One aspect of David Campbell's influence noted by many of the contributors was his embodiment of the ideas which he was communicating; the way in which others experienced the congruence between his selfhood, his values, his ideas, and his practice, which made him an inspiring colleague, teacher, and supervisor. His ability to stay curious, always able to imagine that there might be another way to see a situation, and his thoughtful calmness were experienced as outstandingly useful and, at times, transformative for individuals, families, teams, and institutions.

Interspersed with the contributors are some of David Campbell's own reflections concerning the development of his ideas and practice over time, taken from three interviews carried out in the spring of 2009 with Charlotte Burck. The book begins with his overview of the history of his own systemic thinking and practice in interaction with its development in the UK context.

The first section of the volume concerns therapy and theory. Stephen Frosh draws on his experience as a colleague and a consultee to address the stance that David Campbell took in his therapy, in his collegial relationships, and in his consultation. He elaborates the theoretical underpinnings that inform this reflexive and enabling position, and, in so doing, invites the reader to develop this further. Glenda Fredman identifies some of the significant episodes in her training with David Campbell, and traces the ways in which his phrases have become mantras in the development of her own work, in the course of which she has creatively applied systemic ideas in many contexts. David's own reflections on some questions that have endured and evolved for him over time are included here. In his chapter, Ivan Inger from the USA describes exciting international interchanges with David Campbell and Ros Draper and depicts their parallel developments of a dialogic and decentred position as therapists, and their commitment to this ethical stance. He discusses how he and Jeri Inger have developed this work over time.

Teaching was a professional activity which David Campbell very much enjoyed and conceptualised as a mutual learning process, delighted by the way ideas were generated and applied in these relationships, and the next section of the book concerns supervision and training. Gwyn Daniel identifies various interchanges with David Campbell that inspired her (and also perturbed her) to develop her own work as a systemic supervisor in a different way. She proposes that a supervisor being transparent, alongside taking a position on an issue, can be an effective way of de-centring and managing power ethically. She argues that it is incumbent on all therapists and supervisors to find ways to elicit feedback about how we are experienced and seen by others. Caroline Lindsey, a close colleague of David Campbell's over many years at the Tavistock Clinic, and Rob Senior describe the conceptualisation and delivery of a systemic training programme for child and adolescent psychiatrists, which echoes David Campbell's passion for applying systemic thinking in different professional contexts. Including the voices of trainee psychiatrists, they examine in what ways this has had an influence on psychiatric practice, and address future challenges for the profession and other systemic trainings. As somebody who had been trained by David

Campbell, Barry Mason's chapter describes the impact on his therapeutic and supervisory practice of the centrality placed by David on
the importance of feedback. He discusses his work in training supervisors on helping them to expand ways of including their own ideas
in supervision, in the spirit of developing a "culture of contribution".

Alongside his involvement in other systemic trainings, David
Campbell also carried out research, and taught and supervised systemic research, and his brief reflections on his research activity introduce the next section on research. Yoko Totsuka undertook the
Doctorate in Systemic Psychotherapy at the Tavistock Clinic, and
describes significant moments in her doctoral research supervision
with David as she faced and identified dilemmas during her research
process while exploring young people's experience of their parents'
mental illness. Interestingly, it was David Campbell's interaction with
Valeria Ugazio in Italy, who was researching semantic polarities in
families, that first inspired him to consider the potential of these ideas
and positioning theory. In her contribution, Valeria Ugazio describes
her interesting research with families, which has informed her use of
semantic polarities in her family therapy practice. She considers some
of the differences in the ways she and David developed the use of
these ideas, proposing the significant influence of their personal
contexts, providing a timely reminder to pay attention to our
personal–professional connections.

In reflecting on his development, David identified the co-editing
(with Ros Draper) of the book *Applications of Systemic Family Therapy*,
in 1985, as a significant event in expanding his own applications of
systemic ideas to organisational work and in enabling others to articulate their applications in many different settings. The final chapters
in this volume are particularly concerned with this theme and with
consultation, and begin with his own reflections. It was with
Marianne Grønbæk, who worked as an organisational consultant in
Denmark, that David Campbell developed the ideas about positioning and polarities in organisations. In her chapter, Marianne Grønbæk
describes the process of the development of these ideas, including
positions she and David took in relation to each other's ideas, and
provides examples from her consultancy work, particularly addressing the challenges of identifying the significant polarity and the self-
reflexivity required of the consultant. She discusses the challenges in
keeping in the C (consultant) position when working with significant

issues where others take strong and polarised positions. She comments on how readily David Campbell took this position in many of his contexts, more passionate about ideas and their generativity than about taking positions himself.

Marie Murray draws on one of Ireland's best-loved poets, Seamus Heaney, to explore and expand the meaning of David Campbell's consultative work in Ireland as that of "uncoding landscapes". Her creative employment of this metaphor will translate into many other contexts, as she both celebrates and demonstrates the skill of "making words work well". Angela Abela, Ruth Formosa Ventura, Roberta Zahra De Domenico, and Jenny Zammit convey how David Campbell's consultations and training in Malta provided a profound perturbation and challenge to traditional Maltese ways of thinking, and enabled them to subvert invitations to adopt polarised positions and, instead, to find new ways to connect across differences. Patrick Sweeney demonstrates ways in which he has introduced systemic thinking in his work with the Catholic priesthood in different countries to help manage challenges to the church, and, in particular, to enable reconnections and transformations when relationships had experienced serious breakdowns and rifts.

During the last twenty months of his life, David Campbell lived and struggled with cancer. He demonstrated an impressive openness to talking and writing about his illness and his dying, in a way that seemed to transgress his previous sense of privacy. His daughter Briony, training to be a photojournalist, explored their relationship in the context of his dying through photographs and film, inviting others into this visual dialogue (Campbell, B., www.brionycampbell.com). He also wrote a piece titled "Dying".

> I am actually in the real nightmare of dying with cancer. So what do I think about? It seems to be mainly about letting go. Letting go of everything that made me what I am and everyone who I am connected to . . . I can feel frightened, sad, hopeful, angry and resigned at different times . . . it's confusing. Sometimes, I use ideas to help me and sometimes they don't help, and I just get overwhelmed with unnameable feelings. These are the territories where words prove their limitations and poets may be required, but I will try to put a few things down. One reason I am doing this is that it might help a reader or therapist or a patient reconsider the taboos that we are so uncomfortable talking about. (Campbell, 2009)

What is so well demonstrated in this volume is how such open invitations into dialogue ripple through our conversations with ourselves and with others over time, and that it is in the spaces between ideas that our creativity is most fertile.

References

Bakhtin, M. M. (1981). *The Dialogic Imagination: Four Essays*, M. Holquist (Ed.), C. Emerson & M. Holquist (Trans.). Austin, TX: University of Texas Press.

Bakhtin, M. M. (1984). *Problems of Dostoevsky's Poetics*, C. Emerson (Ed. & Trans.). Minneapolis, MN: University of Minnesota Press.

Campbell, B. http://www.brionycampbell.com/projects/the-dad-project

Campbell, D. (2009). Dying. *Context, June*: 49–50.

Campbell, D., & Draper, R. (Eds.) (1985). *Applications of Systemic Family Therapy. The Milan Approach*. London: Grune and Stratton.

Campbell, D., & Grønbæk, M. (2006). *Taking Positions in the Organization*. London: Karnac.

Campbell, D., Draper, R., & Crutchley, E. (1990). The Milan systemic approach to family therapy. In: A. Gurman & D. Kniskern (Eds.), *Handbook of Family Therapy, Vol. 2* (pp. 325–362). New York: Brunner/Mazel.

Campbell, D., Draper, R., & Huffington. C. (1991). *Second Thoughts. The Theory And Practice of The Milan Approach to Family Therapy*. London: Karnac.

Campbell, D., Reder, P., & Pollard, D. (1983). *Working with the Milan Method: Twenty Questions*. London: Institute of Family Therapy.

Davies, B., & Harré, R. (1990). Positioning: the discursive production of selves. *Journal for the Theory of Social Behavior, 20*(1): 43–63.

Harré, R., & van Langenhove, L. (Eds.) (1999). *Positioning Theory. Moral Contexts of Intentional Action*. Oxford: Blackwell.

Bibliography

Boscolo, L., Cecchin, G., Campbell, D., & Draper, R. (1985). Twenty more questions: selections from a discussion between the Milan Associates. In: D. Campbell & R. Draper (Eds), *Applications of Systemic Family Therapy: The Milan Approach*. London: Grune and Stratton.

Burck, C., & Campbell, D. (2002). Training systemic supervisors: multi-layered learning. In: D. Campbell & B. Mason (Eds.), *Perspectives in Supervision*. London: Karnac.

Byng-Hall, J., & Campbell, D. (1981). Resolving conflicts in family distance regulation: an integrative approach. *Journal of Marital and Family Therapy, 7*(3): 321–330.

Campbell, D. (1975). Adolescents in care. A model for work with the family. *Social Work Today, 6*(9): 265–269.

Campbell, D. (1982). Adolescence in families. In: A. Bentovim, G. Gorell Barnes, & A. Cooklin (Eds.), *Family Therapy. Vol 2*. London: Academic Press.

Campbell, D. (1985). Creating a context for change: an overview. In: D. Campbell & R. Draper (Eds.), *Applications of Systemic Family Therapy. The Milan Approach*. London: Grune and Stratton.

Campbell, D. (1985). The consultation interview. In: D. Campbell & R. Draper (Eds.), *Applications of Systemic Family Therapy: The Milan Approach*. London: Grune and Stratton.

Campbell, D. (1986). Assessment in context of a family system. Tavistock Clinic Paper, No. 26, Tavistock Library, London.

Campbell, D. (1986). Finding meaning in family therapy research. Tavistock Clinic Paper, No. 27, Tavistock Library, London.

Campbell, D. (1990). Social constructionism and live supervision: a slightly different model. Tavistock Clinic Paper, No. 180, Tavistock Library, London.

Campbell, D. (1994). *Report into the Workings of Area Child Protection Committees*. London: Department of Health.

Campbell, D. (1994). Violence in the family and child protection services. Tavistock Clinic Paper, No. 160, Tavistock Library, London.

Campbell, D. (1995). Creating a research team to understand families' experiences of therapy. Tavistock Clinic Paper, No. 161, Tavistock Library, London.

Campbell, D. (1995). *Learning Consultation: A Systemic Framework. With Contributions From Participants in the Danish Seminars*. London. Karnac.

Campbell, D. (1995). Paradoxes in the system: implications for working together. Reprinted in: *Great Britain. Dept. of Health. Young Carers Development Programme*. Workshop presentation, Tavistock Library, London [http://tavi.koha-ptfs.eu/cgi-bin/koha/opac-detail.pl?biblio number=4852].

Campbell, D. (1996). Connecting personal experience to the primary task: a model for consulting for organizations. *Human Systems, 7*(2–3): 117–130.

Campbell, D. (1997). The other side of the story: listening for the client's experience of therapy. In: R. Papadopoulos & J. Byng Hall (Eds.), *Multiple Voices*. London: Duckworth.

Campbell, D. (1998). Ideas which divide the Tavistock: what are they really about? Tavistock Clinic Paper, No. 184, Tavistock Library, London.

Campbell, D. (1999). Family therapy and beyond: where is the Milan systemic approach today? *Child Psychology and Psychiatry*, 4(2): 76–84.

Campbell, D. (2000). *The Socially Constructed Organization*. London. Karnac.

Campbell, D. (2002). Letting go of attachments. In: J. Hills (Ed.), *Rescripting Family Experiences. The Therapuetic Influence of John Byng Hall*. London: Whurr.

Campbell, D. (2002). Models of consultation from European settings: applications to families and organizations. *Family Process Journal website*. AFTA Plenary, Tavistock Library, London.

Campbell, D. (2003). The mutiny and the bounty: the place of Milan ideas today. *Australian and New Zealand Journal of Family Therapy*, 24(1): 15–25.

Campbell, D. (2004). Method in the madness. Re-reading 'Paradox and Counterparadox', twenty-five years on. *Clinical Child Psychology and Psychiatry*, 9(3): 437–442.

Campbell, D. (2008). Locating conflict in team consultations. In: D. Campbell & C. Huffington (Eds.), *Organizations Connected. A Handbook of Systemic Consultation*. London. Karnac.

Campbell, D. (2009). Dying. *Context*(June): 49–50.

Campbell, D. (2009). The best decisions emerge from dialogue. *Context*, (June): 3–35.

Campbell, D. (2012). Can we tolerate the relationships that race compels? In: I.-B Krause (Ed.), *Culture and Reflexivity in Systemic Psychotherapy: Mutual Perspectives*. London: Karnac.

Campbell, D., & de Carteret, J. (1984). Guidelines for clinicians considering family therapy research. *Journal of Family Therapy*, 6: 131–147.

Campbell, D., & Draper, R. (Eds.) (1989–2010). *The Systemic Thinking and Practice Series*, London: Karnac.

Campbell, D., & Draper, R. (Eds.) (1985). *Applications of Systemic Family Therapy. The Milan Approach*. London: Grune and Stratton.

Campbell, D., Draper, R., & Crutchley, E. (1990). The Milan systemic approach to family therapy. In: A. Gurman & D. Kniskern (Eds.), *Handbook of Family Therapy*, Vol. 2. New York: Brunner/Mazel.

Campbell, D., & Grønbæk, M. (2006). *Taking Positions in the Organization*. London: Karnac.

Campbell, D., & Huffington, C. (2008). Introduction: six stages of systemic consultation. In: D. Campbell & C. Huffington (Eds.), *Organizations Connected. A Handbook of Systemic Consultation*. London: Karnac.

Campbell, D., & Huffington, C. (2008). *Organizations Connected. A Handbook of Systemic Consultation*. London. Karnac.

Campbell, D., & Trowell, J. (2005). Narrative perspectives on childhood depression. In: A. Vetere & E. Dowling (Eds.), *Narrative Therapies with Children and their Families. A Practitioner's Guide to Concepts and Approaches*. London: Routledge.

Campbell, D., Dowling, E., Pentecost, D., Bianco, V., & Goldberg-Shaki, H. (2003). Family therapy for childhood depression. *Journal of Family Therapy, 25*(4): 417–435.

Campbell, D., Draper, R., & Huffington. C. (1988/1991). *Teaching Systemic Thinking*. London: Karnac.

Campbell, D., Draper, R., & Huffington, C. (1989/1991). *A Systemic Approach To Consultation*. London: Karnac.

Campbell, D., Draper, R., & Huffington. C. (1989/1991). *Second Thoughts. The Theory And Practice of the Milan Approach to Family Therapy*. London: Karnac.

Campbell, D., Kinsella, K., & Coldicott, T. (1994). *Systemic Work with Organizations. A New Model for Managers and Change Agents*. London: Karnac.

Campbell, D., Reder P., & Pollard, D. (1983). *Working with the Milan Method: Twenty Questions*. London: Institute of Family Therapy.

Gorell Barnes, G., & Campbell, D. (1982). The impact of structural strategic approaches on the supervisory process: a supervisor is supervised. Or how to progress from frog to prince: two theories of change. In: R. Whiffen & J. Byng-Hall (Eds.), *Family Therapy Supervision*. London: Academic Press.

Midgely, G., Gu, J., & Campbell, D. (2000). Dealing with human relations in Chinese systems practice. *Systemic Practice and Action Research, 13*(1): 71–96.

Strickland-Clark, L., Campbell, D., & Dallos, R. (2000). Children's and adolescents' views on family therapy. *Journal of Family Therapy, 22*(3): 324–341.

Reflections on development of ideas: personal and contextual.
David Campbell in interview with Charlotte Burck

Edited by Sara Barratt

When it became apparent how seriously ill David Campbell was in the spring of 2009, Charlotte Burck invited him to take part in a series of interviews about his professional career and the development of his ideas over time. Here, he traces the evolution of his own thinking in the context of the introduction and establishment of family therapy at the Tavistock Clinic and in the UK, his affinity with the ideas from the Milan group, and the concepts which have remained central to his thinking, practice, and training.

CB: How did you come to the Tavistock Clinic?

DC: I had been in continuous education up to the age of twenty-six, needed a break, so came to London. I was very political at that time, post-Vietnam, and felt very angry, so I decided to stay and work for the nationalised health service for a while. I'd known a lot about the Tavistock and had specialised in child psychotherapy. I walked into the Tavistock and told the head of psychology about my research into family interaction patterns, and they happened to have two research sessions. So I started working with transcripts and a year later another job came up working with John Byng-Hall in a social services agency, assessing kids who had come into care.

CB: Do you think the work with John Byng-Hall decided you to go into family therapy rather than child psychotherapy—it sounded as if it was a period when you were involved with both?

DC: Yes, I think so. The job at the assessment centre was part-time, so I got another job as a child psychotherapist in Uxbridge child guidance centre. I really enjoyed that. It taught me how to slow down and listen very carefully, to look for meanings behind the play and the drawings. Something about having a protected space taught me a lot as a therapist. I think the turning point for me was becoming a father. It just didn't make sense to me to separate the child because I could see how much was going on between us as a family, how much Jane and I were influencing the kids and they were influencing us and I found it really interesting. In 1973, a six-session job came up at the Tavistock. John and I were friends and colleagues and we tried to develop a family model in the Child and Family department. Rosemary Whiffen had just come back from America; she had worked with the Ackerman Institute and on some projects in New York City and she was all fired up by these ideas. We were joined by Freda Martin, a Canadian psychiatrist, and others. In 1974, John, Rosemary, and Freda were setting up a training. They got money from the Sheldon Trust, which supported a couple of trainees each year and set up a two-year qualification course. I thought it was most appropriate to join a supervision group so that I could learn more, so I was in Rosemary's supervision group for two years, and, because I was a staff member, I felt ready after that to take a place as a supervisor and provide training myself.

CB: What ideas were you were most interested in at that time?

DC: The first family therapy I had ever seen was a demonstration interview by Virginia Satir in Boston. She had a family on a stage and an audience of 250 people. It was mind-boggling to see this happening. It was very theatrical; her model was based on people expressing their feelings and talking to each other. I would say it was humanist rather than psychoanalytic or structural in those days. That was very influential, and the fact that you could talk to families directly and openly like that made a big impact on me. Then I came here and got interested in John Byng-Hall's ideas about scripts and themes from the past. In around 1975, we ran two conferences here in London with the Ackerman Institute in New York, and we tried to promote family therapy as an ongoing model in the UK.

It was so new and exciting and you look back and think we probably didn't really know what we were doing, but there was a buzz and energy because it was all very new. Then Gill Gorrell Barnes and I organised a third conference at Trinity Hall College in Cambridge. The key speakers were Harry Aponte, and Fred and Bunny Duhl. Harry Aponte was a very charismatic, powerful structural therapist and he made a big impact on me. Being able to get into the midst of family interaction, to observe it, to stop it, to move it around, to comment on things was really helpful in moving me further down that line.

CB: What kind of impact did that have in the clinic for the group of you who were trying to develop that way of working here?

DC: There was an interesting cross-over point: the conferences were organised with plenary presentations and small discussion groups which were managed with an amalgam of a group analytic model and a family systems model. I was a group leader with Sally Box, who was a social worker in the adolescent department and very analytic. I was trying to bring a family systems approach to the discussion. There was some tension there. I think everybody struggled with that. After three years, there was an amicable divorce and the family therapists felt confident enough to go off and do these things on our own.

CB: People will be surprised about some of your earlier influences because you're most known for your writing about connections with Milan, which you started around 1983. Why did you get attracted to those ideas?

DC: The trigger was the book, *Paradox and Counter-Paradox* (Selvini-Palazzoli, Boscolo, Cecchin, & Prata, 1978). They had previously published a couple of articles, but when the book came out I devoured it like a monk reading some medieval manuscript, sentence by sentence. It really touched a lot of important points for me. From my point of view, the Milan approach comes from a political, rather than a therapeutic, tradition. It came out of the move away from asylums and institutions for mental illness and moving people into the community. They were looking for resources in the community and in families; it was a move away from the focus on the individual. I've always been very interested in how society works and how it influences individuals, so that really caught my attention. They were coming from a different branch of the tree from structural family therapy, which comes from a more cognitive or humanist therapeutic tradition. The Ackerman was really based on the development of analytic ideas and the cognitive work of the communications theorists. I thought the Milan group was saying, "How do we make a different society, and how do we deal with mental illness on a broader level? How is it constructed in the way society operates?" I couldn't quite pull off the charismatic, theatrical nature of the structural family therapists, so the Milan approach, in addition to being a sociological, political stance, is much more restrained and you can be effective with the ideas. The method speaks for itself. It carries a process into the family in a way that you don't have to generate with your own personality. So I liked that. I thought, "Here's a way that a quieter kind of bloke can earn a living."

CB: Although Luigi Boscolo and Gianfranco Cecchin are not exactly quiet blokes, are they?

DC: No, that's true. But I wouldn't put them in the same category as Minuchin, Aponte, and Marianne Walters. I got very excited intellectually by the Milan approach because it was the first time I could see systemic ideas being transferred into the practice of therapy; you could ask circular questions or "gossip in the presence of" and there was a conceptual rationale from systems theory about why that should work, why it helps for people to see context, to receive feedback, and so you've got the theory and the practice coming together. It wasn't centred around the dynamism of the therapist, and that was good for me.

CB: Why do you think the Milan and post-Milan ideas have been so important to you over time?

DC: The central idea that comes out of the Milan work for me is to try to understand and observe the way we operate within a feedback loop, within relationships that give us feedback, which we, in turn, feed into; this is how we're constructing the world and building our relationships. I think it's human nature to think that we are the centre of the universe and that things come from us rather than in connection with others. The reason I think it's so important is that there are hundreds of ways you can apply that to organisations and therapy and individual living. I think that they're universal ideas that are always appropriate and always help us advance the discourse.

CB: So some of these are core for you even though you might express them in a different kind of language. How do you think you've seen yourself develop as a clinician?

DC: I've thought about my development in the 1980s. I was looking for a model that I could stake my colours to when the Milan method came along and it suited me. Like the Pirandello play about six characters in search of an author, I felt that I was a "would be" family therapist looking for a model. I was interested in the structural model because Minuchin, Harry Aponte, and Marianne Walters were here and were very influential, but I realised that really didn't suit me as much as the Milan method. I was intrigued by the power of its neutrality.

One of the things that preoccupied me in the early days was getting it right, and that there were methods of interviewing that you had to learn. As I've got older, I've got more confident that I have therapeutic instincts for stepping forward and getting close to people and stepping back and observing. I can still observe what's going on and, in some ways, I want to be more directive than I used to be, rather than so neutral.

CB: How would families you have worked with more recently describe you as a therapist?

DC: I hope they would describe me as a good listener, trying to consider everybody's point of view. I've had comments about getting drawn into one person's story and I have still got things to learn about tuning into women and mothers' experiences, because it's more natural for me to empathise with what the men are going through. The listening is a crucial bit of feedback which I do fairly well but still have ways to go. I think I'm pretty good at talking to, and playing with, children and using their drawings. They say things that others don't say and demonstrate in drawings and play things that are really important for families; I think they would probably say that I am tuned into that. I hope I give the right amount of empathy to their dilemma before moving on. I think when I was in the technique phase I was probably more challenging, but as the years go by I see that if you listen well at the beginning, people will relax and follow you into things that are much more challenging. I've also discovered that the more you give people the idea that you'll just listen till the cows come home, the less they need that.

CB: One way your knowledge has had a huge effect has been through your writing, not only about clinical ideas, but you also started writing about organisations and consultation back in the mid-1980s.

DC: I've always believed in writing as a very worthwhile project. When you have to put something down on paper it's a kind of externalising process. It has an effect of helping you learn something by getting a little distance from it, and you get to know yourself and what you think in a way that you don't when you talk. My dad ran an advertising agency for part of his life and was very interested in writing and how you make an impact with words, and we used to talk a lot about why you would use that word instead of this word. So I was always interested in the way writing can influence. I think the writing is fun if you have something to say and agony if you don't have anything, and that's the problem for me—it's: "Do I have anything that I want to say that is new or helpful to other people?"

CB: You've been pretty prolific over time; you've written eight books, plus editing almost fifty books, as well as chapters and articles.

DC: I've had to find a way to bring it into my life because it's very rewarding for me to be able to communicate to people. The other strand is that I've always been obsessed by how teams work. I grew up in Chicago near a park, and I liked to see what kind of kids were there and make up some teams and play some sport. I used to play different seasonal sports, and I loved the competitiveness and dynamics about how teams work. My parents used to wring their hands and say, "Dave is never going to amount to anything because he doesn't read anything, all he wants to do is play sports." Part of what interests me in organisations is the team and how people work together. It's fascinating how a group of individuals can work together for some higher purpose. I think that's part of the reason that I never left the Tavistock; it changes all the time, people come and go, different courses, different values, different structures set up by the NHS, so it's never the same institution. I think it's a great place to be and as an organisation I think is fascinating.

CB: I was just wondering how you thought being an American has influenced your work?

DC: Being an outsider is a way of keeping a little bit on the edge; you can have your cake and eat it because if there's something going on that I don't like, I can say, oh, those damned Brits, and I can distance myself. But if things are great and things are going well, I say, I'm so proud to be living in London, it's a great country. I think a lot of family therapists are outsiders and need to have a position of being able to step back and view things that are going on. I have one brother who is five years older, and he and my parents had lots of turmoil in the early days of moving round and changing jobs and so on, so I think they made quite a family unit, and then I arrived and thought, "How do I fit in here and why is it that they can communicate so well? I'm five years behind them so I'm trying to observe and catch up." And that has put me on the edge, which I like, it feels creative—you can get in and get out and that's what a lot of therapy is about, it's getting very close and then stepping back.

CB: Do you have other things you want to say about Milan, post-Milan, and your early ideas about consultation?

DC: I think there are three or four ideas that are important in the therapeutic world. The idea of context, feedback loops, creating meaning in language and in dialogue are the kind of universals that were brought to light and made into therapeutic tools by the Milan group. As a teacher or a therapist, I try to make things as simple as I can, but at the same time communicate the things that are very complicated. I try to ensure that trainees have a handle on some kind of tools that they can use to manage what is a very complex, difficult, emotionally demanding job. What I like about the systemic field is that it can be interpreted in many different ways. If somebody asks me to do a seminar, I say, well, what's the context? They might be working in a drug rehabilitation unit, or in social services, or in education. I stop and think, "What are the systemic ideas that would be most helpful in working in that environment and what kind of language would make them accessible?" The systemic model has that flexibility that can twist and turn ideas round to make them fit every context. That could be a criticism, because then it's hard to pin down, but it's also its strength because it makes it very context-relevant. One of my most important ideas is how do I put people into a context in which they can see themselves being part of a feedback loop? So if something comes up as a general theme in a seminar, I might ask, "What do you think about that general point?" So you're constantly linking them back and I'm trying to hold on to these basic ideas whatever the context is, so I don't get distracted too much by content.

CB: And do you think those ideas have had much impact on the Tavistock Clinic over time?

DC: Sometimes I feel irritated that we're not more recognised, but I think it's been important also to be on the edge and to take responsibility for being the "other" in the Tavistock Clinic. It's made us a tighter unit and fight a little bit harder for our ideas, but sometimes I get tired of always having to remind the institution that we're here and suggesting they include our way of thinking. I think we had to make a boundary around ourselves to survive. The psychoanalytic community is fighting a tougher battle in the outside world because psychoanalysis is under attack, and so this becomes a kind of fortress and we represent the outside world for them. My view would be to develop a new model which is psychoanalytic–systemic, but then you'd have to say goodbye to some of your favourite Freudian concepts.

In the child and family department in the late 1970s, there was a group of people that were very interested in family work, but they were also ambitious. I was looking for something that I could own myself. I wanted a trajectory that I could take on for myself and that also fuelled the desire to develop the Milan model as a separate undertaking here. In 1979, Ros Draper and I were very interested in the *Paradox and Counter-Paradox* book, and we wanted to do a supervision group based on those ideas. We had an implicit contract that we were going to try to work according to this model. We would have the pre-session discussions, the reflecting team, and post-session. We were very careful about technique, and that led to some writings about interviewing style and questioning. That really was the launch pad as far as I was concerned. Then Caroline Lindsey, Ros Draper, and myself set up a training course to match the two-year qualification course that John Byng-Hall and Rosie Whiffen had started. That created a lot of tension and bad feeling for a year or so.

CB: Do you think in a way it replicated the way that the Milan group just worked together for that period to develop their ideas?

DC: Yes, you have to be able to see the world in a particular way for that period of time, and because this original supervision group was so dedicated to it, we could support each other very much. We had about ten years in which we used a similar model of a two-year course and did live supervision and seminars; there were written assignments and so on, and I thought it was a really very creative time for me personally and for the Tavistock. Then Ros left and we brought in other people. In 1987, we joined Brunel University to run the first family therapy course with academic recognition in the country, and the first academically recognised Tavistock course leading to an MSC in family therapy. The two courses merged and we placed the emphasis on the supervisor and the quality of supervision, so that people could opt to have a supervisor who had a Milan-orientation where the Milan influence was going to be conveyed.

CB: You did research on identifying significant moments in therapy, so I wondered whether you can identify some significant moments for you in relation to training or therapy.

DC: Well, a significant moment for me was in a consultation interview in Singapore. I was interviewing an Indian family based in Singapore, while behind the screen were the family therapy trainees. I was working with an Indian woman of about twenty who had left a physically abusive relationship. We talked about her relationship with her family, and the shame involved in leaving a marriage, and the implications for the whole family. After a while, I asked her opinion about where she would like to go forward and she didn't seem to understand and asked what I meant; I wondered if there was a language issue or maybe my accent, so I said pretty much the same thing again. She looked at me quizzically and finally said, "I have no opinion about this, it depends on my brother." That hit me like a ton of bricks. I had never expected family influence to be expressed in that way and it made me realise how western my perspective was. It was a significant moment in the sense that it made me much more interested in culture and how people solve problems in a particular culture. It sounds obvious now, but this was the early 1990s, a really significant learning point for me. We had a lot of discussion about what families mean in different cultures.

CB: Are there significant moments that you can identify in relation to your training, David?

DC: Part of the pleasure of training is the privilege of being able to travel and see other cultures and work. I've been going to Norway since 1986, and it's particularly interesting because the Norwegians invite external experts. After a couple of visits, I felt it was a real misunderstanding and that they were doing very interesting creative things that I would bring back to London and use in my training. For example, a group in Oslo were using a particular method of not discussing the case at all outside of the presence of the family, who arrive with a brown file which is the clinician's first exposure to the family problem. The clinician reads the file saying, for example, "It says here that there are eating problems in this family. Is this correct? Would you like to add anything to that?" Their reflecting team discussions are in the presence of the family, and when the family is finished they take the file with them. Everything is transparent. I think that was very creative and progressive and it stirs up a lot of thinking about the way we construct our realities with or without the family. I've brought a lot of things back from other countries and it's got me interested in how to listen differently to what people come up with for their own solutions. So the fun about these foreign visits is to learn about what other people are doing.

CB: How do you think the ideas you brought back from Norway influenced clinical practice here in the UK?

DC: I think systemic thinking is much more widespread here now than it was in the early 1980s. I hear people talk on the news about systemic problems, such as in banking. I think there's more awareness about the need to look more broadly at the connectedness between the different parts of a system. I've heard about people writing different court reports that spread responsibility and blame rather than just locating it in one person or in one agency. The disturbing death of "Baby P" [a child killed by his mother's partner following a long period of abuse during which the local Social Service Department was working with the family] was handled differently than in the past; there was more discussion about responsibility, the process of scapegoating, and how that leads to a poorer service because you can't recruit new social workers. This has been more publicly discussed, and I think we've all had a part in that.

Reference

Selvini-Palazzoli, M., Boscolo, L., Cecchin, G. & Prata, G. (1978). *Paradox and Counter Paradox. A New Model in the Therapy of the Family in Schizophrenic Transaction.* New York: Jason Aronson.

PART I
THERAPY AND THEORY

CHAPTER ONE

Keeping cool in thinking and psychotherapy

Stephen Frosh

I t is a great honour and pleasure to contribute to this volume for David Campbell, whom I knew for thirty years and who was one of the most significant influences on my thinking and therapeutic practice, supporting and supervising me in the limited clinical skills I have, and, latterly, helping me survive the exigencies of academic management through his careful and astute consultation. David's unflappable interest, his personal courtesy and wisdom, and his capacity to think both individually and systemically—to stay neutral and curious, as systemic therapists say—penetrated to the core of what it means to be a colleague, a teacher, and a friend. In a Festschrift book such as this, with contributions from, and also an original audience of, colleagues and students of David, both being categories into which I fall, David's capacity to generate relational warmth was obvious; so, too, is his immense intellectual contribution to the development of psychotherapy and systemic thinking.

The brief for this short chapter is to say something about my own work and the ways in which David's ideas influenced or inspired this, rather than focus on David himself, but the two things are not that easy to prise apart. This is because among the large number of different ways in which David's influence operates, the most pervasive is something relatively intangible, related to, but not dependent on, his teaching or writing. This, of course, is not to underestimate the significance of the *content* of David's work. His promotion and development of systemic thinking, and particularly of the Milan model, was crucial for the flowering of theory, practice, and research in the area, and his many, mainly jointly authored, books and articles (for me, perhaps seminally, the chapter in Volume II of Gurman and Kniskern's *Handbook of Family Therapy* (Campbell, Draper, & Crutchley, 1991)) remain primary source material for anyone wanting to learn this approach. Most of my own understanding of systemic theory and practice has come from this particular stable, with David at the heart of it. Incidentally, or maybe centrally, the *collaborative* nature of David's writing is an important comment on the ethics of his work and its consistency. Wedded to the ideas of openness to discovery, relationality, contextualism, democratisation of expert processes, and collegiality, David rarely "sole authored" his writings. Rather, things were worked out dialogically, in and among people, and often—in his workshops and teaching—this process, with all its necessary hesitancy, was made publicly available for us all to learn from.

In my own writing, despite being too impatient and probably narcissistic to work very successfully with others, I have also been drawn to this democratic principle, although I am probably less sanguine than David and many systemic workers about the means through which it can be achieved. In particular, it has fuelled my critique of a certain kind of theorising which *always finds what it seeks*, because its concepts are imposed as a grid on whatever it comes up against, in a claustrophobically "top-down" way. This is reflected, for example, in some psychoanalytically inflected research that *before it sets out to collect data* already knows that it will find among its research participants a certain kind of wish, a defence against it, and an interpretation that can explain the links. I have argued recently that this kind of use of theory is itself defensive, missing the opportunities that an open engagement with material can give for the production of surprise; in my own sphere of work, psychosocial studies, this risks producing a new orthodoxy just when what is needed is something disruptive and uncertain (Frosh & Baraitser, 2008). How does one maintain this necessary uncertainty, particularly in situations of high pressure, in which, as clinicians or researchers, one might be required to provide answers: for example, to respond quickly to the demands placed upon one by patients, referrers, or funding bodies? The standard and important Kleinian-inflected Tavistock response to this is that it is managed through clinging on to the capacity to live in doubt, the cultivation of Keats' famous "negative capability", "that is, when a man is capable of being in uncertainties, mysteries, doubts, without any irritable reaching after fact and reason" (in a letter to George and Thomas Keats dated 21 December 1817, Gittings, 2002, pp. 41–42). I like, however, to relate to this slightly differently, through the oppositions outlined by Jacques Lacan in his theory of the "four discourses" (Lacan, 1991). Without going into too much detail, it is worth noting, among the contrasts here, the relationships to knowledge embedded in the "discourse of the Hysteric", the "discourse of the Master" and the "discourse of the Analyst". The fourth discourse, that of the University, is returned to below. The first of them incessantly asks questions, pushing for the truth. The second tries to answer these questions from a position of knowledge. The third, the discourse of the Analyst, is a mode of stepping aside, a kind of judo in which the question is returned to itself, and in which the subject of that question—the one from whom it originates—discovers that no one can claim possession of the truth, and, hence, that a certain kind of freedom exists. Uncertainty here becomes a mode of truthfulness. This is not an easy stance to take, in therapy or in pedagogy, because those who come to us do so wanting answers, investing in our knowledge, and seeing themselves as having a right to gain access to it. In this sense, the discourse of the Master is a "lure", attracting the unwary, but, rather than being seen as a way of responding adequately to people's needs (as opposed to their demands), it can better be thought of as a way of propping up one's own claims to expertise.

Despite its very different language, I think the systemic approach works along similar lines, trying to hold off from knowing too much too soon, enacting the uncertainty that should come with claims to understanding, and constantly iterating the importance of context in determining meaning. Circular questions, paradox, reflecting teams, conversational stances, curiosity: the lexicon of systemic technical terms and practices over the past thirty years references an impulse towards the democratisation of therapy in which the therapist tries to step aside from a position of power, even in the face of resistance on the part of clients. One of my PhD students, John Stancombe, showed convincingly in his thesis that the "neutrality" of family therapists was often interpreted by family members as a failure to listen properly. Because their particular positions were not *endorsed*, they were felt to be neglected or rejected. The strong impulse here, fuelled at times by an engagement with sophisticated contemporary theories of power (for instance, Michael White's use of Foucauldian theory (White & Epston, 1990)), is to make the therapist and the patient partners, to equalise their position in a kind of Habermasian exchange of full rationality. That is, one should speak clearly and honestly, drawing the patient into a dialogue based on open principles of exchange, modelling thoughtfulness and non-defensiveness, and so allow a new narrative of experience to emerge. Interestingly, the relational "turn" in psychoanalysis says something similar, with important writers such as Benjamin (2004) building a notion of "thirdness" that emphasises intersubjective exchange rather than expert knowledge. My own view of it, however, is that dialogic attempts to unpick fantasies of expertise run up against both the realities of power and the intense desiring pull of the Imaginary—the wish, that is, for a master who can answer the call of the subject's distress. The discourse of the Master needs quite radical disruption if it is to be undone, and it is difficult to do that in a context in which training regimes, academic and professional accreditation and social expectations promote the bureaucratisation of therapy and its reduction from being an ethical encounter to a *technology* of "treatment". The tricks of the systemic trade are genuinely helpful here, ranging from active processes of self-disclosure to the potentially collaborative engagement of clients with therapists' thinking through techniques such as the "reflecting team"; but the *institutional* context in which this takes place militates against true openness and continues to reinforce an imaginary take on therapy as an "answer", which is bound to fail. This references the other "discourse" of Lacanian theory, that of the University (Lacan, 1991), in which knowledge is flattened and bureaucratised. Knowledge loses its capacity to radicalise; it becomes a passage to gaining credentials rather than a way of pursuing truth. As Lacan said to the students after 1968, in a phrase that seems increasingly prescient in the context of the consumer movement within universities, "You come here to gain credit points for yourself. You leave here stamped, 'credit points'" (Lacan, 1991, p. 201). In the psychotherapies, too, the movement, now very widespread, to accredit trainings with academic degrees has many virtues, but it does raise the spectre of making one believe that a human act of encounter can be reduced to a set of qualifications. What qualifies one to be a psychoanalyst is one of the major fault lines of the Lacanian movement (see Frosh, 2009a).

One can say against this that at least people who come to the institution in which David worked, the Tavistock Clinic, to be seen by members of the systemic team, are "recognised" in the sense of being treated with respect, just as, I believe, are all clients who come to the Tavistock, with its commitment to relational therapy of the psychoanalytic as well as systemic variety. As R. D. Laing once said, *treatment* is understood to signify "how we treat people", how we engage with them *ethically*, and the spirit in which this is done is one in which thoughtfulness predominates over a rush to action and away from the reality of people's pain. Yet, all institutions have their bureaucratising forces, and resisting this in order to open out our procedures in a way that challenges and interferes with the system is a problem for all of us.

However, back to the task. When I wrote that the most pervasive aspect of David's influence on my work is also intangible, I was thinking not so much of his writing and teaching, but of what I think of, with great affection, as his *style*. For someone who generated so much warmth, he was remarkably cool. I mean some pretty obvious things by this, in terms of David's balance and neutrality, his capacity to question and not to be thrown, his adoption of a certain mode of deliberate *slowness* that ensures that no rushing takes place, that time to consider is built into every response. Therapy with David was done in a kind of slow motion, in which what would spread around any system he joined was a new respect for language and for what Rose (2007), in a very different context, rather beautifully calls an "interval of reflection", which she sees as the central requirement of an ethical stance. This interval is technically between "impulse and act", as the moment in which identification and thoughtfulness can occur, in which it becomes possible to imagine a position outside one's own, again a familiar impulse in systemic work. It is also a deliberate act of pausing, a mode of hesitancy that does not lead to a fully formed final statement, but is, rather, an uncertainty to be treasured against the pressure to instantly articulate a response.

What I want to trace here is how these attributes appear in a certain kind of relationship to psychotherapy that I like to think of as "austere"; that is, as difficult and rather relentless, because it refuses to get taken up with the emotionality of the moment of encounter. One of the criticisms that might be levelled against systemic family therapy is that it is too "cognitive", in the sense of being concerned primarily with what people *think* and with the stories they tell about themselves and their predicaments, rather than paying sufficient dues to emotionality and the affective underpinnings of psychotherapy. This links with the kind of reflexivity that distinguishes systemic from psychoanalytic approaches. In the former, the issue is primarily one of externalising the impact of the therapist on the system which she or he joins, and deploying that impact in such a way that the system can be helped to reorientate itself productively. Classically, if one can speak that way about so new an approach, the observing team allows the reflexive impact of the therapist to be brought out into the open, making it amenable as a technique, making the system that is the "original system plus therapist" observable by the system that is the "team plus therapist" in one of those Venn diagrams with which systemic writers like to play. Reflexivity here involves moving outwards from the original system to dramatise the context in which it operates; as the therapist system and client system reflect on the difference they make to each other, so the adaptive propensities of each system can be explored. The psychoanalytic take on this is usually somewhat different, particularly in the Kleinian and object relations traditions and in the new modes of intersubjective and relational psychoanalysis that are increasingly influential around the world. Here, reflexivity refers to the intertwining of subjectivities, as unconscious material from each protagonist in an analytic encounter is passed to and fro, sometimes thought of as entering a space of the "third" for contact and amelioration, but, in any case, reflecting an affective element in the analyst as well as in the patient. The contextualisation here is of something that *flows through* the participants in the exchange and is felt by both of them, perhaps as a movement of excitement or injury. It involves the analyst considering the impact she or he is making on the patient and taking responsibility for that as a way of authorising the patient to move on (Benjamin, 2009).

Both these conceptualisations are powerful, and drawing them together has been one strand of work in which I have been tangentially involved (Frosh, 2009b). Both of them imply a significant level of affective engagement between therapist and client, so when I refer to "coolness" I do not mean *coldness*. But what both of them also insist upon is the requirement to maintain a capacity not to be drawn in by the seductiveness of the other; they are both suspicious of what can happen when one gets too close. That is, the sophisticated understanding of reflexivity present in both systemic thinking and in psychoanalysis acts as a protection against "acting into" the relationship, against, that is, trying to be too ameliorative, too helpful, even, perhaps, too *therapeutic* in one's approach.

I am not against therapy, of course, but I am interested in a very old-fashioned distinction between an *analytic* process, the purpose of which is to examine phenomena through a procedure that elsewhere is called "deconstruction", and a *therapeutic* process that tries to integrate and make things whole. Here, I frequently draw on a quotation from Laplanche that captures the difference between a perfectly legitimate and understandable impulse to make sense of things, and a more austere standing-aside that is less concerned with outcome and more with the sparking off of momentary truths. Laplanche writes, in a discussion about narrative, as follows:

> The fact that we are confronted with a possibly 'normal' and in any case inevitable defence, that the narration must be correlated with the therapeutic aspect of the treatment, in no way changes the metapsychological understanding that sees in it the guarantee and seal of repression. That is to say, that the properly 'analytic' vector, that of detranslation and the questioning of narrative structures and the ideas connected to them, remains opposed in every treatment to the reconstructive, synthesising narrative vector. (Laplanche, 2003, p. 29)

I have used this idea in a number of ways, particularly to offer a critique of narrative approaches both in therapy and in research, where what is given priority is the telling of some kind of integrated story of a person's experience or identity (Frosh, 2007). For Laplanche, this approach is a defence, "inevitable" and "normal" maybe, but in itself not *ethical*, because it gives priority to the ameliorative tendency in therapy over the truth-seeking tendency. I am aware, of course, that this reference to "truth" is itself disturbing and equivocal, and would probably not have been bought into by David or most proponents of systemic psychotherapy, which emphasises above all else the constructionist fabric of truth claims—how they are produced in power relations that operate socially and contextually. But what is being referred to here is the distance that has to be held from a kind of therapeutic impulse to make things better at all costs. That is, "truth", or, maybe better, "truthfulness", has to do with looking things in the eye, with not turning away from the distress and hurt one might see, with not believing that helpfulness is about wishing pain away. I recognise this as an old modernist impulse, with the added postmodern turn of emphasising the fluidity and uncertainty of meaning. More abstractly, I wonder if it is not our role to help people to locate themselves within the complex network of forces that operate on us all: social forces, of course, but also those that inhere in the subject we are starting to call "psychosocial", referring there to the network of criss-crossing relationships in which we are embedded. The "coolness" that I am seeking, that mode of austerity, is one that satisfies itself with this, that stands aside from mastery and punctures the imaginary consolations of specious answers, that maintains what, in some places, is called an "analytic attitude" and, in others, meaning much the same thing, "curiosity".

There is a question here about whether the critique of narrative integrationism implicit in this work applies to systemic psychotherapy, which, for many years, has been interested in a "multiple voices" perspective that actively promotes the idea that adherence to any single narrative is overly constraining and might itself be the source of trouble (Papadopoulos & Byng Hall, 1997).The social constructionism embedded in systemic approaches that, through creative questioning, use of team discussion, or other means, aim to suggest to families or organisations that there might be "other ways of looking at things", is indeed attuned to the dangers of expert pronouncements on "problems" and potential "cures". But what Laplanche is pointing to here is a limitation due not to belief in any *one* narrative as a "master narrative", but, rather, to the mystification produced by narrative itself. As Butler, among others, has argued in various places, most notably in *Giving An Account of Oneself* (2005), it is the *interruptions* to narrative, indexing the breaks in selfhood, that are core to grasping what it might mean to be a human subject; this is true, too, of what it might mean to attempt to appease the suffering of others. Writing admittedly about the position of the psychoanalyst, but with general application to all therapeutic encounters as well as other modes of "ethical" relationality, Butler comments on what is produced in an environment in which the subject seeks narrative coherence, but is faced instead with the realisation that the "other" (the analyst or therapist) is listening out for something else.

The other represents the prospect that the story might be given back in new form, that fragments might be linked in some way, that some part of opacity might be brought to light. The other witnesses and registers what cannot be narrated, functioning as one who might discern a narrative thread, though mainly as one whose practice of listening enacts a receptive relation to the self that the self, in its dire straits of self-beratement, cannot offer itself. (Butler, 2005, p. 80)

"The other witnesses and registers what cannot be narrated", acting *as if* it might be possible to make sense of this, to "discern a narrative thread", but what each of us might need to learn is that forcing experience into narrative form—however many such narratives one tolerates—does a certain kind of violence to it. The multiplication of narratives that is characteristic of much systemic work does not do away with this; in its valorisation of storytelling, it still insists on the simple idea that one might find meaning in suffering, that one might be able to make it make sense. Perhaps, as an extreme response to this, one should take literally Žižek's contention that one should take the story of Job as the appropriate response to trouble. "The greatness of Job", he writes, "is not so much to protest his innocence as to insist on the meaninglessness of his calamities" (Žižek, 2008, p. 152). Narrativising experience, whether through one narrative or many, is an attempt to add meaning to it, and that might well have therapeutic effects, as Laplanche clearly notes. But no narrative or multiplication of narrative can ever quite capture what is there, and the analytic task (using the term generically, not just to refer to psychoanalysis) might better be understood as to reflect back the shards of meaning without trying fully to gather them together. In therapy as well as in other spheres, like teaching, this might be a way of provoking people to move on. "Coolness", here, means being able to tolerate this non-narrativisable core, the recognition that something is always excluded from what we can understand or say. It means finding a way of being and doing in therapy or consultation or pedagogy that is not too strongly affiliated with a particular outcome, but is content to build solidarity with others through a process of waiting and, from time to time, benign interruption. I think much of this was echoed in David's style, even if it would not quite have been his language; it is, in the end, a form of humility.

This brings me to my last strand, that of "psychosocial studies". I define this as follows:

Psychosocial Studies takes issue with conventional distinctions between the 'psychological' and the 'social' and rejects the idea that 'inner' and 'outer' worlds are empirically or theoretically separable. Its object of study is the human subject and the wider social forma- tion, and the affect-laden relations and processes through which each are mutually constituted. It is concerned with the inter-relation between individual subjectivities and individual and group identities, and historical and contemporary social and political formations. (www.bbk.ac.uk/sps/about/)

It will be seen that the emphasis here is on the "unhyphenated" psychosocial, which tries to find a means and a vocabulary for theo- rising the "in-between" as an entity in itself, and, as such, is critical of the distinctions between "inner" and "outer" worlds that are charac- teristic of much psychotherapeutic thinking, as well as of mainstream sociology. Managing this is proving to be a very difficult task, full of contention, but holding off from moving one way or the other, from knowing too soon that x causes y, is part of the needed methodology. Unexpectedly, perhaps, given the relative failure of systemic thinking to have an impact on social theory, all this seems to be very congru- ent with the outlook adopted by David and the systemic team at the Tavistock. While their endeavour always reflects the need to offer a service to families who seek psychological help, their broader context of understanding is precisely that human subjects are not individu- ated entities, but are, rather, constantly constructed and reconstructed in social contexts. The boundaries between what is often thought of as "inner" and "outer" are fluid; as a system shifts, so does the percep- tion and experience of these boundaries; as the lines of flow and force operate, so different subjectivities are thrown up. Why, then, is it that so little of the systemic worldview has so far trickled through to psychosocial studies? In part this might be because the interest in identities and subjectivities that characterises many psychosocial researchers has led them to look primarily to psychoanalysis for a vocabulary that can intersect with the other perspectives in the psychosocial field: for example, with feminist, poststructuralist, and postcolonial thought. It might also be that, to date, very little systemic thinking has moved beyond the therapeutic setting in the way that psychoanalysis has, something which might, in large part, be due simply to the long history that psychoanalysis has had of doing this kind of thing (beginning a century ago with Freud's excursions into social and artistic criticism) (Frosh, 2010). But perhaps it is time to remedy this a little, and develop ways of translating systemic thinking so that it can infiltrate psychosocial studies productively, particularly, perhaps, in intersecting with discursive approaches that focus on how subject positions are generated through their *location* in what amount to systemic, relational fields (e.g., Wetherell, 2008). My own work, provoked by Peter Emerson, has drawn on this a little in trying to think about "critical" narrative analysis, in which the ideas concerning fragmentary texts outlined above are brought together with a strongly relational outlook that owes a lot to systemic practice (Emerson & Frosh, 2004). There is, however, a lot more to do here, with the systemic perspective on how subjectivity is *emergent* in relational contexts being the most promising way forward.

To summarise, I have been suggesting that there is something about "coolness" that can be gleaned across a range of psychosocial, psychoanalytic, and systemic work that offers a way out of a slightly sentimentalised attachment to narrative, yet retains the important ideas of plurality, social construction, and non-knowing. In everything we do, as therapists, teachers, or social researchers, we come up against the complexity and fragmentary nature of human relations and subjecthood, and this can produce an anxious scrabbling after meaning that is best resisted. The demand for answers is, however, great, from patients, students, and social institutions. In standing firm against this, there is much to learn from David's way of inserting himself into the complex multiplicities of systemic life, in which so many things happen, many of which do not seem to make any sense. His mode of being as a teacher, psychotherapist, supervisor, and consultant was to watch this occur, quizzically and hesitatingly, producing formulations only tentatively, allowing things room to shift as the context around them changed. This type of non-knowledge, of holding back, of giving space to what happens, is quite a lesson in humility and understanding, and of the contestation of mastery out of which a provocative, even subversive, practice might emerge.

References

Benjamin, J. (2004). Beyond doer and done to: an intersubjective view of thirdness. *Psychoanalytic Quarterly*, 73: 5–46.

Benjamin, J. (2009). A relational psychoanalysis perspective on the necessity of acknowledging failure in order to restore the facilitating and containing features of the intersubjective relationship (the shared third). *International Journal of Psychoanalysis, 90*: 441–450.

Butler, J. (2005). *Giving an Account of Oneself.* New York: Fordham University Press.

Campbell, D., Draper, R., & Crutchley, E. (1991). The Milan systemic approach to family therapy. In: A. Gurman & D. Kniskern (Eds.), *Handbook of Family Therapy, Volume II* (pp. 325–362). New York: Brunner/Mazel.

Emerson, P., & Frosh, S. (2004). *Critical Narrative Analysis in Psychology.* London: Palgrave.

Frosh, S. (2007). Disintegrating qualitative research. *Theory and Psychology, 17*: 635–653.

Frosh, S. (2009a). Everyone longs for a Master: Lacan and 1968. In: G. Bhambra & I. Demir (Eds.), *1968 in Retrospect: History, Politics, Alterity* (pp. 100–112). London: Palgrave.

Frosh, S. (2009b). What does the other want? In: C. Flaskas & D. Pocock (Eds.), *Systems and Psychoanalysis: Contemporary Integrations in Family Therapy* (pp. 185–201). London: Karnac.

Frosh, S. (2010). *Psychoanalysis Outside the Clinic: Interventions in Psychosocial Studies.* London: Palgrave.

Frosh, S., & Baraitser, L. (2008). Psychoanalysis and psychosocial studies. *Psychoanalysis, Culture and Society, 13*: 346–365.

Keats, J. (1817). Letter to George and Thomas Keats dated 21 December 1817. In: R. Gittings (Ed.), *John Keats, Selected Letters* (pp. 41–42). Oxford: Oxford University Press, 2002.

Lacan, J. (1991). *The Other Side of Psychoanalysis: The Seminar of Jacques Lacan Book XVII.* New York: Norton, 2007.

Laplanche, J. (2003). Narrativity and hermeneutics: some propositions. *New Formations, 48*: 26–29.

Papadopoulos, R., & Byng-Hall, J. (Eds.) (1997). *Multiple Voices: Narrative in Systemic Family Therapy.* London: Duckworth.

Rose, J. (2007). *The Last Resistance.* London: Verso.

Wetherell, M. (2008). Subjectivity or psycho-discursive practices? Investigating complex intersectional identities. *Subjectivity, 22*: 73–81.

White, M., & Epston, D. (1990). *Narrative Means to Therapeutic Ends.* New York: Norton.

Žižek, S. (2008). *Violence.* London: Profile.

CHAPTER TWO

Having a cup of tea with David Campbell: now for something completely different

Glenda Fredman

I am writing in appreciation of David Campbell's contribution to my work as a systemic psychotherapist, trainer, and consultant. I begin with three memories I hold as gifts from my days in family therapy training with David.

Having a cup of tea

It is over twenty years ago. I am talking with a family—father, mother, and two boys—in the Tavistock Clinic, where I am training in Milan systemic therapy. To me, the session is going really well. The parents are nodding and talking with interest and the boys are joining in the conversation. I feel that I understand well what they are telling me. While the conversation is in full flow, there is a knock at the door. "Excuse me," I say to the family, "That is my supervisor—maybe with some thoughts for us." I open the door and there is David. "You're having a cup of tea," he tells me.

I have been training with David for a year, so by now I know this means I have lost what he calls the "creative tension" in the conversation. I am aware of what that tension feels like and also familiar with the comfortable feeling of "having a cup of tea". I have learnt this awareness from David's seriously playful invitations to reflect on action in the moment, as he is inviting me to do here.

From David, I learnt that a collaborative and creative therapeutic process is not about being several steps ahead of the family; it does not involve taking them in a particular direction that I have previously mapped out or pulled from a manual. Rather, holding the creative tension means "leading from one step behind, staying connected to the clients, constantly comparing their feedback with my own point of view and remaining aware of the movement in my thinking" (Campbell, Draper, & Huffington, 1989, p. 27).

Watching David talking with families from behind a one-way screen gave me the opportunity to observe this "creative tension" in action. Having the chance to be interviewed by David, first in supervision as a trainee and then years later in a personal/professional consultation, I was able to experience first-hand this "creative tension". I was able to enjoy the effects of questions that invited me to connect with the ideas I was most familiar with and then to experience the gentle tug of reflexive questions (Tomm, 1988) that took me away from the comfort of the known and familiar to open space for new ways to go on.

This was all going on several years before Cecchin, Lane, and Ray published *Irreverence* (1992) and *The Cybernetics of Prejudice* (1994). Cecchin theorised for us how therapy occurs in the interplay of the beliefs and assumptions (what he called "prejudices") of both clients and therapists. Like Cecchin, David was a master at holding not only his own perspectives, but also the perspectives of the other. For Cecchin, it was in this dialogic space, where the different beliefs and meanings co-exist, that therapeutic change happened.

I now see that David was helping me develop abilities to manage the "tensionality of dialogue" while co-ordinating multiple perspectives with people. I was learning to create and be in that dialogic space with people. It is this process that people such as McNamee (2005) refer to as "therapy as social construction". For the past fifteen years, I have joined others to develop practical theory for working with "the therapeutic relationship" (Fredman, 2007; Fredman & Dalal, 1997; Fredman & Rapaport, 2010; Reder & Fredman, 1996) and 'using our selves in therapy and consultation' (Fredman, 1997; Martin & Stott, 2010). Looking back over the past twenty years, I see that I have been working on the project, started with David, of "How to have a cup of tea creatively". Another memory to illustrate how I began to learn to do this is described below.

And now for something completely different

I am hypothesising (Selvini-Palazzoli, Boscolo, Cecchin, & Prata, 1980) with two other trainees before seeing a family. We have been working for a good half an hour and are really pleased that our hypothesis meets the criteria of a good systemic hypothesis: it is circular, includes all members of the system, and is about relationships. We have not used the verb "to be", but have focused on what people do, think, and feel and we have positively connoted all members of the system to avoid blame or pathologising. David arrives ten minutes before the session, as is the usual practice for our supervisors. We proudly present our hypothesis. Looking impressed, David says, "That's great—now you can put that aside and make a different one . . ." My fellow trainees and I reel. Some of us desperately try to cling to our original hypothesis; others experience feelings of shock, anger, and disorientation when, eventually, we are able to let go of our preferred ideas. Somewhat bereft, we look to David for direction. He invites us to "think of the opposite" and new perspectives start flowing.

Looking back on those times, I recognise that I was learning not only to articulate several hypotheses, but especially to recognise that feeling when I am falling in love with my hypothesis. (Later, David might have called this "taking a fixed position".) I am grateful to him for enabling me to develop practices for letting go of, or "discarding", hypotheses (Campbell, Draper, & Huffington, 1988). Learning from David to think about and hold opposites has helped me to *do* dialectics rather than simply *think* dialectics. This has given me the freedom to play with ideas, embrace them, put them aside, and come back to them from different angles to gain new perspectives. Here, I was learning how to become an observer to my own beliefs and to co-ordinate a multiplicity of views—what in later years we would come to see as therapy as social construction.

Over the years, I have taken these two threads "Having a cup of tea creatively" and "Now for something completely different" and woven them with a third thread from David that connects to another memory.

Now you know this, what are you going to do?

It is towards the end of my training at the Tavistock Clinic. We are discussing Maturana's recently published paper (Mendez, Coddou, & Maturana, 1988) in a seminar with David, Ros Draper, and Caroline Lindsey, our tutors. We trainees are so excited that someone has actually written "there is no objective reality". Phrases like "objectivity in parentheses" and "passion for living together" are tripping off our tongues as we discuss how these ideas both fit with, and also liberate us from, our experience. As our talking reaches poetic heights, David asks curiously, "Now you know this, what are you going to do?" There is a pregnant pause in the conversation. I feel something like I did as a child when climbing down from a tree. I fumble tentatively for a solid foothold, a firm place to anchor briefly and from which to go on. David's words, "Now you know this, what are you going to do?" send me searching for a foothold to ground these wonderful ideas in practice.

David was inviting me to move between theory and practice and back again—to theorise practice and to "practicise" theory. I use the term "practicise" as a counterpoint to "theorise", where "theorise" refers to creating theory out of practice and "practicise" points to generating practices to perform the theory.

Now I see David's question, "Now you know this, what are you going to do?" as his invitation to move from meaning to action, scaffolding us to "practicise" theory.

Managing the tensionality of dialogue

These days, we are going through a phase in our public services where there are strong pulls towards objectivity. Some services require practitioners to single out one person in a family as "the patient" for a diagnosis before a family is eligible to receive a service. Some psychotherapists are expected to approach emotional and relationship difficulties in the same way physicians assess, treat, and evaluate physical medical symptoms. Some services are being developed on the assumption that there is a single treatment approach to fit all people, regardless of age, culture, ethnicity, gender, intellectual or physical ability. As a family psychotherapist and clinical psychologist working systemically in our public health service, these sorts of requirements have sometimes left me struggling to join with the prevailing discourse of the times. To help me with the challenge of working respectfully alongside different discourses, I turn to what I have learnt from David: holding the "creative tension", "moving positions", "alternating hypotheses", and "moving between meaning and action". Weaving these threads back and forth, I repeatedly ask myself, "Now that you know this, what are you going do?" Thus, over the years, I have been able to co-ordinate the multiplicity of views of clients and colleagues, as well as my own, through a process that involves holding on to our own perspectives and letting the other happen to us (Stewart & Zediker, 2000). I will present some of the "steps" I have taken to create "bridges" in conversations between practitioners, colleagues, and clients with the help of an example of my work with twenty-two-year-old Amber and her psychiatrist, Dr P.

I met Amber with her mother and two nurses when she was an inpatient. She had been admitted to a psychiatric ward following what was described as a "psychotic episode". When I introduced myself, Amber avoided eye contact with me. She immediately complained that her nose was green and she did not like the colour. When I asked, "What is wrong with the colour?" and "How long has this bothered you?" she glanced fleetingly at me before singing in a sweet voice the words from a Michael Jackson song, "And I told about equality. / And it's true, / either you're wrong / or you're right. But if / you're thinkin' / about my baby, / it don't matter if you're / Black or White".

Amber's mother was Japanese; her father was from West Africa. Her tuneful words opened space for a rich and moving conversation with them about their family's relationship to skin colour. In our following meeting, witnessed by her mother and the nurses, Amber spoke of her experiences of racial abuse within her extended families and at school.

Amber and I continued to meet when she was discharged from the psychiatric ward. In our early meetings, she kept returning to those first weeks on the inpatient ward, repeating tearfully, "I thought it was the end . . . I had finally gone mad . . . being in there nearly killed me . . ." By our fifth meeting, she was pleased with how things were going. She had begun to reclaim her life from "the black cloud" (Amber's words), had made new friends, was exhibiting her college sculpture project exploring her ethnic identity, and had two part-time jobs. I was, therefore, surprised when, at our sixth meeting, she said she felt "like giving up . . . what's the point . . . I'll probably end up in a loony bin anyway . . ." Amber told me that the "hopeless" feelings had returned shortly after her routine psychiatry clinic review when "The doctor said I have to take more pills . . . I thought I was getting better . . . but obviously I am getting worse . . . I must have been imagining it."

Although I had informed Amber's psychiatrist, Dr P, of her considerable improvements in response to the "strength-based approach" we were taking, he had increased her antidepressant medication. Amber had worked very hard to counter the stigmatising effects of the inpatient admission and diagnosis of "depression with psychotic features". Therefore, I felt frustrated on her behalf, as I saw how the increase in medication began to erode her newfound confidence and positive view of herself. As my frustration grew, I viewed my psychiatry colleague's approach as impeding the process of therapy and found it challenging to collaborate respectfully with him.

As doctors, nurses, psychologists, social care workers, or therapists, we spend many years learning how to be good practitioners according to the values, principles, and ethical codes of our professions. Over time, our professional values become woven with our professional identities and the stories we tell of ourselves as practitioners and people. Thus, we can develop loyalties to our professional stories, elevating many of the theories we are taught to truths. Trying to hold on to our commitment to work ethically, to be a good practitioner and a good person according to our professional discourse, can draw us into blame or criticism of other people or practices that challenge our worldview, especially if that challenge speaks negatively to us of who we are as a person by undermining our core values. I think David would say that it is at times like this that we are most prone to "take a position" and could benefit from moving positions and holding the tension between positions. I found myself taking a strong critical position that negatively connoted Amber's psychiatrist when I learnt of the effects of his increasing her medication, and turned to practices inspired by David to help me go on.

From blending to bridging

McNamee (2004) challenges systemic and family therapists to "see a model, technique or even a theory as a discursive option" (p. 236), rather than to try to merge models into one meta-narrative. Later (McNamee, 2005), she suggests "bridging" incommensurate models rather than trying to make incommensurate discourses commensurate, and proposes that "bridging requires coordination". It was Pearce (1991) who distinguished "commensurable" from "incommensurable" theories or discourses. Belief systems that are "commensurable" share a common logical or rational structure and meaning system, allowing the possibility of point-by-point comparison (or translation). When belief systems are "incommensurable", on the other hand, their basic beliefs are seen as essentially contradictory, so that the different ideas cannot be logically accommodated in a coherent and internally consistent meaning system. Therefore, the absence of a common structure makes point-by-point comparison (or translation) illogical. McNamee puts forward Cecchin's (1987) "curiosity" and "irreverence" (Cecchin, Lane, & Ray, 1992) as postures the therapist might adopt to "construct bridges" across incommensurate discourses. For McNamee, it is the process of bridging, rather than trying to blend into one discourse that opens space for what Bateson calls the "difference that makes the difference". It is this bridging that we call "co-construction".

Over the years, I have worked towards creating the sorts of "bridges" in conversations between practitioners, colleagues, and clients that McNamee refers to. Treating all theories as potential "knowledges" that take their place among other cultural, religious, communal, or personal "knowledges" has enabled me to move between, and "hold the tension" of, different positions. Instead of identifying any particular theory or discourse as the best way to work or think, therefore, I position myself, and invite colleagues and clients, to evaluate the different "knowledges", theses, or stories according to how they fit with our personal and professional contexts (Fredman, 2004). For example, rather than suggest that practitioners give up their preferred theories of loss and mourning, I invite them to add a range of different theories to their repertoire of stories and practices, including their personal and cultural stories about death and dying, and to evaluate the fit of these stories with different contexts (Fredman, 1997).

Approaching our professional training as culture

Thus, I approach our professional trainings as one of our cultures, alongside the cultures of our ethnicity, gender, age, religion, and sexuality, which construct what it is we know, how we come to know it, and what we are allowed to include in our knowing. Drawing on Ricoeur (1996), Lang (2005) says "we cannot translate; we can only be guests in each other's cultures". The medical model informed my psychiatry colleague's practice. My work with Amber was informed by systemic and constructionist approaches. Rather than try to find a common language to translate one approach into another, or work out ways to blend approaches, I asked myself, "What might I do and how might I be if I were a guest in Dr P's culture?"

Approaching our professional training as one of our cultures implies acknowledging that there is no universal theory to account for problems necessarily acceptable or familiar to all cultures. Taking the position that no "worldview" is superior to another, however, is not the same as taking a position of moral relativism, whereby all perspectives are seen as equally desirable. Since each discourse we adopt shapes our experience and, thereby, enables or constrains what we feel, think, and do, I recognise that I might differentially affect people's sense of belonging and self-worth if I privilege one discourse over another while engaging with people. Therefore, I try to reflect on, evaluate, and take responsibility for the consequences of adopting different practices, not only for myself, but also for people involved and for our relationships. According to McNamee (2004),

> selecting a theory or technique as a practical option (as opposed to a truthful option) for action enhances our ability to be relationally engaged with clients. We become sensitive to their stories as well as our own stories in ways that allow us to be responsive and relationally responsive. (p. 237)

Below I discuss my approach to developing the sort of "relationally responsive" abilities McNamee is talking about that involve becoming reflexive to our discourses and contexts and using our beliefs and discourses as a resource.

Becoming reflexive to our discourses and contexts

Dr P's approach to Amber challenged my professional principles and values that favour collaborative practice and a focus on competence. I found myself using warlike language, such as "sabotage", as well as expressions like "undermining" or "discrediting" to describe how his practice with Amber had affected the progress of our work together and challenged my professional identity.

Using this sort of adversarial language tends to position us in unwanted competitive or blaming relationships with colleagues, thus potentially interfering with collaboration at the expense of our clients' well-being. Lang (2005) reminds us that working aesthetically involves respectful working not only with clients, but also with other practitioners involved. Therefore, our challenge is to consider how we can exist alongside models of practice and within professional and agency contexts that have expectations that challenge our ethical positions. My intention is to position myself to facilitate positive working relationships with colleagues which open space for constructive and creative contributions to the well-being of the people with whom we work.

I have found that reflecting on the discourses that shape our practice can enrich our work and professional relationships (Fredman, Johnson, & Petronic, 2010). Therefore, I start by "stepping back" to locate my views, prejudices, pre-understandings, and practices in the different discourses that organise my practice with people. I reflect on my own positions and try to consider the perspectives of other practitioners working with the client as well. I ask myself how and why they and I are pulled towards one practice or another with questions such as: "What are the different professional/service contexts informing our work with Amber?" "Are we acting out of similar or different contexts?" "What are the taken-for-granted assumptions about what counts as competent and ethical 'professional' behaviour coming from our different professions/work contexts?" (Madsen, 2007). "How do these assumptions affect our decisions/actions with Amber?" "What discourses do our contexts pull us towards or away from?"

I reflected that the junior psychiatrist, Dr P, who had increased Amber's medication, was probably following prescribed assessment protocols and working according to clear diagnostic criteria, for example the *DSM-IV* (American Psychiatric Association, 1994). I assumed that he was reporting to the consultant psychiatrist ultimately responsible for his work. Therefore, he would be pulled towards focusing on deficits and using problem-solving and expert practices, the predominant approach in the psychiatry service. I noted that my systemic psychotherapy training pulled me towards different "collaborative" and "possibilities" practices with which Amber had engaged particularly well. I was also aware that "deficit", "expert", and "protection" discourses are dominant in public mental health services for adults and receive more institutional support than the "strength-based", collaborative approach.

Stepping back and examining the values and assumptions informing both my approach and that of my psychiatry colleagues enabled me to create some distance from my dilemma and from my experience of frustration. Hence, I was able to notice how the different discourses were "pulling" my psychiatry colleague and me towards different practices with Amber. Thus, I moved towards "externalising" the respective discourses (Madsen, 2007), whereby I saw the "discourse" and not the psychiatrist (or his consultant) as responsible for the dilemma.

If we let go of the idea that there is a right or wrong discourse and acknowledge instead the wide range of possible stories and practices, then the responsibility falls to each of us to consider which practices to adopt and the possible consequences for everyone involved as we adopt one practice rather than another. To help me contemplate the consequences of following one discourse or another, I consider questions such as: "In what ways does this language or vocabulary enhance or diminish how these people value themselves and each other?" "If I choose this discourse, how will it inform my relationship with this person?" "How will it enhance or constrain our being together or their being with each other?" "How will our actions differ if we use this metaphor or another?" Addressing the consequences, opportunities, and constraints of adopting different discourses leads us into ethical considerations about how we treat people within the different forms of discourse and, hence, whether we bring forth enhancing rather than diminishing stories of identity, positive rather than negative experiences of relationships, and whether we create collaborative rather than isolating experiences for people.

Recognising that the psychiatrist and his consultant did not invent the "deficit" discourse enabled me to move beyond a blaming, critical stance. I offered to join Amber at her next meeting with the psychiatrist to explore how we might work together in Amber's interest while staying loyal to our respective discourses. My intention was to create opportunities for the psychiatrist to witness Amber's positive developments. I also hoped to develop an understanding of the logic informing the psychiatrist's actions to help me introduce alternative ideas or practices without compromising his preferred ways of working.

Using our pre-understandings and discourses as a resource

Cecchin, Lane, and Ray (1992) point out that "excessive loyalty" to a specific idea pulls us away from taking personal responsibility for the moral consequences of our practice. On the other hand, when practitioners reflect on their own presumptions and examine the pragmatic consequences of their own behaviour, they take a position that is both ethical and therapeutic. Therefore, they propose adopting a posture of "irreverence" that involves juxtaposing ideas that might seem contradictory to enable practitioners to stay with "doubt" in the face of certainty and, hence, attain self-reflexivity.

I approach the discourses, stories, and pre-understandings out of which we act as "resources" (Fredman, 1997; Fredman & Dalal, 1997) to this process of self-reflexivity. (Like Martin and Stott (2010), I use Andersen's word, "pre-understandings", rather than Cecchin, Lane, and Ray's (1994) "prejudices", since the term prejudice can mean "injustice" or "intolerance", and so can carry a negative connotation. Also I prefer "pre-understandings" to "beliefs" or "cognitions", as these terms can imply something internal, non-relational, and divorced from their context.) Instead of construing our assumptions as obstacles to overcome, therefore, we can use clients' and our own pre-understandings to guide therapeutic conversations. We can also use our cultural beliefs and stories as resources, treating them as alternative theories alongside our professional theories. Thus, we can "play with different levels" (Cecchin, Lane, & Ray, 1992) of our beliefs and stories as resources to therapeutic conversations.

Before I joined the meeting with Amber and Dr P, I spent some time on a self-reflexive exercise I have developed to create flexibility in my thinking when I am prone to become attached to a position or am unsure how to go on (Fredman, 1997; Martin & Stott, 2010). My intention was to use this practice to help me open space in the meeting with Amber and the psychiatrist, whereby both the psychiatrist and I might take different positions with Amber about her future treatment.

The problem here is about (my hypothesis is) . . .
For things to improve, what needs to happen is . . .
I strongly believe that . . .
The therapist must be sure to . . .
The therapist must never . . .
It is OK for the therapist/client to . . .
The therapist needs to take responsibility for . . .
It is the client's/therapist's right that . . .
In relation to this issue, I am the sort of person who . . .

Figure 1. Sentence completion task to generate pre-understandings.

The first part of this exercise involves a sentence completion task I developed to invite a position, bring forth pre-understandings, and prompt statements reflecting our moral order (Figure 1 above). This task is intended to generate a repertoire of ideas, not right or wrong, but that could be more or less useful as a resource to the practitioner. Therefore, the intention is to complete the phrases quickly, with a "gut" response, resisting the urge to take too much time for deliberation.

Completing the sentences helped me generate a repertoire of my pre-understandings and threw light on my moral order in relation to the positions I was taking to the psychiatrist's approach with Amber. My pre-understandings included:

– The psychiatrist is seeing Amber out of context. He has not paid attention to her developments and is focusing only on medication and symptoms and not the whole person.
– He needs to see Amber in context, learn about her recent developments, and notice her abilities, not just her symptoms.
– Amber is doing very well and increasing her medication is inappropriate.
– I should make the psychiatrist aware of Amber's strengths and improvements.
– I must never undermine the psychiatrist.
– I need to support and enable Amber to assert herself with her doctor.
– I need to ensure that the work with Amber is ethical.
– Amber has the right to ask questions and get information so she has informed consent.
– I should take Amber's position when I think she has not been given a voice in her own treatment.

The next step involves choosing one of these pre-understandings to work with and noting its implicit rule or the actions it points towards. I selected my pre-understanding, "I should make the psychiatrist aware of Amber's strengths and improvements".

The next step involves identifying the contexts that inform and give meaning to the selected pre-understanding with questions such as: "Where does that idea come from?" "Who else agrees?" "Who tells me that?" Then we go on to generate further stories from our other personal/professional contexts with questions such as: "What does my *training* say about this?" "What is my *culture/religion/community/family* view about this issue? Is there a story?" "What would my *team/colleagues/supervisor/manager* say?" "From a *gender* perspective, what are the rules for men/women about this in my cultures?"

I recognised that my pre-understandings in relation to Amber's treatment came from many different contexts of my life. Reflecting on my family and culture, I recalled many stories of encouragement to focus on resilience and strength. As a child growing up in a post-Holocaust Jewish family, I was audience to many stories of survival and resilience passed down through my family and community. I recalled my grandmother singing, "When you're smiling . . . the sun comes shining through . . ." and my mother singing, "Always look on the bright side of life". My team's, supervisor's, and manager's perspectives also encouraged a resilience-focused, appreciative approach. When I asked myself the question, "What are the rules about this for men/women?", I began to wonder whether Amber would have responded differently to her doctor if he were a woman. Then I found myself thinking about power in our relationship, too. Although we were both women, I was a lot older than Amber and the "professional" whose questions she answered. I began to wonder whether she was giving me what she thought I wanted to hear in our conversation. I began to wonder if she felt she had to sing along to my tune.

Thus, this process opened space for different positions to come into view and, with them, other stories emerged. A different story that came to light included an episode in my adolescence when I failed my driving test for the second time. My mother tried to encourage me not to dwell on what to me was a total disaster. I recalled wanting to linger in my misery with my mother joining me there and my disbelief that she could not see this "disaster" as anything other than a tragedy. I was grateful for the emergence of this story, since it extended my repertoire in ways I anticipated might be useful to future conversations with Amber and the psychiatrist.

The last question in this process is one that comes from David: "What is the *opposite* view (to this pre-understanding you have selected)?" Again, it includes reflecting on the context informing this (opposite) perspective with questions such as, "When might I take this view?" and "Who would agree?"

I formulated the opposite to my pre-understanding ("I should make the psychiatrist aware of Amber's strengths and improvements") as "I should stand back and let Amber's doctor do his job—I should listen more to Dr P's perspectives on her problems." I thought my systemic supervisor would agree with this perspective. He might suggest I join the appointment to learn how the doctor works so that I can understand his (professional) logic. David, too, might suggest that I notice the position I am taking and begin to consider, "Why is it personally so important for that doctor to take that position?" (Campbell, 2008, p. 88)

As David might have anticipated, this process opened space for me to stand back and, as Cecchin might have said, "become an observer to my own beliefs" so that I came to see the positions I was taking as just positions. By following this process, I was able to juxtapose different, perhaps seemingly contradictory, ideas from a range of different contexts, mine, Amber's, and the psychiatrist's, towards developing the sort of self-reflexivity Cecchin, Lane, and Ray (1992) describe and, thereby, "practising" irreverence. New perspectives emerged and I was able to join the meeting with Amber and Dr P in a curious and collaborative posture.

By joining the psychiatric review meeting, I gained a new perspective on the psychiatrist's decision to increase the medication. He seemed to be following a prescribed assessment protocol. He asked Amber orienting and investigative questions (Tomm, 1988) designed to help generate clear descriptions of symptoms that he could then match against diagnostic categories or syndromes: for example, "*Do you feel sad, depressed or empty? Sometimes people find that they feel more low in the morning than later in the day—is that the case for you? How is your sleep/appetite? Have you lost weight? What about your energy? Do you feel tired?*" These sorts of questions seemed to elicit accounts of pathology (Mendez, Coddou, & Maturana, 1988) from Amber. As their talks progressed, I noticed Amber's demeanour change and her preferred version of herself as "hardworking" and "creative" fade from the picture. She was sinking further into her chair, lost eye contact with the psychiatrist, and her voice grew quieter and quieter, so that she was barely audible.

Mindful that this was a psychiatric appointment, I was careful to stay respectful to the psychiatrist's discourse. At all times, I deferred to his expertise. With more of an understanding of his logic and the pressure of his context on his practice, I tried to open space for the psychiatrist to connect with other, more life-enhancing stories concerning Amber, thereby creating the opportunity for him to witness her progress. I spoke politely to the doctor.

Glenda: Excuse me, Dr P. I am wondering if you can help us. Amber is having a bit of a problem trying to save money at the moment.

Dr P: What's the problem?

Glenda: Well doctor, you see, Amber is trying to save money to study sculpture abroad. She received a very high grade for her exhibition—what was it you got again, Amber?

Amber: Distinction.

Glenda: Is that the highest grade—the best?

Amber: (sitting up in her chair) Yes.

Glenda: (to the doctor) But things are so expensive these days. Even though Amber has two jobs—where are you working again, Amber?

Amber: The Palladium [theatre].

Glenda: Oh yes—Amber is an usherette at night and also works in the local launderette two half-days.

Dr P: (to Amber) Do you think you are doing too much?

Amber: I don't know . . .

Dr P: So what's the problem with money?

Glenda: Well, Amber also likes to be fashionable. And she works near Covent Garden with all those wonderful shops tempting attractive young women who are earning—did you get that leather jacket in Covent Garden, Amber?

Amber: (smiling and stroking the collar of the jacket) No—I got it at a charity shop.

Glenda: Picking that out in a charity shop takes a creative eye . . . what do you think Doctor?

Doctor P: (awkwardly) Yes . . .

Glenda: Dr P, Amber has been asking me about the medication, the pills. I said we should discuss them with you. I was not sure if you think she would need so many pills . . . since she has made all these developments. Can you help us with this?

Dr P: (reading the medical notes and clarifying the current dosage with Amber). Do you want to cut down your medication?

Amber: I don't know. If I stop the pills . . . will I get worse?

Dr P: Well—we could review you earlier next time—say about six weeks—and see how you go. If things are still going so well . . .

Glenda: Are you saying that Amber is doing well—that doing well at college and keeping up the jobs and having these plans for more studying is a good thing? And that in six weeks you will talk about the pills again?

Dr P: Yes. (To Amber) What is the problem with money? Why don't you put it in a bank account or give it to your mother to look after for you?

Without creating an excessive demand on his time, I tried respectfully to involve Dr P in a more relational conversation with Amber that included systemic practices like contextualising her symptoms (tiredness, lack of sleep) in positive stories of her everyday life, bringing forth her competence and connecting Amber to her relationships with college, work, and family rather than focusing on her as only an individual. Thus, I was able to engage in dialogue with Amber that was coherent with the aesthetics of systemic practice without compromising her doctor's ability to work according to his medical ethics and standards of competence.

And now you know this, what are you going to do?

In our last conversation, David said two things that have stayed with me, "I see you as the next generation", and "I am going to push on with more (drug) trials. I still want to work with you on emotion—our work is different." I replied, "I want to do that—let's do it." Although David tried, we never had the chance to speak again. Now I am left to have that conversation without David here—to imagine, to invite his voice, and to take his position as well as my own.

I wonder what David would have said if he had been observing this conversation with Amber and Dr P from behind a one-way mirror? Would he have commented that in some ways we were indeed having a cup of tea—yet also participating in something completely different? Would he have recognised that I was trying to honour the professional culture of my psychiatry colleague by staying reflexive to both our discourses and contexts and using our contexts and discourses as a resource to the conversation? Would David have noticed my efforts to manage the tensionality of dialogue by bridging our different discourses, rather than trying to blend the different perspectives? Would he have been interested in the curiosity with which I connected to the different positions I was able to take?

I take David's words, "I'd like to work with you on emotion—our work is different", as an invitation to create a polarity to invoke a difference to make a difference. I hear his words, "I see you as the next generation", not as a directive to run with the baton he has passed me, but as a gift of encouragement to hold the creative tension of that difference, from which we can find new ways to go on.

I return to those early guidelines from David and I wonder—have I been having a cup with of tea with David Campbell while writing this chapter? If so, where would I go "now for something completely different"? David's voice comes to me, "Think of the opposite." Then I find myself saying to myself "OK, Glenda—now that you know this, what are you going to do?" I hold myself back from thoughts or comments that diminish the difference between us, such as "Our work is not so different", or "It is quite similar". Instead, I position myself to invoke the polarities, to push David's ideas to the extremes, to push the ideas he attributes to me to extremes. I press myself to say, "What is the opposite of my ideas and of his?" "If I put his practices at one end of the continuum and mine on the other, what would other positions along this continuum look like?" New possibilities to go on start forming and I am able to leave this chapter now and look forward to the emergence of the next possibility . . .

References

American Psychiatric Association (1994). *Diagnostic and Statistical Manual of Mental Disorders (DSM-IV)*. New York: American Psychiatric Association.

Campbell, D. (2008). Locating conflict in team consultations. In: D. Campbell & C. Huffington (Eds.), *Organisations Connected. A Handbook of Systemic Consultation* (pp. 79–97). London: Karnac.

Campbell, D., Draper, R., & Huffington, C. (1988). *Teaching Systemic Thinking*. London: Karnac.

Campbell, D., Draper, R., & Huffington, C. (1989). *Second Thoughts on the Theory and Practice of the Milan Approach to Family Therapy*. London: Karnac.

Cecchin, G. (1987). Hypothesising, circularity and neutrality revisited: an invitation to curiosity. *Family Process, 26*(4): 405–413.

Cecchin, G., Lane, G., & Ray, W. A. (1992). *Irreverence. A Strategy for Therapists' Survival*. London: Karnac.

Cecchin, G., Lane, G., & Ray, W. A. (1994). *The Cybernetics of Prejudices in the Practice of Psychotherapy*. London: Karnac.

Fredman, G. (1997). *Death Talk: Conversations with Children and Families*. London: Karnac.

Fredman, G. (2004). *Transforming Emotion. Conversations in Counselling and Psychotherapy*. London: Whurr.

Fredman, G. (2007). Preparing our selves for the therapeutic relationship. Revisiting 'Hypothesizing revisited'. *Human Systems: The Journal of Systemic Consultation and Management, 18*: 44–59.

Fredman, G., & Dalal, C. (1997). Ending discourses: implications for relationships and action in therapy. *Human Systems: The Journal of Systemic Consultation and Management, 9*(1): 1–13.

Fredman, G., & Rapaport, P. (2010). How do we begin? Working with older people and their significant systems. In: G. Fredman, E. Anderson, & J. Stott (Eds.), *Being With Older People: A Systemic Approach* (pp. 31–60). London: Karnac.

Fredman, G., Johnson, S., & Petronic, G. (2010). Sustaining the ethics of systemic practice in contexts of risk and diagnosis. In: G. Fredman, E. Anderson, & J. Stott (Eds.), *Being With Older People: A Systemic Approach* (pp. 188–210). London: Karnac.

Lang, P. (2005). Plenary. Transforming worlds, language and action. Making people's lives better. International Conference, KCC Foundation, Canterbury, July.

Madsen, W. (2007). Sustaining a collaborative practice in the "real" world. In: *Collaborative Therapy with Multi-Stressed Families* (pp. 323–353). London: Guilford Press.

Martin, E., & Stott, J. (2010). Using our selves in work with older people. In: G. Fredman, E. Anderson, & J. Stott (Eds.), *Being With Older People: A Systemic Approach* (pp. 61–86). London: Karnac.

McNamee, S. (2004). Promiscuity in the practice of family therapy. *Journal of Family Therapy, 26*(3): 224–244.

McNamee, S. (2005). Curiosity and irreverence. Constructing therapeutic possibilities. *Human Systems: The Journal of Systemic Consultation and Management, 16*: 75–84.

Mendez, C. L., Coddou, F., & Maturana, H. R. (1988). The bringing forth of pathology. *Irish Journal of Psychology, 9*: 144–172.

Pearce, W. B. (1991). On comparing theories: treating theories as commensurate or incommensurate. *Communication Theory, 1*: 159–164.

Reder, P., & Fredman, G. (1996). The relationship to help: interacting beliefs about the treatment process. *Clinical Child Psychology and Psychiatry, 1*(3): 457–463.

Ricoeur, P. (1996). Reflections on a new ethos for Europe. In: R. Kearney (Ed.), *Paul Ricoeur: The Hermeneutics of Action* (pp. 3–87). London: Sage.

Selvini-Palazzoli, M., Boscolo, L., Cecchin, G., & Prata, G. (1980). Hypothesising, circularity and neutrality: three guidelines for the conductor of the session. *Family Process, 19*(1): 3–12.

Stewart, J., & Zediker, K. (2000). Dialogue as tensional, ethical practice. *Southern Communication Journal, 65*: 224–242.

Tomm, K. (1988). Interventive interviewing Part III: Intending to ask lineal, circular, strategic or reflexive questions. *Family Process, 27*: 1–15.

Relationship to questions over time: David Campbell in interview with Charlotte Burck

Edited by Sara Barratt

CB: What questions have persisted for you around family therapy across time? Do you think there are some questions you keep coming back to?

DC: I'm sure that my questions are much more relational than they were when I started, because my training was as a clinical psychologist specialising in child psychotherapy when the child had already been identified as having the problem. By the time they came to me, I had to struggle to raise the family profile and would always be asking questions that looked at a context of relationships around a problem. One of my top ten articles is the one by Anderson, Goolishian, and Winderman (1986) about the problem being determined by the way it is constructed by the professionals. I've also been influenced by some of Karl Tomm's (1987a,b, 1988) early papers about interventive interviewing, and a lot of my questions are meant to push people into a different way of thinking, so if they say it's black, I'd ask about the white, and if the kid is wonderful, well, what about the times they're not wonderful, and so on. I do a lot of looking for opposites, and that has really come together for me in terms of the thinking about positioning theory, in that people take positions in relation to the positions not taken, which is something that's really important in the way I work with people. I think the more solution-focused people have influenced me to take the hypotheses that the families generate themselves more seriously and to get into their own narrative about problems. As a child psychotherapist, I held on to ideas about containment and support, and I think it is important for therapists to be present and available for people to give them the confidence that we can work this through together. I think sometimes we get a little bit too fond of our own theories and think change comes about because of some of our complicated ideas, when it's just about being a trustworthy supportive person. I try to see feedback loops, and whenever I'm talking to anybody I am thinking, what's the feedback that they have been getting that leads them to say this, and what might other people say about this point you've just made. Those kind of questions are really interesting to me.

CB: Can you say a bit more about how you craft a question, because you have a very fine ability to ask questions in different contexts?

DC: One of the mantras that runs through my head is the diagram Bateson put in *Mind and Nature* (1980) about finding meaning, acting on the meaning, and the action leads to another level of meaning, which leads to further action. I think that's such a wonderful template to have in mind because it always makes it possible to ask a question to move through the diagram, so, if people say this is what we think is going on, I would ask what that suggests we should do, what's the activity based on that understanding? That would lead me into the next question. If people are in the activity side of Bateson's ladder and they've decided to set up a community service, I'd say that's fine, but let's step back and be reflective and look at what it means. Now we've moved on to another understanding in relation to what are we going to do next, or tomorrow, or whatever time frame is appropriate. I think I've developed sensors for not letting people slide away from that ladder, and sliding away from the ladder is acting before you understand the meaning or settling for a meaning without really analysing the action and consequences of it, so I think it's important that there's somebody who is trying to keep people to the task. There are lots of interesting theories that come from Bateson and other people about group dynamics and the tendency for groups to fall off task and become more primitive and competitive, so a lot of my work has been based on helping people stay task focused and not to get into the rivalries and the competitiveness that they do otherwise.

CB: I suppose systemic therapy is sometimes critiqued for having too much flexibility. What is your view is about that?

DC: To go back to the Bateson schema, family therapists are probably happier on the activity side of the ladder and maybe not as interested in the meaning analytic side. That's probably a fair criticism, but somebody has to, for example, act on a new idea that has just come out of the field of anthropology, or try a new technique and see whether it helps. Family therapists tend to like to be creative and exploratory, and there are others in the field who are happier slowing it down and analysing; they may be more research orientated and want to look at what's going on and make some hypothesis about it. I don't think the criticism is negative as long as we're aware that we're on the Bateson diagram and that we've taken a position somewhere.

References

Anderson, H., Goolishian, H., & Winderman, L. (1986). Problem determined systems: towards transformation in family therapy. *Journal of Strategic and Systemic Therapies*, 5(4): 1–13.

Bateson, G. (1980). *Mind and Nature. A Necessary Unity*. Toronto: Bantam Books.

Tomm, K. (1987a). Interventive interviewing: Part I. Strategizing as a fourth guideline for the therapist. *Family Process*, 26: 3–13.

Tomm, K. (1987b). Interventive interviewing: Part II. Reflexive questioning as a means to enable self healing. *Family Process*, 26: 153–183.

Tomm, K. (1988). Interventive interviewing: Part III. Intending to ask lineal, circular, reflexive or strategic questions? *Family Process*, 27: 1–15.

CHAPTER THREE

The road taken: a brief history of a dialogic family therapy

Ivan B. Inger (in collaboration with Jeri Inger)

On the road with David Campbell

We first met David Campbell in 1981, when we were involved in international interchanges with him. We were attracted to David's rendition of the Milan approach and his modest, low-key way of being. He has been enormously influential and collaborative to our work, offering a Maturanian, "third eye", which we have carried with us on our journey as we have teased out the nature and nuances of psychotherapies and, in particular, systemic psychotherapies.

In our contacts with David, we questioned the popular role of the family therapist as highly visible, central, and instrumental. We supported more facilitative, non-charismatic roles and interactions: more on the order of a Sullivanian (1953a,b) "participant–observer" and keeper of the continuity and coherence of conversations. Our bias has consistently been toward attending to the ethics of practice and the resulting local ethos created in the exchanges.

Current beliefs and practices

Family therapy, from our perspective, consists of complex bio-psycho-social exchanges in language and action that take place within socially defined and ritualised discourses. Therapeutic exchanges, regardless of how complexly packed their ideologies, or how linguistically elegant, emotionally appealing, or intellectually forceful, all take place within a local meaning-making context, even though different family therapy models extensively borrow metaphors and rhetorical devices from the sciences, philosophy, spiritual, and religious constructs. They have divided into self-defined cohorts, often using different language and subscribing to different principles and belief systems; they do not subscribe to a unified or consensually agreed upon body of knowledge or methods of procedure.

Our work has led us to rely on local beliefs, organised tautologies, unverified theoretical constructs, customs, rules, and habitual practices of social conduct (mores). Family therapeutic exchanges offer ways of creating and understanding meanings through dialogue, of healing ruptured emotional attachments and connections, and reconciling conflicting beliefs and actions. These exchanges can create conditions for the formation of relational couplings, which promote mutuality and reciprocity in a context that creates a safe-enough environment for sorting similarities and differences of meanings, beliefs, and ideologies. Family therapy can be a vehicle for the interplay between the content (the various issues, topics, positions, or questions dealt with in speech, discussion, or writing) and the process (a series of actions directed toward a particular aim or outcome) of interaction. This creates a third dialogue, one that is inclusive, empathic, and reflective, and can construct a "between" among participants. Such a "between" is an amalgamation of the new meanings arrived at as a result of reciprocal interactions of speaking and listening. Family therapy affords the opportunity to reconcile these sometimes antagonistic interests, both within and among individuals in their contexts of daily living.

The family therapist continuously uses herself/himself as a person embedded in the social milieu of the therapy within which she/he participates. The self of the therapist resides within that milieu. Family therapy practices deal primarily with beliefs, intentions, desires, and commitments, and operate within the parameters of subjectivity. Objectivity, as a compartmentalisation or special use of self, is more illusionary than operative fact (Inger & Inger, 1990). Family therapists are within the culture, not outside it.

De-centring the therapist

We encourage a shift away from the family therapist as *the* centrally responsible agent for therapy in favour of a shared and stratified responsibility among all participants in therapeutic exchanges. Thus, the therapist is consciously preoccupied with a de-centring position in the dialogue. Through encouraging shared responsibility (and ascendance of the family's ability to reorganise and re-create meaningful relationships), the balance of the hierarchy shifts in favour of family members. We believe that being-in-the-moment, helping co-construct the therapeutic context (Inger & Inger, 1990, 1994), is one way to encourage a relationship through the development of a safe-enough, authenticating, and trustworthy environment. Resilient family therapy outcomes depend on this process as much as on the content of the dialogic exchanges.

Our commitment is to understand the meanings, beliefs, attitudes, and prejudices of the family as they unfold and are expressed, and we take the inclusive/empathic position, which asks us to suspend judgements for the moment. We participate in tautological and metaphoric conversations. We work at the local level of thinking and acting, and use the family's language to focus on the interactions.

The de-centring therapist position begins with the initial contact with the family. We ask, "How can we be *useful to all* of you?" Framing the question in this way indicates that the family will make that determination, and we will not begin by dominating the conversation. It opens a space for family members to tell why they have come and what they want to accomplish. It also affords us the opportunity to witness each person's story, which positions family members to give their testimony and hear the testimony of others. Thus begins a process of talking and listening to one another and offers a way to give voice to novel ideas about what they are telling each other. It is their contributions to the dialogue that make it possible for the individual stories to become a coherently shared story, but not necessarily a homogeneous one. Our role in this dialogue is to continue to weave back and forth among the contributions of the individual members of the family. We stress the notion of meeting, not therapy, as there is not a consensus yet on why they are here or what they want to accomplish. This most often leads to differences in who wants to be here and what each person thinks is the reason(s) for being here.

A brief example: the power dilemma.

Recently, a family, consisting of adult children, a mother and stepfather, came for an initial meeting. The mother had called to make the appointment and indicated they had been having conflicts for years and needed to sort them out.

At the beginning of the meeting, after introductions, the oldest daughter announced she was here to deliver a letter and leave. The therapist asked other family members if they knew of this ahead of time. All said no. The daughter was asked why the surprise element. She responded,

"I don't care what they think."

"Why?" asked the therapist?

She responded, "None of them care about me or have ever cared about me."

The therapist then asked, "Do you care about them?"

Her response: "I wouldn't be here if I didn't."

The therapist reflected, "So you don't care and you do care?"

She replied, "Both."

The therapist asked rhetorically, "So that is why you are staying?"

The therapist then turned to the family and asked, "Does anyone care about her?"

They all responded that they did. She began to cry. The therapist then asked, "Who in the family could show her caring?"

All froze. The therapist asked, "Is there anyone you want to care for you at this moment?"

She replied, "My fucking mother and father."

The therapist queried whether this was her biological mother and her stepfather.

"Did you mean him?" asked the therapist.

"Hell no, not him. He's the cause of all this. All of them have taken to him and rejected me and my father."

There are many choice points in the first few minutes for the therapist. In this case, the choices were whether to let the daughter read the letter and leave, to let the other siblings have a voice, to use the initial power of the therapist to influence where the conversation would go. The therapist already made an intervention by asking the family if they knew about this letter and whether this was a surprise or not, rather than its contents. This was a conscious choice, because the therapist's intent was to be inclusive and open the door for others, so this power move on the part of the sister would not prevail. The intent was to slow down the conversation, which started out explosively. The use of power here was for the purpose of making it safe for the sister to remain after her threatening introduction. The therapist made a further intervention by opening up the conversation about "caring", using the word the daughter already used in the negative and then the positive. Her "both . . . and" response about caring signalled to the therapist that she would probably stay. This semantic intervention was designed to help the conversation move away from a threat toward a dialogue about the relationships that might be driving the sister to make such a bold bid for attention.

Often, the first few minutes of an initial interview are crucial in determining whether or not there is likely to be a successful therapy. That is why the therapist must be prepared to be the calming influence, the voice of compassion and safety, but with a firmness that indicates a confidence and a familiarity with the problems at hand.

The stepfather became enraged and started yelling. The therapist asked the family, "Is this usual?'

"Happens all the time," a brother said.

He stood up, went over to his sister, and gave her a tissue to wipe her eyes. He turned to the family and said, "See, this is what always happens. She wants and gets attention, and the rest of us suffer. No more. I'm fed up with this."

The therapist mused, "I am a stranger in this conversation, but I am wondering if this is your usual way of loving one another or is this unique to this moment? I'd like to know so I can figure out how to participate with you."

Mother pipes up, "It's usual all right. We do love each other, but we sure don't know how the hell to show it."

Daughter: "That's because you only love him, so the rest of us have to fight over what's left over."

From that point on, the letter was dropped and the family took up the question of love, being left out, how to appeal to one another's compassion and interest, how to show it, and whether or not that would be possible.

The therapist, in this situation, used a nuanced form of power to present opposing ideas and feelings to open space for the family to talk about their dilemmas in ways they have not been used to that might offer them ways out of their dilemma of repetitiveness and redundancy. These are initial de-centring acts that allow the therapist to participate in novel ways, rather than as referee, interpreter, or controller of conversation and emotion.

The "how" of de-centring

De-centring the therapist is a multi-partial position that opens dialogic space for the family to explore and reflect on their interactions and not privilege the views or biases of the therapist. The therapist is free to disagree with the family's views and to offer contradictory ideas, but all are offered in a non-confronting, non-authoritarian, non-judgemental manner. The de-centring therapist's disagreements must be vocalised and formulated as hypotheses and opinions, not unquestioned expertise.

We have developed ideas for guiding our actions as de-centring therapists and to concentrate on the *how* of social exchanges. This position helps co-construct a way of interacting that is different from the one the family typically employs (Inger & Inger, 1990). It is, admittedly, an inductive process that can initially create confusion and uncertainty. By offering novel ways of thinking and feeling about their "problems" and "dilemmas", the family is offered a potentially different interactional repertoire. In the first instance, this can be confusing, provoking negative thoughts and emotions among family members that they might have avoided or not considered.

Taking a position as a de-centring therapist (Inger & Inger, 1990, 1994) requires the therapist to begin orientating awareness to how he perceives the other(s) in the present, and how he thinks, feels, and anticipates what is about to occur in the ensuing interactions. Buber (1965) coined the phrase, "bending toward the other". This is a way of "realizing" the other in his particular existence, even the encompassing of him, so that the situations common to him and oneself are experienced from his, the other's, end (Buber, 1965, p. 23). The de-centring position involves accepting what is being said by others and attending to the other from the imagined perspective of the other. Accomplishing that perspective constitutes an act of inclusion which can be defined as exploring what the other is experiencing, feeling, intending, thinking, and believing, while simultaneously retaining one's own set of beliefs, feelings, etc. Acts of inclusion require suspending judgement (conclusions) and imagining how the other wants to be received (understood). Also, awareness of the other's experience of what is transpiring in the moment is part of the initial process of engagement.

As one moves within a dialogic perspective, the de-centring therapist engages in asking questions that are orientated toward helping the family clarify, among themselves and with the therapist, the meanings they attribute to one another, the differences and similarities they experience in the dialogue, and what values they place on what they say and hear from others. The focus is on the family's renditions and ability to speak and hear one another in new and different ways.

Being in dialogue from a de-centring position, therapists observe their own thoughts and feelings, and anticipate new and different thoughts and feelings that occur as a result of interacting with the family. This requires the therapist to observe recurrent patterns of thoughts and feelings that surface and formulate reactions with the family as they become solidified within the therapist's awareness. This act is one of using dialogue as a realising function by formulating questions to the family about what the therapist is experiencing and how that is congruent, antagonistic, or neutral for family members. In this position, the therapist asks the family for feedback, accepts that feedback, and continues to explore the same subject in a mode of curiosity. The de-centring therapist maintains this attitude of "bending toward" the family's views, emphasising language that has the potential for positively connoting those views.

Tripartite roles and functions

We weave and move among three, sometimes conflicting, at times complementary, roles and functional perspectives, depending on what and how the family presents to us. These fall into the categories of management, counselling, and psychotherapy.

Management functions

The management function involves helping to create a safe-enough environment within and beyond the meeting with the family. We attempt to ensure that they understand the scope and limits of our meetings, and have an idea of our intentions. For some families, our management role is central to their reasons for seeking therapy, and this form of interaction can take up the bulk of the encounters with them. The therapist cannot move out of that role if safety and daily living crises remain dominant in their lives.

Counselling functions

The second function is that of counselling, a role that reflects an attempt to assist the family in solving or dis-solving particular problems. This function includes helping as mediators, giving feedback, and opening up new avenues of thought and action for the family to discuss and try.

Psychotherapeutic functions

The third function is a psychotherapeutic one in which we help to create novelty in the way the family thinks and acts toward one another, rather than continuing to interact in repetitive and redundant ways. In this role, we perform the function of expanding the family repertoire about their significant and problematic differences. Sometimes, we suggest ideas that are confusing, antagonistic, and not readily understandable, in order to create possible new scenarios of as-yet-not-considered alternatives to the way they have been thinking, feeling, and interacting. We often take the position of inclusion and empathy as a way of helping to create a dialogic perspective in which the family can explore new thoughts, feelings, and actions. This role allows the therapist more latitude in operating from a de-centring position.

The meta-process

Regardless of the role we take with the family, the meta-context we strive for is one of a safe-enough dialogic space which includes being careful witnesses to the family as individuals and as a collective, who, through their contributions, give testimony to their pain and suffering. We see our participation as respectful, compassionate witnesses to the private world they live in. It is our obligation to make sure that all members of the family can be heard in their own voice. As Friedman states,

> Entering the private perceptual world of the other and temporarily living in the other's life suggests empathy in the narrower sense of losing one's own ground, whereas communicating one's sensings of the person's world with fresh and unfrightened eyes and checking as to the accuracy of one's sensing, suggests inclusion, which remains on its own side of the dialogue even while swinging over to the other. (Friedman, 1985, pp. 199–200)

We had some disagreements about the hierarchical role of the trainer and consultant during the training programmes we co-led with David and Ros Draper (Inger, 1998). Their position was that the trainers had responsibility for the format and implementation of goals for the exchange. Our position was that we should begin with an "open space" to be filled in by the participants and we, as organisers, were not responsible for promoting particular "content" for the participants. We struggled with these differences throughout the workshops. Looking back on this experience together, David Campbell had shifted toward a more egalitarian perspective regarding the role of the family therapist, and we shifted toward his nuanced leadership position regarding training and consultation. We continued to discuss the ramifications of how therapists, trainers, and consultants organise themselves and take positions depending on the contextual requirements they face. Both ways of thinking and acting have merits in different training, consultative, and therapeutic contexts. It was not "one size fits all". We agreed with David that the difficulties of being in these various roles centred on how we conceptualised our roles, positioned ourselves, and performed them. The task was to continuously reflect about their appropriateness at the time and in the place we invoked them.

Together, we spent much time discussing the ramifications and consequences of acts of overt and covert power. We agreed that power, in one form or another, is immanent in social exchanges, and that covert power could be as influential as overt acts of power. David Campbell and Ros Draper were more comfortable in leadership roles than we were. There were many discussions with all the participants about issues of hierarchy, power, and influence. David Campbell notes, "My own view is that therapists must commit themselves to an 'ethic of dialogue'. In other words, ethical positions are socially constructed through an exchange of dialogue" (Campbell, 2003, p. 21).

We were in agreement that, although manifest in quite different ways, central to each of our work has been a commitment to immersion in dialogue. For us, psychotherapy is,

> . . . a way of being in the world of relationships, not a set of applied techniques. It reflects a commitment to the process of conversation, not the content or outcome of that conversation. It represents an attitude of give and take, for all participants, while maintaining respect for different positions. It requires reflection upon the consequences of actions of all participants in dialogue. Responsibility for the genuiness or authenticity of dialogue is part of the dialogue itself, not a special characteristic of a given person. (Inger, 1993, p. 301)

Our framework invites the therapist to hold on to simultaneous (often competing or antagonistic) meanings: one's own and that of others. Authenticating dialogue comes from held positions that are revised and reconstructed in dialogue, and then carried beyond the context of psychotherapy. If the therapist and client use these reconstructions beyond the therapy context, then change can be continuous, becoming part of their repertoire in different contexts outside the therapy room.

David Campbell continued his work on de-centring the therapist in favour of the ascendance of the family's ability to re-create meaningful relationships. As he said,

> I am more interested, today, to observe the way the therapist creates . . . the 'therapeutic context' . . . and I frequently ask myself such questions as: Does the relationship at this moment seem sufficiently therapeutic, i.e., is everyone in the room . . . safe and able to trust . . . (Campbell, 1997)

His work represented a movement away from charismatic, instrumental roles of the therapist toward those who practise with an attitude of humility and self-reflection in the pursuit of therapeutic discourse: "I am convinced the purpose of therapy is to allow the family to explore new possible meanings until the problems lose their original meaning" (Campbell, 1997).

David Campbell spent his career promoting the therapist, consultant, and supervisor role as one that legitimises the beliefs of those participating in dialogue.

Comments on future developments

The family therapy field has gone through many phases and periods of heightened and enthusiastic effort, all of which have contributed to the different ways of thinking and practising the trade. We have witnessed and been part of the breakaway from the psychoanalytic movement, scientism and instrumentalism, constructivism and social constructionism as foundational beliefs, conversationalism and collaboration, philo-socio-political versions of therapy, to the present, in which evidence-based efforts are more prominent.

In spite of the many studies that promote manualised, laboratory-developed methods of therapy, countervailing perspectives have continued to be more persuasive for us. Beginning with Strupp, Fox, and Lessler (1969), Duncan and Moynihan (1994), Stubbs and Bozarth (1994), Bohart and Tallman (1996), Silverman (1996), Bohart and Greenberg (1997), Bozarth (1997), Shapiro and Shapiro (1982), Wampold (2001), and others, these analyses have promoted the "common factors theory" of psychotherapy. These researchers have concluded that therapists of all theoretical persuasions are successful to the extent that they promote trustworthy relationships and involve the clients in the construction of the experience. They claim that interventive techniques play a minuscule part in the outcome of psychotherapies. These and other researchers have concluded that the "active client" determines outcome, not the therapist. Furthermore, these researchers conclude that the main variable for success from the client's perspective is the active support of the therapist, who provides a safe environment and uses the client's frame of reference in participating in the dialogue. Finally, these researchers have found that by providing a safe place, the clients can explore and experience new ways of expression and new ways to relate to others (Silverman, 1996).

Seligman (1994) and Imel and Wampold (2008) suggest that the common factors across therapeutic practices account for success or failure of therapies. That leads back to the conduct of the self of the therapist as critically important. It is this idea that could bring together the disparate views and practices that divide us. Theory, ideology, territoriality, and the like serve divisive purposes. The commonalities among the different persuasions, on the other hand, could lead to a unified set of principles of practice and conduct. To that end, we might have to co-construct a consensus about what counts in our efforts to help relieve the pain and suffering of others. We could testify among ourselves to the cost of continued competition and lack of courage to come together to face the inefficiencies, redundancies, and power issues that divide us.

The future of the family therapy movement lies in whether we can heal ourselves from the isolation, competitive spirit, rigidly held stances, and fear of the other. The future could take us to consilience (Wilson, 1998), if we could embrace a common sense of purpose (mission), goals, roles, and best practices, no matter where they take us or whose ideas ostensibly belong to whom.

David Campbell and Marianne Grønbæk, in their book, *Taking Positions in the Organization* (2006), provide ideas about how organisations and their members can change to reconcile closely held positions through the process of transcendent positioning. The way to move away from polarisation is through a third way. As Harré says in his Foreword to the book, "A transcendent position, from which the contradictory positions can be viewed, makes possible the transformation of first-order dialogue into second-order dialectic, facilitating radical repositionings" (Harré, 2006).

Can we, as a diverse, competitive, and fractured field, take heed from our own ideas and, for example, embrace some of these principles and apply them to our own field? Do we practice what we preach, do we walk the walk and talk the talk that we promote to others—our clientele (students, clients, consultees, etc.)? Do we promote second-order practices, but act in first-order ways among ourselves? We do not need more or new techniques. We need more coherence among ourselves and our beliefs and practices, so that we can better serve those who rely on us for authenticity, resilience, and trustworthiness.

Conclusion

Over the years, we have become more and more comfortable with having less and less ambition to change others and more and more ambition to help others grapple with their own ideas, dilemmas, and conflicts until they arrive at constructive ways to be with one another. We have stopped biting off more than we can chew. We have become convinced that promoting our means to our ends confuses others and helps them retrench, rather than re-think or re-do.

Our personal and professional relationship with David Campbell stands out as a beacon of light showing the way to collaborative, co-operative ways of being in personal, teaching, consulting, and therapeutic conversations, ways that contravene the tendency toward authority, control, hubris, and closed or template-driven thinking about ourselves and others.

References

Bohart, A. C., & Greenberg, L. S. (Eds.) (1997). *Empathy Reconsidered: New Directions in Psychotherapy.* Washington, DC: American Psychological Association.

Bohart, A. C., & Tallman, K. (1996) The active client: therapy as self-help. *Journal of Humanistic Psychology, 36:* 7–30.

Bozarth, J. D. (1997). Empathy from the framework of client-centered theory and the Rogerian hypothesis. In: A. Bohart & L. Greenberg (Eds.), *Empathy Reconsidered: New Directions in Psychotherapy* (pp. 81–102. Washington, DC: American Psychological Association.

Buber, M. (1948). *Israel and the World. Essays in a Time of Crisis.* New York: Schoken Books.

Buber, M. (1965). *I and Thou.* New York: Charles Scribner's Sons.

Campbell, D. (1997). The other side of the story: the client's experience of therapy. In: R. K. Papadopoulos & J. Byng-Hall (Eds.), *Multiple Voices: Narrative in Systemic Family Psychotherapy* (pp. 15–40). London, Duckworth.

Campbell, D. (2003). Mutiny and the bounty: the place of Milan ideas today. *Australia and New Zealand Journal of Family Therapy*, 24(1): 15–25.

Campbell, D., & Grønbæk, M. (2006). *Taking Positions in the Organization.* London: Karnac.

Duncan, B. L., & Moynihan, D. W. (1994). Intentional utilization of the client's frame of reference. *Psychotherapy, 31*: 294–301.

Friedman, M. (1985). *The Healing Dialogue in Psychotherapy.* New York: Jason Aronson.

Harré, A. (2006). *Taking Positions in Organizations.* London: Karnac.

Imel, Z., & Wampold, B. (2008). The importance of treatment and the science of common factors in psychotherapy. *Handbook of Counseling Psychology* (4th edn) (pp. 249–262). Hobokon, NJ: John Wiley and Sons.

Inger, I. (1993). A dialogic perspective for family therapy: the contributions of Martin Buber and Gregory Bateson. *Journal of Family Therapy,* 15: 293–314.

Inger, I. (1998). A cross-cultural consultation and training exchange. *Journal of Systemic Therapies,* 1(17): 45–61.

Inger, I., & Inger, J. (1990). *Co-Constructing Therapeutic Conversations: A Consultation of Restraint.* London: Karnac.

Inger, I., & Inger, J. (1994). *Creating an Ethical Position in Family Therapy.* London: Karnac.

Seligman, M. (1994). *What You Can Change and What You Can't.* New York: Knopf.

Shapiro, D., & Shapiro, D. (1982). Meta-analysis of comparative therapy outcome studies: a replication and refinement. *Psychological Bulletin,* 92: 581–604.

Silverman, W. (1996). Cookbooks, manuals, and paint-by-numbers: psychotherapy in the 1980s. *Journal of Humanistic Psychology, 33*(2): 207–346.

Strupp, H. H., Fox, R. E., & Lessler, K. (1969). *Patients View their Psychotherapy.* Baltimore, MD: Johns Hopkins University Press.

Stubbs, J. P., & Bozarth, J. D. (1994). The dodo bird revisited: a qualitative study of psychotherapy efficacy research. *Applied and Preventive Psychology*, 3: 109–120.

Sullivan, H. S. (1953a). *Conceptions of Modern Psychiatry*. New York: W. W. Norton.

Sullivan, H. S. (1953b). *The Interpersonal Theory of Psychiatry*. New York: W. W. Norton.

Wampold, B. E. (2001). *The Great Psychotherapy Debate: Models, Method and Findings*. Mahwah, NJ: Lawrence Erlbaum.

Wilson, E. O. (1998). *Consilience: The Unity of Knowledge*. New York: Alfred A. Knopf.

PART II
SUPERVISION AND TRAINING

CHAPTER FOUR

Passions and positions: selfhood in supervision

Gwyn Daniel

S upervision, unlike therapy, tends mostly to be discussed and written about in instrumental language. Yet, as all of us who practise it know, it is an intensely emotional business and one which calls up and challenges our sense of selfhood just as intensely as does therapy. In this chapter, I will explore some ways of understanding what we bring of ourselves to the process of systemic supervision, how it affects, and is affected by, the relational contexts in which we supervise and, in particular, how our ideas about ourselves are constructed and performed in relation to the theoretical positions we take when we supervise, consult to, or train clinicians. A tradition of openness and spontaneity, as well as an aspiration to be transparent and collaborative, has been part of the cultural practice of systemic supervision for years, so finding ways to reflect on our "supervisory selves" should be well embedded in our practice; however, two factors make me think that it is a subject that would repay closer inspection. One is that not a great deal has been written about the self of the supervisor compared, for instance, with the self of the therapist (Flaskas & Perlesz, 1996). The other is that, in the training of systemic supervisors, it is so often in the domain of selfhood that the most creative and exciting "learning edges" are to be found. These learning edges often cluster around the personal resonances arising from the question of power, authority, and expertise, which raise fresh dilemmas not always provoked in the journey to become a therapist. While David Campbell never wrote specifically on this subject, I have found many of his ideas invaluable in support of my own forays and I use them to frame this paper.

In editing papers and writing about processes in supervision (Burck & Daniel, 2010), I have been struck by the fact that, while the "second order supervisor" deconstructs assumptions about power, expertise, and authority, and engages with multiple ways of enhancing the learning and creativity of supervisees, the complex emotional processes enacted between them have received less attention. Psychoanalytic approaches have often been called upon to explain group processes (Clarke & Rowan, 2009; Granville, 2010). In exploring the emotional processes in systemic supervision, Spellman and Smith (2010) have looked at the reverberations for groups of intense emotions arising as a result of episodes in the clinical work, and Dutta (2010) has connected such an episode to both the personal narrative and the theoretical stance of the supervisor.

When the preoccupation of the supervisor is with managing his or her relationship to the power dynamic, some dilemmas might arise. Just as therapists might position themselves as "non-expert" and non-directive collaborators in the lives of their clients, likewise trainers and supervisors might try hard to identify themselves as co-participants in learning, and attempt to de-centre their own position as a means of divesting themselves of universalising power. But what does this aspiration for "de-centring" mean in practice? Conversations with trainees on supervision courses often reveal deep anxieties about the power and authority of the supervisor, with fears that the supervisor's beliefs and ideas, if expressed too robustly, will inevitably prevail over the supervisee's. This sometimes leads to new supervisors restricting the range of self-expression available to them. However, as I will argue in this chapter, being more overt about our personhood as supervisors might, paradoxically, contribute to a de-centring of our position and to an easing of anxieties about our power.

At some level, of course, the power of the supervisor is inescapable (Brecelj-Kobe & Trampuz, 2010). It resides in the clinical or managerial responsibilities we hold, our evaluative role within training institutions, or, even if none of these factors obtain, in the perceived expertise and experience that leads a clinician to choose a particular supervisor. The very act of paying someone to be one's supervisor invests that person with the status of having something valuable to offer. From the perspective of the supervisee, the person of the supervisor is likely to be crucial. Many of us look back on our own experiences of training with powerful memories of the authority and charisma of our supervisors, or, indeed, with negative feelings about an insensitive, ineffective, or dictatorial supervisor. How we think about "charisma", or other ways of exerting influence, is invariably something we are much more aware of when others have power or influence over us than when we ourselves are in positions of power. The disowning of our own power and influence might not, therefore, do justice in any way to the actual experience of those we supervise. So, perhaps if we try too hard to find a position that accords with a postmodern stance of de-centring the supervisor, or, worse, start to believe we *have* found it, we might lose the imperative to find out how we are seen by others and miss out on the possibilities for harnessing this kind of feedback.

This question of ability and willingness to elicit and respond to feedback is crucial in considering the extent to which there is a correlation between the theoretical model espoused and the way that a therapist, supervisor, or trainer projects his or her authority. For example, many renowned presenters interact with their audiences in ways that run directly counter to what they are teaching. Those most committed to a collaborative approach to therapy might be least amenable to being challenged or questioned, and some show a distinct unwillingness to engage in dialogue or respond to feedback. This could be connected to an arrogant assumption of expertise, a messianic belief in their "message", or perhaps to a lack of confidence in their ability to engage with feedback. The ability to build ideas by responding to unexpected or discordant feedback, to develop, critique, or elaborate ideas in the moment and through dialogue, is a much rarer gift and requires a particular mindset which is linked to, but goes well beyond, a theoretical position. Cecchin, for example, had the ability when presenting his work to enact Bateson's (1973) concept of feedback as "news of difference" and to bring his thinking to life as he responded to feedback. So, I maintain, did David Campbell, although in later years he couched this in dialogic rather than cybernetic language. David's intense interest in expanding theoretical ideas, in developing their potential for practice, in questioning and interacting with others, rather than fixing a therapeutic "product" that could become ring-fenced as "his own", all lent themselves to a genuinely dialogic style. As he wrote in "Family therapy and beyond: where is the Milan systemic approach today?" (1999),

> When I come to write an article like this, I can only produce a monologue based on my own ideology and as a result I simply cannot take my ideas too seriously. What I do take seriously however is the process of dialogue. My own ideas become interesting to me when I see them making some impact on another person and then I become interested in the way I am influenced by that other person.

Although I never received clinical supervision from David, I can testify from training and other contexts to the effect of being part of that expansive dialogic process.

David has explained his preference for curiosity through descriptions of his experience as a younger child with a brother five years older, and of his need to keep asking questions to challenge the certainties of those positions in his family that seemed to have already been laid down in advance and that, therefore, constrained what he could do (Campbell & Grønbæk, 2006).

There are fascinating and fruitful links to be made between our life experiences, our narratives of self, and the theoretical positions we adopt as therapists and supervisors (Daniel, Eyres, Majid, & Williams, 2010), and, given this, there are, inevitably, tensions and contradictions in the ways that we, as supervisors, actually perform our roles in relation to the theoretical models we aspire to. While our aim, in my view, should always be to enhance and expand the personal, relational, and professional resources and stances available to the therapists we supervise, we also act from certain ideas about who *we* are, about aspects of ourselves that we choose to highlight or keep hidden, and from the repertoire of relational activities that we feel comfortable with. When we perform authority, curiosity, "decentring", or other supervisory stances, we are acting in accordance with our own precepts about how we should be, but also in a dialogue with what we can call our own "hinterland", cultural, social, gendered, and familial, which gives meaning to, or is challenged by, these activities.

I often find myself wondering whether, for the postmodern supervisor, there is such a thing as an ideal "postmodern personality". What might this consist of? One might see this as someone who always maintained a fascination, an attraction, and a living curiosity about the idiosyncrasies of others' lives, who "de-centres" him or herself, or, as we have seen above, someone who is always able to take a new position in response to feedback, whose own beliefs and principles are perhaps less in evidence, because they are more interested in expanding and deconstructing those of others.

A postmodern supervisor could, as Ungar (2006) suggests, be one who takes on different identities in relation to the exigencies of the evolving dialogue with the supervisee; in his words, "depending on what the supervisee wants or needs". This assumes an ease in holding to multiple identities. However, the selfhood of the trainer/supervisor is much more than a conduit for gauging the needs of supervisees, or a tool for being attuned to the emotional climate of the group, or for reflecting on processes of mirroring between families and therapeutic teams. All these attributes can be seen, as Ungar's prescription suggests, as rather instrumental ways of thinking about selfhood. It is interesting that in relation to systemic therapy, subjectivity is so often conflated with that rather strange expression "Use of self", as if there were an instrumental core self available to be used or not used. And what happens, in this "use of self" process to the bossiness, the passions, and the certainties, the enthusiastic exuberance that can take flight and inspire us to hold forth at length about our own ideas? Or, conversely, our fears, conflict avoidance, or confusion? How do we manage our relationship to our own strongly held views? While supervisors have passions, egos, fears, vulnerabilities, etc., what we learn most from the literature are the more instrumental "doings" as systemic supervisors set up creative contexts for learning and develop ingenious exercises to enhance the reflexivity of their supervisees, while their own thoughts and feelings might remain less accessible.

Clearly, supervisors are more likely to describe those activities that can be generalised in order to be of use to other supervisors, but the attempt to de-centre the supervisor's position can ignore the likelihood that those at the receiving end might tell a different tale. They might talk about how inspiring, exciting, or wonderful their individual supervisor is, how much they learnt from watching them at work, or how lucky they were to have had this particular person. Or negative versions of all of these. Thus, supervisors cannot exactly de-centre themselves simply by developing creative structures for equal participation in the learning process. In fact, the more they do so, the more they might underline their expertise. For example, a supervisor's use of reflexive questioning to explore an aspect of a trainee's development might simultaneously enable the trainee to reflect from new contexts on their own practice, but also lead to an increased admiration for the skill of the supervisor in asking these questions, an admiration that can increase a sense of the distance between them. The supervisor has expertise to be owned and shared, and, in my opinion, the emphasis, rather than worrying about too much about constraining this expertise, should be on how supervisors and supervisees can interact to bring out the best in all of them.

In this context, I find that the question of which of our strongly held beliefs we make overt and defend as supervisors and which we treat as more "contingent" and place alongside other equally valid ideas is a crucial area for supervisors to explore. Some strongly held beliefs, such as a commitment to justice, to high ethical standards of clinical practice, openness to the views of others, a belief in dialogue and inclusion, are easy to incorporate in the ethos of a systemic supervision group. Other beliefs have a more challenging edge, where we can be less sure about their place and the extent to which we feel entitled to state them. Our attitudes to religion might be one of these (Mason, 2012) or those with a strongly political component.

When I was doing my clinical training in the 1980s, my dissertation was on feminism, which, although I had felt it as a core part of my identity for many years, seemed in that context to be quite a risky topic. David Campbell supervised this work, and I remember him describing feminism as a "passionate position" and that I rejected this description because I felt that he reduced it only to a personal dimension—one of many possible passionate positions—when I located it, as I still do, as a fundamental stance relating to justice and a critique of the power practices that underlie gender transactions. He was enormously helpful to me in developing my ideas, but, in his David way, enacted a caution around what these ideas might mean to him. I was aware of a covert wish on my part that he would somehow "get it"!

As a supervisor now, I might have a profile as someone who promotes thinking about gender (Burck & Daniel, 1995). My experiences and responses are, thus, influenced as much by how others see me as by my own views about gender and their evolution over the years. Indeed, the climate within which we debate issues of gender has changed since I did my training. I am interested in all the complex intersections between gender, class, culture, and sexuality. As well as applying feminism to gender relations, I find feminist critiques very helpful in addressing other forms of power imbalance, stereotyping, and "othering" (Daniel, 2012). Sometimes I am surprised to find that, compared with ten years ago, when a group and I are preparing for a session, I might not have included gender in my hypothesising at all. On other occasions, I find that I become so fixated on gender patterns in family or wider system interactions that I find it hard to question something that seems so utterly obvious and familiar. In the first case, I usually find that other members of the group will supply the missing ideas about gender. In the second, I will usually reflect out loud as to why I am so passionately attached to a gender hypothesis in this case, opening up a space for others to challenge me. The key issue for me is that the more strongly held and certain are the positions we hold, the more incumbent on us it is to be accountable for these views and to place them within the wider contexts in which our personal and professional worlds intersect.

Returning to David Campbell's statement that "my own ideas become interesting to me when I see them making some impact on another person", what are helpful ways for supervisors to be free to enjoy their expertise, share their passions, and, at the same time, demonstrate that they are alert to feedback and, as a result, engaged in their own learning process, a process which informs and changes them as much as it promotes supervisee's learning?

I will highlight three ways of thinking about this, all of them areas where David Campbell made a contribution.

Contexts and reflexivity

As Boscolo and Cecchin frequently commented in their account of the development of second order positions (personal communications), a new context, that of inviting trainees to observe their therapy, created observer positions which brought forth an intense interest in the beliefs and ideas and activities of the therapist, rather than what the family were doing. This challenged the therapists to reflect on their own influence and the "realities" they were creating as they worked. In the same way, the development of training courses for supervisors has created new contexts for the supervisor's ideas, position, influence, and persona to be subject to similar explorations and reflections.

This is not only because the process of learning to supervise inevitably brings forth for the trainees intensely personal resonances about power, authority, responsibility, and evaluating others, but also because it creates similar perturbations and new reflections for the tutors. The Tavistock Clinic's Systemic Supervision course, set up by David Campbell, Caroline Lindsey, and Charlotte Burck, involved, for many years, the live supervision of live supervision. David Campbell and Charlotte Burck wrote,

> trainee supervisors are often very interested to explore with tutors how they themselves use personal resonances in a reflexive way and they ask questions about how and on what occasions a supervisor can use self disclosure. This has pushed our own development as supervisors and trainers in clarifying use of self in the supervisory tasks. (Burck & Campbell, 2002, p. 67)

One course component includes members observing experienced supervisors as they carry out live supervision in clinical training, and then interviewing the group and the supervisor about their experience of this process. Having, on several occasions, been one of the supervisors observed and interviewed, I know how powerful it is to be questioned about why we do what we do and, even more importantly, to have the experience of seeing ourselves as the supervisee and others in the group see us. Being live supervised in a training context involves what is usually an intense experience of being the object of scrutiny, under the normalising gaze of the supervisor. While the supervisor is, of course, under the gaze of the supervisees, this is likely to be at a more covert level and is often less available for feedback. I have been very interested in finding ways to expand ideas about self and relational reflexivity (Burnham, 2005) to think about how therapists or supervisors, especially when they are in positions of power or of cultural dominance, can see themselves through the eyes of others (Daniel, 2012) This has been inspired for me both by feminist theories (Benjamin, 1988, 1998; Butler, 1990, 2004) and by what the post-colonial theorist, Edward Said, wrote in another context, which is about the experience of exile. He wrote about the moral importance of looking at our own home with an exile's eye; this means that the more settled and secure our position is, the more incumbent on us it is to find a way to view ourselves as a potentially vulnerable and displaced "other" (Said, 1993). I take this idea into the supervisory context to explore ways of reversing the gaze. As well as having outside observers, there are many ways we can do this; expecting to have to give an account of our interventions is a crucial one. This can, however, easily be forgotten when we and our supervisees seem to be agreed on our theoretical orientation and when we feel we have shared sense of direction. Part of my work has been to provide systemic supervision to groups of psychiatric registrars in psychoanalytic training, a context in which I am in a clear theoretical minority. I have, thus, an obvious context in which to experience all my own most cherished and passionately held systemic ideas as contingent and of having to be accountable for them. I have to observe my own ideas, stances, and interventions as they are seen by a group who have a very different tradition of thinking and acting in therapy. I have, paradoxically, found this liberating, since it diminishes the risk of the supervisor's ideas being automatically privileged (Daniel, Eyres, Majid, & Williams, 2010).

Social constructionist and dialogic ideas

Can the ideas of the self as located within relational contexts create opportunities for supervisors to be confident about expressing themselves more freely? A quotation from Shotter was used by David Campbell (2000) in *The Socially Constructed Organization*:

> I act not simply "out of" my own plans and desires . . . but also in some sense "in to" the opportunities offered me to act. . . . And my action in being thus situated takes on an ethical or moral quality. I cannot just relate myself to others around me as I myself please. The relationship is ours, not just mine, and in performing within it I must proceed with the expectation that you will intervene in some way if I go "wrong". (Shotter, 1993, p. 144)

This both highlights the ethics of a relational view and also, somewhat optimistically, assumes that feedback loops will operate between people to constrain utterances that do not fit or are oppressive, wounding, or inappropriate. At some level, it is, of course, true that feedback operates in this way, but we need also to take into account the way power operates and how very subtle or indirect might be the attempts on the part of supervisees to give feedback so that their signals might, indeed, not be picked up. Such counter-narratives might be very slow to appear, if ever. Therefore, it has to be continually worked at. How can we think about the way supervision groups can influence supervisors and be alert to the diverse and very creative, if opaque, ways that supervisees might have of offering such interventions? Addressing this with supervisees through questions such as "What would be all the different ways you might find as a group and as individuals of letting me know you didn't agree with me?" is helpful here.

This connects both to Mason's ideas about relational risk taking (Mason, 2005) and to another "David Campbellism" which has stuck with me. It was addressed to a trainee therapist, but I have found it invaluable as a supervisor: "How can you find a way of taking a clear position and showing at the same time that your position is open to being challenged?" (Campbell, personal communication, 2004).

However, how amenable we are to feedback from supervisees about their experience of our supervision, how alert we are to group process, how adept we are at giving an account of ourselves and the ideas behind our interventions generally bears a strong relationship to many contexts in our lives which influence our feelings of security about our identity so that we can withstand criticism, stay with confusion, or acknowledge that we have made a mess of things. While trainee supervisors can really struggle with feeling confident enough or secure enough in their identity to invite feedback, it is important not to think of this only as a linear process: that is, as we become more experienced and confident, we become more confident about our skills in eliciting feedback. As in therapy, as we start to feel that we have been able to embrace a new self-narrative, to discover alternative ways of being in the world and in relationships, we also become aware of contexts that can be powerful enough to pull us back into ways we do not want to be. This can happen in relation to a particularly challenging therapeutic session or to conflict within a group, both occasions for supervisors to feel anxious or incompetent. I find it helpful on such occasions to pay attention to what messages I am giving myself about how I should be acting and to be alert to any tendencies to try to impose a way of thinking.

Here, I find ideas from dialogism helpful, in particular Bakhtin's ideas about dialogue only happening when each party is coming to the conversation free from the control of the other, or does not try to fuse the other into "one-ness".

So, for me, that would mean being very alert to the edge between, on the one hand, taking a clear and passionate position about matters of relevance to the lives of supervisees and clients and, on the other, drifting too far into the rhetorical devices of persuasion, so that openings for dialogue and disagreement are closed down. This is, of course, much more likely to happen with those beliefs we feel passionate about, but, in my experience, the more overt we are about them and the contexts they emerge from, the more possibilities there are for others to take a different stance and, thus, expand and enhance the dialogic process.

Regarding the self of the supervisor, Bakhtin's idea of double-voiced dialogue—words that contain within themselves a possible dialogue even before the actual dialogue has taken place—is extremely useful. In an individual's utterances, the voices of social groups and institutions can be heard. Even when another is not present, there is hidden dialogicality, since "The second interlocutor is invisibly present" (1981). Rober (2005) has used this concept of hidden dialogicality to develop ideas about the therapist's inner conversation. This, it seems to me, can be helpfully expanded to encompass more than the emotional reactions evoked in the therapist/supervisor. It also includes the way we "evaluate ourselves from the standpoint of others" (Bakhtin, 1990), both in the sense of the social and cultural "voices" present in the dialogue and in the immediacy of our interactions.

Boyd (2010) has used Bakhtin's concept of ventriloquation—the process through which one speaks through the voices of others—to evoke past and imagined audiences to supervisees' speech acts, enabling increased manoeuvrability as clinicians and team members. For supervisors, too, these processes can be helpfully explored. What is the imagined audience for the supervisor? Is it family, current relationships, cultural allegiances, professional identity, institutional context? To give a personal example, I frequently find myself reflecting on whether I am being "too much" of a presence in a supervision group or not active and authoritative enough, not having enough of an effect. In reflecting on why it might be this polarity that organises me, I might become aware of my critical reaction to my father's tendency to hold forth in a didactic and rather self-indulgent way, coupled with a fear that I might be rather similar, since I, too, enjoy "holding forth". This tendency will, however, be played out in relation to another inner voice which both rebels against and is somewhat organised by my mother's subtle but powerful messages not to get "above myself". All of these responses are embedded in a nexus of class, gender, and cultural influences from past and present.

Sometimes the voice that organises us is that of the inner "ideal supervisor", which might, according to our theoretical model, be interrogating us along the lines of: "Am I attending to the emotions in this session? Do people feel safe enough? Are they challenged enough? Am I avoiding anything? Am I being inclusive/collaborative enough? Am I attending enough to gender/cultural difference? Does my feedback to this person address their own style of learning?" When running workshops for supervisors, I have found it helpful to access ideas about our inner "ideal supervisor" and consider how they might organise us. Then, when we explore the dilemmas that particular supervisors are experiencing with their groups or with individual supervisees, we look both at how the "ideal supervisor" supports or constrains us and think about the personal resonances of these constructs for the supervisor. The supervisor can use these reflections to find a new position in relation to their dilemmas, and this can be fed back implicitly or explicitly into the supervision group.

Positioning

This has been one of the most popular and persuasive ideas in recent years to find resonance for systemic therapists and supervisors alike, due in large measure to David Campbell's innovative work in applying these ideas, originally developed by Harré and Langenhove (1999) to consultation with organisations (Campbell & Grønbæk, 2006). In supervision, the complementary poles of "expert supervisor who knows everything" and "supervisee who knows very little" are readily available as positions to step into and can easily be maintained by all participants, despite our declaratory postures and best intentions. The concept of semantic polarities provides us with experiential tools to unsettle rigid complementarity and move into more fluid and nuanced framing of such polarities as "the supervisor has the expertise for supervisees to learn from" at one pole, and "supervisor and supervisee both have equal amounts of expertise" at the other. Inviting a supervision group or a group of trainee supervisors to take positions along this continuum and to reflect on how their positions have evolved and might evolve over time can be useful, especially if the supervisor, too, takes positions. If, as can happen, there is a stampede for the centre ground, then people can be invited to reflect on what their experience might be at each end of the continuum and what contexts would invite them into either end.

As a reflexive tool for supervisors and supervisees to explore their struggles, their ideas about selfhood and professional dilemmas, positioning theory can be invaluable, especially as it invites us so well into the interactional; in other words, what each participant actively does to maintain the others' position. There is always a risk, however, of reducing these ideas to overly simplistic formulas. For example, virtually everything that goes on in families or groups can be described, blandly, as positioning or being positioned, and the notion of semantic polarities might reify positions too much by delineating a continuum that might suggest an imperative to move between positions within this framework. However, another of David Campbell's helpful mantras in working with difficult processes within supervision groups, which would help us militate against any such tendency towards the facile, is to "just keep talking about the complexities of the relationship" (personal communication, 2004). He always made it clear that it is the conversations about positioning, rather than the positioning itself, that invites creative thinking.

One way to connect the two ideas—of semantic polarities and of complexity—is to think about how we might individually occupy positions which can embrace complexity and then become aware of those times when these more nuanced positions can be whittled down to a unitary and rigid stance in the face of positions taken by others. The degree to which I will take a complex, exploratory, multi-faceted approach to gender, or a more rigid, essentialising one, will be governed by the dialogic context and the positions taken by others. In my practice as a systemic therapist and clinical supervisor, I aim to move quite flexibly between the semantic polarities of, for example, optimism and hopefulness/caution and pessimism about change, conveying a sense of hopefulness and optimism about a family's desire for, and commitment to, change while simultaneously holding another, perhaps more sceptical, position about less positive outlooks, less benign intentions, or about the losses involved in change. In the context of supervising the group of psychoanalytic specialist psychiatric registrars, whose training led them to be alert for resistance or beneath-the-surface negative communications, I found this latter position so thoroughly occupied by the majority that I temporarily abandoned the complexity of my own position and found myself starting to take a position and occupy territory generally reserved exclusively for "Pollyanna"—the girl from the novel of the same name (Porter, 1913), who was relentlessly and naïvely optimistic about everything. Noticing that I was starting to do this and commenting on it led not only to a discussion of our mutual interactions, but also to a fascinating conversation about how we chose the therapeutic modalities we did and what were the personal influences on our theoretical preferences.

In considering the selfhood of supervisors, I became very interested in how supervisors deal with experiences of shame and failure, especially in the public arena of working with groups. In a chapter co-written with Grania Clarke and Reena Nath (Daniel, Clarke, and Nath, 2010), I explored the experience of feeling a failure as a supervisor. Writing about this involved holding a unitary position for longer than felt comfortable; that is, choosing to highlight all the things I thought I got wrong. This self-imposed constraint in one aspect of a much more complex whole was, however, a very helpful learning experience, because it made me aware of how utterly compelling was the narrative of professional pride and success and how very much I yearned to highlight the things I had done well! However, for supervisors to be able to acknowledge their mistakes and reflect on how they had come to make them is an absolutely invaluable experience, no matter how ghastly it might feel at the time. It is a powerful demonstration of learning from feedback, of developing the confidence to find new positions and recover from mistakes, which can, paradoxically, enhance our own confidence in taking risks and, thus, help us to feel freer to act spontaneously.

Conclusion

In this chapter, I have drawn upon a number of ideas that I have found especially helpful in reflecting on the selfhood of supervisors.

Those which have influenced systemic therapists and supervisors in recent years have included narrative, dialogic, and positioning theories, but I have found feminist and post-colonial theories invaluable in sharpening our understanding of how we might be seen in the eyes of others, the bedrock of an ethical position as well as a systemic approach. Here, although cybernetic theories have been somewhat neglected in our field in recent years, the idea of feedback is crucial. Focusing on feedback—how it operates, how it situates actor and acted upon, and how systems can be put in place for enhancing it—is, it seems to me, crucial for the exploration of the self of the supervisor. Freedom to be spontaneous, to take risks, to be passionate, and, above all, to make mistakes involves a concomitant responsibility to be accountable and to keep finding ways to elicit and respond to feedback. This includes being highly attuned to what constraints there will be on the giving or receiving of feedback, an attunement that is a crucial accompaniment to the inevitable power dynamics of the supervisory process. In the current professional climate, where therapists are engaged in carrying out manualised interventions and where model compliance might, therefore, have an increasingly high priority in supervision, there is the risk that the skill of eliciting and acting on feedback becomes less valued or important.

A final comment on the ways that supervisors and trainers both rely on and can be surprised by the feedback they receive comes from the context in which this chapter was conceived, the *Festschrift* for David Campbell. Many of the ideas I and others discussed have been nurtured within his arc of influence and disseminated by him with exquisite clarity, but, with typical modesty, David expressed astonishment that this was so, not having had, by definition, the experience of his own effect and influence. So, in order to know this, we have to rely on feedback. Most of us will have to find other ways of acquiring this awareness other than by attending our own Festschrift, and yet David's response to the event was powerful proof of his wisdom in being mostly excited by learning how his ideas have, over the years, resonated with others.

References

Bakhtin, M. (1981). *The Dialogical Imagination*. Austin, TX: University of Texas Press.

Bakhtin, M. (1990). Author and hero in aesthetic activity. In: M. Holmquist & V. Lipianov (Eds.), *Art and Answerability: Early Philosophical Essays*. Austin, TX: University of Texas Press.

Bateson, G. (1973). *Steps to an Ecology of Mind*. St Albans: Paladin.

Benjamin, J. (1988). *The Bonds of Love*. New York: Pantheon.

Benjamin, J. (1998). *Shadow of the Other*. London: Routledge.

Brecelj-Kobe, M., & Trampuz, D. (2010). The power of delegated authority and how to deal with it. In: C. Burck & G. Daniel (Eds.), *Mirrors and Reflections; Processes of Systemic Supervision* (pp. 267–285). London: Karnac.

Boyd, E. (2010). "Voice entitlement" narratives in supervision: cultural and gendered influences in speaking and dilemmas in practice. In: C. Burck & G. Daniel (Eds.), *Mirrors and Reflections; Processes of Systemic Supervision* (pp. 203–223). London: Karnac.

Burck, C., & Campbell, D. (2002). Training systemic supervisors: multi-levelled learning. In: D Campbell & B. Mason (Eds.), *Perspectives on Supervision* (pp. 59–80). London: Karnac.

Burck, C., & Daniel, G. (1995). *Gender and Family Therapy*. London: Karnac.

Burck, C., & Daniel, G. (Eds.) (2010). *Mirrors and Reflections: Processes of Systemic Supervision*. London: Karnac.

Burnham, J. (2005). Relational reflexivity: a tool for socially constructing therapeutic relationships. In: C. Flaskas, B. Mason, & A. Perlesz (Eds.), *The Space Between* (pp. 1–17). London: Karnac.

Butler, J. (1990). *Gender Trouble*. London: Routledge.

Butler, J. (2004). *Undoing Gender*. London: Routledge.

Campbell, D. (1999). Family therapy and beyond: where is the Milan systemic approach today? *Child Psychology and Psychiatry*, 4(2): 76–84.

Campbell, D. (2000). *The Socially Constructed Organization*. London: Karnac.

Campbell, D., & Grønbæk, M. (2006). *Taking Positions in the Organization*. London: Karnac.

Clarke, G., & Rowan, A. (2009). Looking again at the team dimension in systemic psychotherapy: is attending to group process a critical context for practice? *Journal of Family Therapy, 31*: 85–107.

Daniel, G. (2012). With an exile's eye: towards a position of cultural reflexivity (with help from feminism). In: I.-B. Krause (Ed.), *Culture and Reflexivity in Systemic Psychotherapy: Mutual Perspectives* (pp.91–113). London: Karnac.

Daniel, G. Clarke, G., & Nath, R. (2010). Times past, present and future: revisiting a supervision group experience. In: C. Burck & G. Daniel

(Eds.), *Mirrors and Reflections; Processes of Systemic Supervision* (pp. 163–183). London: Karnac.

Daniel, G., Eyres, M., Majid, S., & Williams, A. (2010). Systemic ideas in action: supervising across a theoretical divide. In: C. Burck & G. Daniel (Eds.), *Mirrors and Reflections; Processes of Systemic Supervision* (pp. 359–380). London: Karnac.

Dutta, S. (2010). Exploring emotions: a critical incident for a supervisor. In: C. Burck & G. Daniel (Eds.), *Mirrors and Reflections; Processes of Systemic Supervision* (pp. 103–119). London: Karnac.

Flaskas, C., & Perlesz, A. (Eds.) (1996). *The Therapeutic Relationship in Systemic Therapy*. London: Karnac.

Granville, J. (2010). Minding the group: group process, group analytic ideas, and systemic supervision—companionable or uneasy bedfellows? In: C. Burck & G. Daniel (Eds.), *Mirrors and Reflections: Processes of Systemic Supervision* (pp. 123–139). London: Karnac.

Harré, R., & Langenhove, L. V. (1999). *Positioning Theory*. Oxford: Blackwell.

Mason, B. (2005). Relational risk taking and the therapeutic relationship. In: C. Flaskas, B. Mason, & A. Perlesz (Eds.), *The Space Between* (pp. 157–170). London: Karnac.

Mason, B. (2012). The personal and the professional: core beliefs and the construction of bridges across difference. In: I.-B. Krause (Ed.), *Culture and Reflexivity in Systemic Psychotherapy: Mutual Perspectives* (pp. 163–179). London: Karnac.

Porter, E. H. (1913). *Pollyana*. Boston: L C Page.

Rober, P. (2005). The therapist's self in dialogical family therapy: some ideas about not-knowing and the therapist's inner conversation. *Family Process, 44*: 477–495.

Said, E. (1993). *Culture and Imperialism*. London: Vintage.

Shotter, J. (1993). *Conversational Realities: Constructing Life Through Language*. London: Sage.

Spellman, D., & Smith, G. (2010). Three gasps behind the screen: exploring discourses of emotion in systemic supervision. In: C. Burck & G. Daniel (Eds.), *Mirrors and Reflections: Processes of Systemic Supervision* (pp. 79–102). London: Karnac.

Ungar, M. (2006). Practicing as a postmodern supervisor. *Journal of Marital and Family Therapy, 32*(1): 59–71.

CHAPTER FIVE

From Milan to the Tavistock: the influence of systemic training on child and adolescent psychiatrists

Caroline Lindsey and Rob Senior

Introduction

This chapter will describe a study involving child and adolescent psychiatric trainees that explored the impact of systemic training on their child psychiatric practice as consultants. The training aims to provide them with the knowledge and skills to practise systemically with the families and wider systems that they will encounter in their work as future consultants. The course has evolved over fifteen years, influenced by the changing contexts of both psychiatric and systemic training

Applied systemic practice

Applied systemic practice may be defined as the systemic understanding and skills that we bring to our work when we are not acting formally as systemic family therapists, but are making a clinical, managerial, training, or supervisory intervention in another role or setting. We consider that an important aspect of applied systemic practice is the introduction of systemic ideas to professionals from other disciplines to enhance their practice in their fields. Before family therapy was established as a profession, family therapy training was seen as adding an important therapeutic paradigm to core professional skills. We suggest there is still a need to offer systemic skills to people who are not going to become career family therapists. There are those who do formal family therapy training while intending to remain in their core profession. However, for many professionals, such as social workers and doctors, there is a benefit in having the training tailor-made for the professional role in which they will apply the systemic training. One example was a course for general practitioners and primary health care professionals (Launer, 2002; Launer & Lindsey 1997) at the Tavistock Clinic. This systemic training, "Narrative-based Primary Care", enabled GPs and primary healthcare professionals to give meaning to their "five minute" consultations, using skills based on an understanding of context, curiosity, circularity, and co-created conversations. The subsequent dissemination of this course among general practitioners, consultants, and medical educators around the country demonstrates the contribution that systemic thinking can make to medical practice more generally.

Systemic training for child and adolescent psychiatrists

The original idea was to provide child psychiatrists with the tools to work as family therapists. In time, it became just as important that they learnt to apply systemic ideas to their daily work, irrespective of the task, be it working with a family, prescribing medication, consulting to the network, or preparation of a court report. The key concepts of systemic thinking taught included understanding the meaning of context, the use of curiosity and self-reflexivity, the distinction between linear and circular thinking, and interventive interviewing (Tomm, 1988). The training offered an alternative form of thinking and interviewing to the psychiatric model. As trainers, while we did not explicitly use the language, we addressed Campbell-inspired polarities between biological psychiatrist and systemic psychotherapist, between positivist scientist and postmodern constructivist, between certainty and doubt. We adopted a "both . . . and" perspective on the issues of psychiatric diagnosis, history taking, and intervention. Future psychiatrists need to be able to talk several "languages", including "evidence-based" practice, have the capacity to put objectivity in parentheses, in Maturana's terms, and to hold a "not knowing" position alongside their learnt knowledge (Maturana, 1988). This entails the ability to tolerate uncertainty and cultivating curiosity in the interest of developing a co-created understanding in conversation with families and others.

Since many were already familiar with psychodynamic thinking, which informed their interviewing style, we found ourselves making clear distinctions from the psychodynamic model to enable the trainees to learn to practise systemically. As we became less defensive of the systemic model and conceived it as overarching, there was less room for conflict. We became flexible, finding it helpful, for example, to incorporate psychodynamic thinking as hypotheses into our family work.

Live supervision in a team context was a unique experience for most trainees, providing a transparency not common in their other clinical practice. The use of reflecting teams took the process of openness and the achievement of multiple voices in a co-created therapeutic process a step further. As in other psychotherapeutic endeavours, we were confronting the pain and distress of the people who came to see us, finding ways to make meaning of it for them and for ourselves. Live supervision allowed the impact of the work on us as practitioners to be explored and used to enrich our work together.

There were multi-layered contexts for the course, relating to its organisation, its uni-disciplinary nature, and the separation of personal–professional development training from the supervisory role, and to the broader psychiatric training and practice.

The group, diverse in terms of age, gender, and ethnicity, was uni-disciplinary. This ran counter to family therapy training tradition. All our trainees were working in multi-disciplinary teams elsewhere and so would have been open to the challenge of assumptions and prejudices by other professionals. Multi-disciplinary training is valued for the opportunity it provides for exploring difference and capitalising on the strength this brings to learning.

The rationale for our decision, as trainers of both child psychiatrists and family therapists, was to ensure that child psychiatrists acquired systemic skills by having systemic training integrated into their psychiatric training. We knew that few would commit themselves to the professional family therapy training. Our systemic course was probably unique among psychiatric training schemes.

Further, we knew of instances where challenging and undermining beliefs were expressed about the "medical model" and psychiatric practice to psychiatrists in multi-disciplinary training designed for people intending to make systemic family therapy their chosen profession. This might create an unsafe learning environment for our psychiatric trainees. This was not the only story, of course; other psychiatrists found their medical expertise valued alongside the others in the group.

By contrast, training a group of child psychiatrists enabled us to hold in mind and to explore freely the integration of systemic ideas and practice with other aspects of the child psychiatric role and task. We could set the idea of diagnosis in the context of family relationships and the wider mental health system, and discuss the implications of making or not making a diagnosis. For example, with a child with obsessive–compulsive disorder (OCD), we worked with the family members around their relationship to the child and the OCD and its meaning for them, at the same time offering medication and cognitive–behavioural therapy, the effect of which was also thought about in terms of its meaning for them as a family. We could explore the influence of our medical and psychiatric beliefs and assumptions on thinking about the meaning of the difficulties which families presented. As trainers, we could both challenge the potentially pathologising aspects of the psychiatric model and find it helpful as one way of conceptualising and communicating about a problem.

This was a safe setting in which to explore these issues, free from a sense of a more fundamental challenge to the trainees' role as doctors. We do not know whether, on the other hand, they might sometimes have been constrained in their thinking by the power inequalities between us; could they disagree with the supervisor if he is also the medical director overseeing the whole psychiatric training?

Personal–professional development (PPD) is fundamental to family therapy training (Hildebrand, 1998). The PPD sessions entailed exploration of genograms, trigger families, and intra- and interpersonal issues raised by the family work. It also addressed issues of professional identity, power, responsibility, and authority. PPD raised a dilemma in that, as supervisors, we were also assessors for the child psychiatric training. It was important that our future assessment of their suitability to qualify as child psychiatrists was not influenced in their minds or in ours by a confusion of roles. It was essential to maintain the boundary of confidentiality around their personal discussions in PPD. By contrast with family therapy trainees, who come together weekly and work elsewhere, ours were participating in a full-time, 3–4 years' child psychiatric training together. To address these dilemmas and to safeguard our professional relationships, we asked a colleague systemic family therapist to provide PPD. This also added a third perspective to their experience. However, the arrangement created a challenge in the group when, as supervisors, we could not always understand the responses to particular clinical situations in terms of the trainees' personal experience. They sometimes chose to share the connections with us, or helped each other based on the understanding they had gained from the PPD sessions. We created other opportunities aside from the formal PPD to work on self-reflexivity together. A further issue was that some of our trainees were in psychoanalysis at the same time. This introduced a tension about the best place to explore personal family and professional identity issues. Despite these drawbacks, PPD remained central to developing self-reflexivity in a group context, to examine the fit between each trainee's self as a family member, as a professional with a family, and the connection between the two.

Another context was the Royal College of Psychiatrists' curriculum for training of child and adolescent psychiatrists in therapeutic modalities. In the past, trainees had been expected to learn a range of therapeutic modalities. In 1999, a revised curriculum viewed family systems therapy as a treatment modality alongside individual psychotherapy, behavioural, cognitive, and group therapy. They recommended basic experience in all modalities, basic competence in at least two areas, and encouragement to pursue specialist competence in one area. This fitted with our original ideas about the need for child psychiatrists to have family therapy training. In 2008, the competency-based curriculum (Royal College of Psychiatrists, 2008) for specialist training addressed training in psychological therapies using a skills-based approach, including many ideas that fit with the goals of systemic training. The therapist is expected to be a reflective practitioner, behaving respectfully and taking account of the power differentials in a therapeutic relationship. The therapist is responsible for maintaining boundaries, showing respect for others' contributions to a treatment package and being non-discriminatory. Three levels of competence comprise "under supervision", "competent" (the ability to work independently expected of a consultant), and "mastery" (the expertise to supervise, teach, and develop new ideas). The competent practitioner will be able to deliver therapy, plan and conduct therapy under supervision, plan and conduct an appropriate course of therapy in two of the four core modalities, and be able to use supervision. Theoretical knowledge and technical ability is expected and an emphasis on engagement. It goes some way to recognise the wider applicability of therapeutic skills in the clinical encounter. Thus, it supported the shift that we had made from offering family therapy training to also equipping trainees with a systemic lens to view the whole range of their work as child psychiatrists.

Managing the delivery of psychological treatment within a complex network of agencies is another requirement. Our course addressed this by working with networks under supervision and bringing cases from the workplace for consultation. Participants learnt consultation skills while reflecting upon their current work in context. Cronen and Pearce's theory of the "coordinated management of meaning" (Cronen, 1994) was invaluable in understanding the complexity and interrelatedness of the multiple contexts in which the child psychiatrist works.

The significance given to good therapeutic practice by the Royal College curriculum marks a change in attitude to the importance of therapeutic intervention since 1999. The Child Psychiatry Faculty did previously value acquiring therapeutic skills, but the emphasis on competent practice and self-reflexivity is new. It is also reflective of changing attitudes towards "talking therapies" within the mental health field and the outside world. This may mean that trainees taking our course now feel more authorised to do so than previously. In the past, having specific therapy training fitted the cultural expectations of the Tavistock. Now, they will be gaining the skills expected of the modern child and adolescent psychiatrist. Our training practice at the Tavistock, undervalued by the "orthodox" psychiatric school for years is now validated.

A further contextual change was represented by *New Ways of Working for Psychiatrists* (Royal College of Psychiatrists and the National Institute for Mental Health, 2005), which promoted best use of the skills, knowledge and experience of consultant psychiatrists by concentrating on service users with the most complex needs, acting as a consultant to multi-disciplinary teams, and "promoting distributed responsibility and leadership across teams to achieve a cultural shift in services". It invited a willingness to embrace change and to work flexibly with all stakeholders to achieve a "motivated workforce offering a high quality service". These ambitions are very systemic in their aspirations but involve a particular positioning of psychiatrists in the discourse about money, skill mix, and models of mental health. As psychiatrists, we had to consider how to position ourselves in relation to these changes in expectation in the external world and to help our trainees position themselves. As National Health Service (NHS) funding cuts target mental health services, we think the integration of psychiatric and systemic identities will provide survivor skills.

The contribution of systemic training to child psychiatric practice

In 2004, we decided to explore the effectiveness of the training from the perspective of our ex-trainees. Three or four trainees participate in the weekly half-day training, over a year, led by two consultant child and adolescent psychiatrists who are systemically trained. We invited thirteen male and female psychiatrists, most of whom were now consultants, to contribute. For reasons of confidentiality, no further details of the sample will be given. We designed a questionnaire to gain feedback about the effect of the training on the participants' current practice, curious to learn how they would rate, on a five-point scale, what we felt were the seven key components of the course (Table 1). In addition, we asked them to describe how these components had affected their daily practice as child and adolescent psychiatrists.

Results of the enquiry

The most popular components of the course were training in systemic interviewing, use of live supervision, training in a small peer group, and clinical work in a team. Teaching of the theoretical framework had more varied feedback. The trainees had relatively few opportunities to discuss their theory reading in seminars because of the time constraints of the course and its emphasis on clinical work. The use of

Table 1.   The following is a list of components of the training that we would like you to evaluate with regard to the effect they have had on the quality of your daily practice as a child and adolescent psychiatrist on a scale of 1–5, with 1 as not useful at all, and 5 as very relevant indeed.

On a scale of 1–5					
	1	2	3	4	5
1. Training in a small peer group of child and adolescent psychiatrists	–	–	–	4	9
2. Clinical work in a team	–	–	1	5	7
3. Use of live supervision	–	–	1	2	10
4. Use of video	–	1	4	6	2
5. Teaching of theoretical framework	–	1	2	4	6
6. Personal professional development	–	2	3	3	5
7. Training in systemic interviewing	–	–	1	1	11

video was less popular, largely because it was so difficult for the trainees to find time to review the tapes and, thus, make use of the material. When there were opportunities for video review in the group, it was seen as a useful learning exercise for developing skills and facilitative of work with the families. There was a more varied response to the personal professional development sessions, influenced in part by some trainees who found PPD in conflict with their analyses.

Training in systemic interviewing

Using the Milan method in a post-Milan form, informed by social constructionist and narrative ideas, we taught hypothesising, circularity, and the use of curiosity, both formally and, mainly, through role-play practice in the early stages of the course.

"Role play is very useful—I learn best when doing it myself."

We were open to discussions about alternative ways of conceptualising and intervening, but emphasised the need to practise the form of systemic interviewing which they had come to learn. Remaining neutral and curious and asking circular questions was a change from their usual way of working. Taking a non-interpretative stance, following feedback, and being sensitive to the use of language needed practice.With most groups there was a shift about half-way through the year, when they had developed the ability to conduct a systemic interview. The use of the reflecting team (Andersen, 1987) was seen as supportive of the development of these skills and enabled participation in the therapy by more team members in a "hands on" fashion. We had a pre-session discussion, mid-session break, and a post-session discussion, often using a reflecting team for the supervisory process. Our aim was that each trainee would work with at least two cases over the course of the year.

Feedback about the benefit of training in systemic interviewing was positive.

"This has been invaluable as a tool in my clinical skills sense."

and

"Very helpful—will continue to be relevant in varied work group setting and family work."

Its value in understanding the therapist's role and in becoming more confident about facilitating change was commented upon.

"I feel more confident now about ways of introducing change in family systems and my role in the room."

The need for ongoing supervision and practice to maintain the newly acquired skills was noted. Not everyone went on to work in settings that enabled their continuing family therapy practice.

"I've found this skill quite hard to hold on to and could do with further practice."

Use of live supervision

Most trainees had not had live supervision previously. Considerable anxiety was usually expressed about it initially. Feedback confirmed that live supervision was challenging but that the benefits to learning in terms of being empowered and confident outweighed this. The advantages of being able to respond differently to families at the time, rather than at a future session, were valued.

> "Though initially daunting—in the long term, not only was this a very empowering approach, but also enabled clinical difficulties to be tackled head on with direct help and support, e.g., how to confront parents who were behaving in an emotionally abusive fashion towards their son."

> "It helped build up confidence in one's own practice. Good to have immediate feedback/supervision."

Learning through observation was seen to be helpful. In order to focus on this, we asked different team members specifically to follow the process of therapy by observing members of the family or the therapist and recording key points.

> "Learn a lot watching other people."

> "Very helpful to note in detail reactions of family members and our own reactions to what went on in the room."

Supervision is a task that all child psychiatrists are asked to perform in their daily work. The experience of live supervision contributed to the trainees' development of this role, in addition to which we facilitated them in supervising each other as the course drew to an end.

> "The immediacy and honesty of the experience of live supervision has (both in front of and behind the screen) made me feel less daunted and more open about 'supervising' my own and others clinical work. I've still a long way to go with this!"

Training in a small peer group of child and adolescent psychiatrists

The comments about working in a small peer group supported our vision in establishing a uni-disciplinary training to integrate systemic thinking and practice with child psychiatric practice.

> "Most of our training is with colleagues from other disciplines, so this represented a unique opportunity and difference to think directly about a systemic approach to more speciality child psychiatric issues."

It also confirmed the advantage of being in a peer group for training purposes, which was, in some ways, less threatening than a multi-disciplinary group.

"This has advantages as a trainee at the Tavistock because it is within a peer group that we are familiar with and therefore feels comfortable."

It offered an opportunity to consider their roles and developing identities within a systemic framework of thought, which included exploration of beliefs, attitudes, and prejudices in relation to families and wider systems. We used reflecting teams for supervision and consultation and also for facilitating reflections on experiences of learning and training.

"Excellent opportunity to share, learn and think with peers about our roles, and the particularities of our previous training and future work as psychiatrists."

"Helped me feel clearer about my professional/discipline identity."

They enjoyed the chance to work together clinically, which was an almost unique experience within the training.

"The common background of previous clinical experience was a good base from which to learn together and also helped in translating what was learnt into practice."

Clinical work in a team

Working in a clinical team was new for some and not for others, influencing how they saw the experience.

"Very interesting to work clinically together as we didn't elsewhere in the clinic at the time."

And, by contrast,

"Most of my placements allowed for this so not unique to the systemic training but I feel that being experienced in working as a team is one of most relevant things in my daily practice."

They commented on the benefit of gaining multiple perspectives and the part team-working plays in the development of respectful listening.

> "Essential—more minds can be better than one in developing ideas about family. Learning to listen, respect colleagues' viewpoints etc."

The idea of the whole being greater than the sum of the parts was reflected in this comment on the ability to intervene more effectively in a team working together.

> "This enabled me to see the value of working in a team. It was helpful to be shown how the different perspectives of team members could be brought together in order to move things forward. Also a sense of how anxiety in relation to complex clinical situations can be thought about within a team has stayed with me."

Teaching of theoretical framework

At the start of the course, there was a more intensive overview of the theoretical framework, and thereafter, a slot for a reading seminar based on selected papers. We relied on trainees' ability to make time for this reading. Despite the limitations, it seemed as if the reading complemented the course in a helpful way.

> "I think this training really allowed me to become familiar with theory and I use it as a model to understand families."

> "Essential to understand context. Definitely helps me in my work and in communicating with some other disciplines here."

Personal professional development (PPD)

PPD produced a wider range of responses than the other course components. For some, it was a creative space to explore their responses to families and their own beliefs about family life and the wider professional issues.

> "This has been enormously helpful. It's helped shape a sense of professional identity and thinking about my own and other families has provided a personal perspective with which to approach the work."

For others, it seemed intrusive and replicative of work being done in their own psychoanalyses.

"I did not find this as useful or accessible for me as the clinical work. Perhaps because I was concurrently gaining largely from thinking about many of these issues (more privately) in my own personal analysis. I was uncomfortable with sharing such personal information in a work setting."

Specific work around wider cultural contextual issues was unique to PPD work.

"Allowed one to become clearer about trigger families and how to manage although being in analysis I think meant there was not much added to personal issues I'd already explored. But helpful in exploring issues of race, gender, religion."

PPD, more than any other aspect of the course, brought forth the interpersonal dynamics of the group, often, but not always, productively.

"This had strengths and weaknesses. The positive aspect was spending time thinking about how one's family history correlated with one's practice, the difficulty was being dependent on one's peers in rather a vulnerable situation."

Use of video

The use of video always carries anxiety in the initial stages of training.

"Some initial concern this may 'inhibit' families not a significant problem."

It was a useful tool to learn to use in a range of ways.

"Although not used often in my daily practice I was glad to have experience so I feel able to use it when relevant."

"Useful for supervision purposes and record keeping and seeing oneself (can be painful but helpful!) and tracking processes."

We also asked three further questions and gave space for any further comments or feedback.

*Do you consider that you have maintained your systemic/family
therapy practice?*

With the exception of one trainee who went on to work as an individual psychoanalytic psychotherapist, the others saw themselves as
applying systemic thinking and practice in their work, using words
such as essential, integral, invaluable, and incorporated.

> "Yes, I see this as an essential part of my training and practice"

> "It has given me another method of clinical working—plus, perhaps
> more importantly for me at present, is part of my thinking now in
> work across systems and groups of all kinds."

Not everyone was practising as a family therapist, but they were
using it as part of their daily work.

> "I use the skills in assessment interviews and in follow-up family
> interviews. Also useful in team meetings!"

> "I may still use interviewing techniques, still try to see all of the family
> and still make assessment of wider network that supports the
> family / child I see."

Some, who wanted to practise more formally, were finding it hard
to access or create a systemic team and supervision.

Have you developed your systemic/family therapy practice?

Six of the trainees were continuing to participate actively in family
therapy workshops or supervision; some had aspirations for the
future or had conflicting work or personal priorities.

*Are there ways in which you would like to continue to
develop your systemic practice?*

Three trainees wanted to do a formal training at some point; most felt
the need for further opportunities to maintain their practice

Other comments or feedback

Of the twelve comments about the training, ten were extremely positive; the other two were feedback concerning the questionnaire. There

were two comments that focused on how systemic thinking and practice complements psychiatric practice.

"I think systemic thinking and application are essential to good psychiatric practice. It is a useful framework that complements the essential bio-psychosocial model that we have been trained to use. It is helpful in formulation of cases and identifying interventions. Less useful when considering diagnosis or risk but certainly useful for risk management."

"Systems theory counterbalances the influence that years of medical training have on the way we think. Helps us think of the many things that may explain the problems as opposed to the *one* thing (as we are trained to do in medicine)."

The course was seen as benefiting all aspects of the child psychiatrist's work, which also related in the trainee's mind to the specific focus of the course on their needs.

"It can't be overestimated how important this was as a training experience. The families we saw were representative of the kind of families I continue to see and the way of thinking and working remains highly applicable in many areas not just clinical work. It's rare to be offered a therapeutic training that specifically focuses on the needs of trainee child psychiatrists."

It was seen as providing tools to tackle the most challenging aspects of their work.

". . . some of most useful experiences in it was how to handle and defuse difficult scenarios with families or engage difficult families without reaching an impasse. Allowed me to develop flexibility and creativity in these situations."

The timing of the course within the overall training was often debated.

"I think it is an essential part of our training as child psychiatrists and the earlier the better. One year is a good period I feel as we have opportunities to expand in the training."

The opportunity for skills development in a group setting was probably unique in the training.

"This training was one of the most valuable experiences in my training, for its intense focus on interviewing skills and interactions and the opportunity to share experiences and learn together."

Discussion

The feedback was gratifying. It demonstrates what can be achieved in half a day over a year. The trainees are to some extent a self-selected group, highly motivated to participate and engage with the training. Even so, it is noteworthy that the training had contributed to their abilities to carry out their daily work as consultants. This was an important aim of the course, believing as we did that a systemic approach could enhance psychiatric practice and protect professionals from burn-out. It is known that this arises, among other factors, from lone working; systemic practice cannot happen in isolation. The course remains popular and relevant.

From our enquiries, it seems that many child psychiatry training schemes aim to have opportunities for trainees to achieve Level 2 in family therapy if they wish (i.e., competent to practise and to provide supervision on simple cases). This is probably an outcome of the competency-based curriculum described earlier. The pressures arising from that curriculum also mean that few trainees today will have time to do a masters training.

Building on Burton and Launer's (2003) work in teaching systemic supervision skills to medical educators, there has been an introduction of systemic skills or "conversations inviting change" in general practice and some local undergraduate medical trainings. Adult psychiatric trainings have shown little interest in developing systemic components to their training despite the evidence base for family intervention in many adult mental health predicaments. This is disappointing. If consultant psychiatrists have not been introduced to systemic ideas during their training they will be unlikely to value those ideas in their teams later. The relatively greater attention paid, for example, to pharmacological interventions perhaps inevitably tips the balance in that direction. Again, we would want to take a "both . . . and" position. Systemic ideas are potentially of enormous value when addressing pressing issues of treatment concordance or compliance, as well as addressing the contribution of the "family" to recovery.

As supervisors, this training was a constantly stimulating and challenging experience. We were in several roles at once. In general family therapy training, one is still also a psychiatrist, but this is not in the foreground. In this setting, we were conscious of the need to "perform" both as a systemic practitioner and also as a competent psychiatrist. There was a pressure that arose from the wish to ensure each trainee had a satisfying clinical experience of systemic practice and gained skills in a short period of time. We struggled with the balance of discussion and practice. Reflecting team work was a helpful tool, since it could address both and was appreciated by the families.

There were multi-layered contexts to this training. As supervisors, we had constantly to think about where we were positioning ourselves within these contexts and to help our trainees to see how the contexts were shaping the meaning of what we were doing together. We were working in the NHS; some families chose to come, others were sent, and others wanted the expert opinion they believed the Tavistock Clinic could provide. This was a local Child and Adolescent Mental Health Service (CAMHS), so the cases we saw reflected the range of child mental health and family problems.

We took a systemic approach to all our work, but always held a "both . . . and" position in relation to our thinking and practice. This allowed us, for example, where appropriate, to consider the use of psychoactive medication or cognitive–behavioural therapy (CBT) approaches within our overall systemic intervention. There might be disagreements as to the best way forward, when some felt that a child should be seen individually for psychotherapy or CBT rather than in the family group. At other times, the issues centred on the importance of seeing the case from a biological perspective diagnostically. Tension was created in cases where there seemed to be child protection concerns, arising out the question of whether and when to act and its impact on the therapeutic process. We tried to resolve these issues by holding on to our overarching systemic view, maintaining curiosity and asking questions, while offering what seemed to be the most appropriate intervention.

We had half a day to offer the best learning experience for our trainees while offering a clinical service. This meant that time had to be found outside the course when families needed urgent help. We faced the dilemma of how and whether to explain to families that the team behind the screen were all psychiatrists and debated how letters should be signed, since we were intending to work as family therapists! As trainers, we were offering a new way of thinking and working to professionals who were already highly trained in their chosen profession. The process of relearning the ways they talked to families was anxiety provoking and challenging at times, although rewarding ultimately. Their seniority meant that they learnt quickly, but were also capable of critique based on their other knowledge, which pushed us as supervisors to clarify and extend our own understanding.

As systemic family therapy trainers, we find the feedback from our course has significance for training generally, especially in the light of developments in CAMHS services, particularly the government's commitment to "Improving Access to Psychological Therapies for Children and Young People" (www.iapt.nhs.uk). Family therapy might be a specific modality in future waves of IAPT implementation, but we would suggest that all therapists aiming to contribute to this initiative should be able to work in a systemically informed way. This could entail offering other specific interventions, like CBT or Webster–Stratton parent training from within a systemic framework. Family therapists can make this way of working accessible through their brief practice and training courses, supervision opportunities, and day workshops for all practitioners working with children, young people, and their families. In this way, practitioners, irrespective of profession, can potentially think and practise systemically, even though few will become family therapists. The important components of our post-Milan systemic training which can be replicated are that it is brief, focused, and skills based, contextualised, clinical, involving teamwork with both a clear theoretical model and interviewing method and the integration of other relevant models and interventions. It builds on the expertise and knowledge of the participants, enabling the integration of personal beliefs, meaning-making, and methods within an overarching reflective systemic framework.

Dedication

Caroline Lindsey

This chapter is dedicated to the memory of my friend and colleague, David Campbell. I met David in a role-play at the Tavistock–Ackerman Clinic Family Therapy Conference in 1974. We became colleagues in the family therapy team in the Department for Children and Parents at the Tavistock Clinic in 1976. Our work together continued for the next thirty years, and, even during David's last illness, we shared our enthusiasm for jointly newly found skills in EMDR and talked about working together. I believe that the subject matter of this chapter—training child and adolescent psychiatrists in systemic practice—would have been dear to David's heart, since he was interested in making systemic thinking accessible to professionals working in diverse contexts. The clue to his ability to influence people from so many different fields lay in his non-judgemental attitude towards everyone he met, his compassionate and facilitating style, and sense of humour, which enabled him to teach and communicate with the very many people whose lives he influenced for the good. David's capacity for therapeutic optimism was part of the secret of his success as a therapist, trainer, and supervisor. His love of ideas and enthusiasm for seeking another way to think about an issue led to his great creativity and innovation in the field of systemic practice. His ability to take on new ideas was nowhere more evident than in his response to the introduction of the Milan Group's model of systemic family therapy. This had a far-reaching effect on our work at the Tavistock Clinic (Cecchin, 1987; Selvini-Palazzoli, Boscolo, Cecchin, & Prata, 1980). Together with Ros Draper, David and I established the Milan Systemic Training in Family Therapy. Later, David, Charlotte Burck, and I set up a systemic training for supervisors at the Tavistock Clinic and had the privilege to present our work at the Milan School for Systemic Therapy 25th Anniversary Conference. The key concepts and practices introduced during that period remain the foundation underpinning the systemic training offered to child and adolescent psychiatric trainees in the Tavistock training scheme.

Acknowledgements

We would like to express our appreciation to our colleague, Charlotte Burck, for her contribution to the success of the training.

References

Andersen, T. (1987). The reflecting team: dialogue and metadialogue. *Family Process*, 26: 415–428.

Burton, J., & Launer, J. (Eds.) (2003). *Supervision and Support in Primary Care*. Oxford: Radcliffe.

Cecchin, G. (1987). Hypothesising, circularity and neutrality revisited: an invitation to curiosity. *Family Process, 26*: 405–413.

Cronen, V. E. (1994). *Coordinated Management of Meaning: Practical Theory for the Contradictions of Everyday Life*. Norwood, NJ: Ablex

Hildebrand, J. (1998). *Bridging the Gap. A Training Module in Personal and Professional Development*. London: Karnac.

Launer, J. (2002). *Narrative-based Primary Care: A Practical Guide*. Oxford: Radcliffe Medical Press.

Launer, J., & Lindsey, C. (1997). Training for systemic general practice: a new approach from the Tavistock Clinic. *British Journal of General Practice, 47*: 453–456.

Maturana, H. (1988). The search for objectivity or the quest for a compelling argument. *The Irish Journal of Psychology, 9*: 25–82.

Royal College of Psychiatrists (2008). *A Competency Based Curriculum for Specialist Training in Psychiatry: Specialist Module in Child and Adolescent Psychiatry*.

Royal College of Psychiatrists and the National Institute for Mental Health in England Supported by the Changing Workforce Programme (2005). *New Ways of Working for Psychiatrists: Enhancing Effective, Personcentred Services through New Ways of Working in Multidisciplinary and Multi-agency Contexts. Final Report 'But not the End of the Story'*.

Selvini-Palazzoli, M., Boscolo, L., Cecchin, G., & Prata, G. (1980). Hypothesising, circularity and neutrality: three guidelines for the conductor of the session. *Family Process, 19*: 3–12.

Tomm, K. (1988). Interventive interviewing: Part III. Intending to ask lineal, circular, strategic or reflexive questions? *Family Process, 27*: 1–15.

CHAPTER SIX

Towards a culture of contribution in supervisory practice: some thoughts about the position of the supervisor

Barry Mason

Introduction

In this chapter I wish to develop some previous thinking (Mason, 2005, 2010, 2011) about the expertise of systemic supervisors. In particular, I wish to highlight the need for supervisors to extend their range of feedback to supervisees, and some ways in which this might be done. At the same time, while I acknowledge that the term "culture of contribution" suggests a two-way process, consistent with Wiener's (1948) notion of mutual influence, I will (not least because of the need to keep the chapter to a certain length), particularly concentrate on the practice contribution of the supervisor. Further, I will illustrate some of my thinking with reference to the results of a small survey addressing feedback with members of a cohort of the advanced training programme in supervision at the Institute of Family Therapy in London.

Expertise

Almost twenty years ago (Mason, 1993, p. 192), I offered another way of looking at the "not knowing position" (Anderson & Goolishian,

1992). While I found the not-knowing position extremely helpful, not least in the intrinsic respect for the contribution that clients could make to the therapeutic process, I also felt that it was in danger of marginalising the expertise of the professionals. I suggested that professionals take a position of "authoritative doubt" (Mason, 1993, 2005), the ownership of expertise in the context of uncertainty, and that we should not throw the baby out with the bathwater.

A year earlier, Cade (1992) had written an article entitled "I am an unashamed expert". In Batesonian (1979) terms it was an excellent example of "serious play"—in this case, tongue in cheek with serious intent. It was a comment on what Cade saw as a desperate rush by some family therapists (taking a position of not knowing) to disown anything that might resemble an identity of expert. Further challenges to the not-knowing position have ensued, among them Rober (1999, 2005) in relation to the self of the therapist and his or her inner conversations and to the extent that they become outer; Larner (2000) and the holding of a position of "knowing not to know"; Bertrando and Arcelloni (2006), and Bertrando (2007), who believe that therapy is a dialogue and that part of that dialogue is the contribution of the therapist's thinking in addition to the expertise of the clients. In some ways, I prefer the notion of not getting into premature certainty (Stewart, Valentine, & Amundsen, 1991) to the not-knowing position, because it implies (for me, at least) that the clinician or supervisor is clearly approaching therapy and supervision with some ideas that they think might be useful without marginalising the clients' perspectives. Anderson (2007) has acknowledged that, "I've not always been good at articulating what not-knowing is". However, my sense (from watching the work of many clinical teams and supervisors—mainly, but not exclusively, in a training context) is that there can still be a reluctance to own therapeutic and supervisory expertise in the form of "this is what I am thinking"; "these are some suggestions I have" (Mason, 2005, 2010). In essence, what we are doing when we do this is that we are taking a position, not as truth, but as part of a contribution to developing useful ways of moving forward. As David Campbell has written in his contribution to the introduction of *Taking Positions in the Organization* (Campbell & Grønbæk, 2006), he might say what he feels "and invite others to take a position in relation to mine" (p. 6). David and Marianne kindly invited me to make a speech at the book launch of *Taking Positions in the Organization*. In praising the book's elegance, clarity, and usefulness, I ended my speech by saying that I was struck by a culture which seemed to be embedded in the book. I called it a culture of contribution. This comprises (a) curiosity, and (b) the giving of our thinking and ideas. Each aspect exists in a relationship of mutual influence.

As positioning theory (Langenhove & Harre, 1999) has become more influential in the systemic field, so practitioners have had to consider that the taking of a position might, at times, be a requirement for constructive practice. As Boston (2010) has pointed out, supervisors involved in the clinical training of family therapists exist within a hierarchy and it is unethical for us to act as if that might not be the case. And, as she further highlights, being hierarchical and being collaborative are not mutually exclusive.

Feedback

In a book highlighting the legacy of David Campbell, it is important that I say something briefly about David's influence on me concerning the need to keep the idea of feedback central in thinking and practice. From being a trainee of his (and Ros Draper) in the early 1980s, the need to pay detailed attention to, and utilisation of, feedback was something that particularly struck me about the way David practised as a supervisor and as a therapist. The attention to the importance of feedback is a consistent theme in his (and Ros Draper's) writing (Burck & Campbell, 2002, p. 60; Campbell & Draper, 1985, p. 1; Campbell & Grønbæk, 2006, p. 6; Campbell, Caldicott, & Kinsella, 1994, p. 15; Campbell, Draper, & Huffington, 1988, p. 11, 1989, p. 9). Indeed, they (Campbell, Draper, and Huffington) considered feedback "to be the single most important intervention to enable organizations to manage change productively". They added, "Feedback is the lifeblood of any system" (Campbell, Draper, & Huffington, 1988, p. 14). This can also apply to smaller units, such as a supervision team.

Towards a culture of contribution

A movement towards the developing of a culture of contribution in supervision, or therapy, or team, or organisations is essentially about the sharing of expertise. This ownership and sharing of our expertise in its two different forms, as highlighted earlier, is what I now see as central to my therapeutic and supervisory practice relationships. Each of us in such relationships contributes to the generation of any useful therapeutic and supervisory dialogue that might emerge (for example, the sharing of hypotheses and the influence of each hypothesis on the other (Bertrando & Arcelloni, 2006). It is consistent with one of the basic tenets of systems theory—the notion of mutual influence (Wiener, 1948). This has been put elegantly by Kraemer and Schlicht (2005) in relation to therapy, but is easily transferable in thinking about the context of supervision and the supervisory relationship.

> Our goal is an informed spontaneity in which respect for our own experience is as important as respect for the patient's. Therapists know what they know, and patients too know what they know. When both are free to acknowledge this they may learn something new, "the difference that makes a difference" (Bateson, 1979). (Kraemer & Schlicht, 2005, p. 19)

This opening up of dialogue, the taking of a position of opening oneself up to the potentially useful ideas of "the other" (without disqualifying the potential usefulness of one's own ideas) so that each may learn, is central to the notion of a culture of contribution. If a "collaborative approach" (Anderson & Goolishian, 1992) can also be seen in this way, I do not have a problem. However, as Young and colleagues (1997) at The Bouverie Centre in Melbourne have suggested, clients invest therapists with a constructive ownership of power. Therapists who view a collaborative approach, in part, by withholding their knowledge—thus attempting to limit their power (as if it were intrinsically negative) from the therapeutic relationship—are in danger of only "concealing its visibility" (Guilfoyle, 2003, p. 334).

Fine and Turner (1997, p. 231) make a useful distinction between position power and knowledge power. By the very nature of their role, supervisors have a responsibility to "mind the power" (Fine & Turner, 1997, p. 229), to be part of the safeguarding of a constructive use of power in the service of clients. It is an ethical position. Knowledge power, a position which acknowledges the specialist expertise that supervisors might have, is seen by Fine and Turner as a useful contribution to the supervisory relationship as long as it does not veer into "a positivist belief in foundational or universal truth"

(1997, p. 231). This is all well and good as long as supervisors, particularly in the training context, do not pull back from contributing their knowledge as ideas to be considered; the importance of making space for the circulation of ideas, as Fine and Turner have put it (1997, p. 235), although their belief (as that of Anderson and Roberts (1993)) that all ideas have merit, is, somewhat ironically, an absolutist one. All of us at some time or another have ideas that do not have merit and there are plenty of ideas, I would strongly suggest, that for me have no merit at all: for example, the idea that men are intrinsically superior to women in terms of universal human rights. Gender and other "social graces" (Burnham, 2010; Burnham, Alvis-Palma, & Whitehouse, 2008) need continually to be kept in focus in terms of using power constructively (Ayo, 2010; Bond, 2010; Boyd, 2010; Brecelj-Kobe & Trampuz, 2010; Burns & Kemps, 2002). I should add at this point that I see it as important that, in owning our "position power", we take on the responsibility of using that power to contribute to a context where supervisees increasingly feel able and comfortable to challenge the supervisor. This is particularly important in a training context. I make a point of saying at the beginning of such supervisory relationship contexts that I welcome supervisees coming in with their different (to mine) perspectives. It was something David Campbell encouraged. This challenging of me will not necessarily happen immediately, as a culture is built up over time. However, one way to help foster this aspect of a culture of contribution (I first started doing it in 1991) is to ask a supervisee to interview the supervisor about the supervision they have been giving (Mason, 2002). In a group context, I might also ask for other supervisees to voice their reflections (Andersen, 1987) about the supervision.

A culture of contribution in supervision: helping trainees to contribute their knowledge

Since 1998, I have been the Chair of the advanced training programme in the supervision of family and systemic psychotherapy at the Institute of Family Therapy, London. During that time, other members of staff and I have noticed a pattern evident across all cohorts: the trainees are much more comfortable contributing their expertise to the supervision process with the use of curiosity than also contributing expertise with the giving of their ideas and knowledge. There is now an expectation, part of the assessment process, that both aspects of their expertise are important to their supervisory development and practice. Feedback from trainees has indicated that this "both . . . and" emphasis has contributed to them feeling much more at ease with their own authority, and they have also consistently reported that their supervisees have felt that the supervisory contribution of both forms of expertise has been beneficial for them. Recent comments from some trainees in reflecting on their learning on the course has highlighted that one of their biggest and most useful shifts had been to experiment with using their power constructively by contributing their ideas, other peoples' ideas, suggestions, and tips. There seemed to be an initial fear that by the giving of their knowledge they would be, as one person put it, "being disrespectful of the supervisee's perspective", rather than also choosing to think of it as a different position for the supervisee to consider. Taking Campbell and Grøn-bæk's (2006) semantic polarities approach, this could be seen in either of the following ways, depending on perspective:

- to offer my ideas might be seen as marginalising the expertise of the supervisee,
- to offer my ideas might be seen as contributing to the expertise of the supervisee.

All supervisees on the training are, therefore, asked to experiment with difference, to take a risk in going outside their comfort zone (Wilson, 2007, p. 47), not least in experimenting with voicing their knowledge in a direct way—for example, "I have a suggestion"—in addition to an indirect utilisation of their knowledge through the use of curiosity.

Giving feedback

On the supervisor training, trainees are visited in their agency and observed supervising in "live" team supervision, video supervision, and group and individual retrospective supervision. At the end of the visit, verbal feedback is given, and this is followed up with written feedback. In common with many other courses, trainees are given the opportunity to offer their own feedback to the staff member's comments. There is a culture *per se* on the training of course members being encouraged to give feedback to staff, and each other, throughout the length of the course.

My concern about a collaborative approach (see above) has led me more recently to the formulation of six areas of feedback to utilise in supervision (and, indeed, therapy). The idea of these six aspects (arising from my observations of therapeutic and supervisory practice) originally started off as an aid to helping reflecting teams add to their interventions of curiosity and wondering by including the giving of some of their thinking and ideas. What I had begun to notice was that families, couples, and individuals would often give indications that they would welcome the therapist's ideas and suggestions, and would sometimes become frustrated when they did not get them. In an effort to be respectful and collaborative and "not knowing", therapists were, I felt, doing clients a disservice by not offering ideas and suggestions that might be potentially useful with which to engage. Just as those of us who are involved in the academic assessment of students can be in danger of using too narrow a range of marks in assessment (usually between 50% and 75%), the idea I was having about feedback involved going beyond the usual parameters. I wanted to encourage the use of a greater range. I then realised this idea did not relate only to reflecting teams and reflecting processes, but also to supervision.

The six aspects

The six aspects are:

- this is what I heard/am hearing
- this is what I noticed/am noticing/observed/am observing
- this is what I am curious/wondering about
- these are some questions I have
- this is what I think
- this is what I suggest/recommend.

The supervision training at IFT

The programme has been in existence since 1998. As part of the training, trainees lead a supervision group in their agency or professional community. During the period of the programme, they are visited twice by a member of the course staff. The course staff member mainly observes, but might also come in at times with more direct ideas for the trainee supervisor to consider. The group usually consists of three or four people plus the supervisor. The form of supervision activity is a mixture of "live", group, individual, and retrospective (including video retrospective). After each visit, the course member is given both verbal and written feedback. The six aspects are utilised in this feedback. Examples are given below.

Verbal feedback

At the end of the visit to the agency, I will, as a staff member, initially be curious and ask the trainee how they viewed their supervision during the clinic; what did they like about how they supervised and what did they think they could have done differently? I might also ask about their reactions to any interventions I might have made to them during the supervision and whether such interventions from me were a help and/or a constraint. After I have explored feedback through the use of my curiosity, I will usually share some of my observations and comments, including suggestions, which are then written up and sent to the trainee. At other times, I might ask the trainee at the beginning of our discussion whether they would prefer to make some comments first about how they were thinking about their supervision, or would they prefer for me to give my thoughts. Sometimes the answer is the former and sometimes it is the latter.

Written feedback

The following are examples of comments given in written feedback to trainees. I have added, in square brackets, how the written feedback relates to the six aspects:

> "My immediate impression (first visit) was that you had no problem about leading the group—owning your position as the supervisor. It also struck me that you clearly had a mandate from the group to supervise." [This is what I noticed.]

> "Be careful about asking too many 'do you think type' questions [this is what I suggest] as it often closes down answers to a yes or a no."

"I felt you were concentrating too much on the clinical session itself rather than the supervision of the (videotape) session. It was as if you were wanting to be the clinician rather than the supervisor." [This is what I think.]

"I heard you supervise a lot using curiosity (this is what I heard) but not much of the bringing in of your own ideas. Given this is something we have been talking about, how come you held back on giving some of your thinking—in the break towards the end of the session? [This is what I am wondering about; this is a question I have.] I agree with you that the conversation we had after the clinic was useful. I'd ask you to ponder further the idea that to give some of your own thinking (and other people's thinking, for that matter), in addition to your respectful curiosity, is not non-collaborative. My guess is, from what I heard and observed today, that your supervisees would really value your expertise and experience via your thinking and suggestions." [This is what I think and suggest/recommend.]

(And on my next visit.) "I heard you supervise differently today. [This is what I heard; this is what I noticed.] The balance between showing your expertise through the use of curiosity and the showing of your expertise through the sharing of some of your knowledge seemed to me to be well received by the members of the group. [This is what I noticed; this is what I think.] Did you get this sense?"

"I'm wondering whether it would be useful to give some tips to the supervisee who saw the family today—some tips about how to elicit themes from content. [I am wondering about; I have a suggestion.] I have a question: what kind of feedback does she want from you about her clinical work? If you haven't already done so, maybe it would be useful to explore that with her. [I have a suggestion/recommendation.]

"The last piece of supervision I saw you do today was very skilful. You were able to be both curious and give your ideas and suggestions; you explored the supervisee's understanding of his practice and related this to theory. You explored the relationship with help and the therapeutic relationship, and you managed to address the self of the supervisee—linking issues in the case material to his experience in his family of origin around gender equality. You also addressed cultural aspects of parenting styles and offered some useful suggestions about how he could address this area more effectively in the clinical work." [This is what I noticed, heard.]

"I think you are very good at offering a clear structure. There is a calmness about your supervision and a seriousness about the task in hand, while at the same time injecting, and responding to, humour across the supervisory relationship. [This is what I noticed.] There are times when I thought you could have challenged more than you did, particularly around your supervisee's dilemmas, the therapeutic relationship and self. [This is what I noticed. This is what I think.] The latter was particularly evident in the discussion of the article when both supervisees volunteered personal issues that you didn't address. I wondered at the time whether this was because I was present, and in our discussion after the clinic you indicated that this was so. [This is what I observed; this is what I was wondering about.] However, A and B (the supervisees) took the initiative and raised the personal connections themselves, so you might have explored that more. [This is what I noticed; this is what I think.] You could have negotiated with them as to whether they wished to go into these issues further by just asking them. [This is what I think.] If you have a dilemma like this it is useful to ask yourself—can I just do the obvious here and ask them directly?" [This is what I suggest.]

A small survey of the 2010–2011 cohort

The widening of the range of giving feedback has, as previously indicated, become a fixture of the teaching on the programme. The group consisted of eleven experienced family therapists—nine women and two men—and was culturally mixed.

The questionnaire

The questionnaire was given to each member of the course at the beginning of the programme and again at the end of the programme. Eight people responded at the beginning of the course and nine people responded at the end of the course. The responses, below, are based on mean averages. Some respondents added brief comments in the space for such at the end of each question, but most did not. All questions ended with the following request in parentheses: "Please put in rank order—the most preferred as number 1, and the least preferred as number 6."

The questions

The following areas were addressed:

1. The trainee supervisors' preferred form of giving feedback to their supervisees.
2. The form of feedback from their own clinical supervisor outside the course and whether the trainee perceives this as their preferred form of receiving feedback.
3. The preferred form of written feedback from staff in relation to their supervision on the course.
4. The preferred form of verbal feedback from staff in relation to their supervision on the course.
5. The preferred form of giving feedback when the trainee is part of a clinical reflecting team in their home agency.

The responses

The trainee supervisors' preferred form of giving feedback to their supervisees

At the beginning of the course, a pattern emerged of trainees giving supervision with an emphasis on stating what they had heard their supervisees say, what they found themselves wondering about, and highlighting some questions they had of the supervisee. The least preferred forms of giving supervisory feedback were the last two in the list—the supervisor saying what they were thinking, and the giving of suggestions/recommendations. The latter was the least preferred by a wide margin.

By the end of the course, there had been a shift. The most preferred form of giving feedback was the contribution of their own thinking; the giving of suggestions had also risen in the order to be the third in the list. Written comments made by the trainees on the questionnaire suggested that by the end of the course: (a) they were more comfortable with owning the part of their expertise that allowed them to share their knowledge more directly; (b) feedback from their supervisees indicated that they preferred a conversation that included different ways of contributing in the supervisory relationship. As one trainee put it:

> "I have become far more comfortable in putting forward my own perspective. Feedback from my supervisees suggest that they appreciate a dialogue containing both my thinking and their thinking. Earlier on in the course I had kept my thinking and suggestions to myself. I

felt much more confident at asking questions about what they were thinking."

Another trainee wrote,

"I think that our pre-and post sessions have become richer (since I added more of my thinking and suggestions). I believe it's very valuable for supervisors to express their thoughts and opinions about a situation and make recommendations/suggestions to their supervisees. I believe this is part of the educative part of supervision."

It is important to add that many of the supervisees also stated that while the balance had changed regarding the giving of feedback, by the end of the course they used all of the six aspects. As another trainee wrote,

"I like all of these six aspects to appear in my supervision to others, rather than have a preference that would exclude the remaining others."

The form of feedback from their own clinical supervisor outside the course, and whether the trainees perceive this as their preferred form of receiving feedback

This was one of the most striking responses. At the beginning of the course, as noted above, the preferred form of giving feedback was mainly concerned with offering what the supervisor said, what s/he observed, and what s/he was wondering about. The trainees' preference from their own clinical supervisor was for feedback of a more direct kind. They stated as their main preference that they wanted to hear the supervisor say what they were thinking. By the end of the course, the trainees, as noted above, had shifted their preferences and there was more congruence with the feedback style they wanted from their own supervisor.

The preferred form of written feedback from staff in relation to their supervision on the course

The responses to questions (3) and (4) in the list above were similar in some respects. The preferences at the beginning of the course for both written and verbal feedback from staff were almost identical. Trainees wanted staff to offer feedback via observations, what they had heard, and what they were wondering about. More direct feedback from staff was placed as least preferred. This was interesting for the staff because, in our position as trainers and assessors, we had the view that we needed to place the giving of more direct feedback higher than the trainees. It quickly became apparent that the form of feedback we subsequently started giving to them when we visited their clinical supervision projects was, without exception, well received. By the end of the course, the trainees indicated in the questionnaire that they had found the more direct feedback from staff helpful, in addition to the comments about what we had observed and heard and were wondering about. What the staff were thinking was placed as the number one preference for trainees. Suggestions and tips for practice also moved higher in their preferences, from least preferred to third preferred. As one trainee put it at the end of the course:

> "I have always appreciated knowing what supervisors/assessors think and why and what they recommend. I like direct, specific feedback and this is what I received. I have a preference for conversational/discursive processes and enjoy debating issues rather than sitting quietly and not saying anything; this gets me to think, reflect and learn. Direct, clear feedback enables me to engage with debate when I feel it is necessary."

The preferred form of giving feedback when the trainee is part of a clinical reflecting team in their home agency

As the initial idea for the extending the range of feedback had come from my observations of reflecting teams, I included a question addressing this area, since many of the trainees were often part of the reflecting team discussions in the clinical work. A similar pattern emerged to one that is now evident from the responses to the previous questions. At the beginning of the course, the preference was for what was noticed, what was heard, and what was being wondered about. The more direct thoughts and suggestions took up their usual position at the end of the line, so to speak. By the end of the course, there had been a small shift. The "this is what I am thinking" type of feedback had risen to become the third preference. The offering of suggestions was still placed sixth—by a wide margin.

I would make a suggestion here. If a collaborative perspective involves taking into account preferences of the clients, then it is perhaps worth being more direct with clients and asking them what kind of feedback they would prefer. My experience, both clinical and supervisory, is that families are not asked. Reflecting teams I have been part of and observed (and I acknowledge that I might be generalising) tend to adhere to the feedback of wondering, hearing, and noticing. Yet, many clients give indications that they would like more direct feedback in the form of ideas, advice, and suggestions. One of the trainees indicated in the survey that "this tool [six aspects of feedback] has been very influential in my team and we have adopted a more rigorous approach regarding feedback as part of reflecting processes."

In summary and conclusion

In thinking about the results of this small survey, I was reminded of something David Campbell and Charlotte Burck (Burck & Campbell, 2002) have written in relation to training family therapy supervisors. They note that "It takes time for trainees to develop their own authority, to be able to assert their point of view" (2002, p.79). While I would probably favour the word contribute rather than assert, I would concur with this view. The IFT supervision training has, in part, addressed this issue by having an expectation of supervisors that they will experiment with using a range of ways of giving feedback; that they will experiment with difference.

One of these differences is to help trainees contribute their expertise and feedback in the form of knowledge and ideas, in addition to (my emphasis) the contribution of their expertise through questions—the latter being something that many family therapists are extremely good at. An idea of the fostering of a culture of contribution has been highlighted. It can be said to be a collaborative approach without the handcuffs. The handcuffs have been used, I have suggested, to marginalise a particular aspect of expertise, that of the ownership of knowledge within the context of utilising a wider range of feedback: the taking of positions.

In *Taking Positions in the Organization* (Campbell & Grønbæk, 2006), David Campbell noted that it was important to ask the question, "Where do I position myself?" (p. 6). He added that he would use himself (where he placed himself and where he was placed) to contribute to the development of the opening up of new perspectives (p. 6). For me, David's approach to his work highlighted that, while we may have our preferred ways of seeing, let us also try to help open up, not close down, as wide a range of positions as possible—positions that might be potentially useful to us in our supervision. It is in this spirit that one perspective of the fostering of a culture of contribution in supervision, the perspective of the supervisor, has been presented in this chapter. This perspective exists in the context of helping to create a culture where the supervisee can also contribute from a position of curiosity and knowledge. Finally, the results of a small survey of trainees in supervision suggest that development of the ownership of expertise can be helped by utilising a wider range of feedback than they had previously used.

Acknowledgements

I would like to acknowledge my appreciation to Viv Gross, Sue McNab, John Burnham and Maeve Malley—fellow staff on the supervision training at IFT; as well as the supervision course trainees on the 2010–2011 cohort: Karen Burgess, Sue Cruickshank, Hazel Hyslop, Georgia Iliopoulu, Nigel Jacobs, Patrick Kuhn, Monica Lynch, Alison Martin, Sarah Reeves, Bernadette Sharr, and Gill Stevens. I also wish to thank Corry de Jongh, at the Clanwilliam Institute in Dublin whose enthusiasm for the six areas of feedback, and exploration with her supervisees, provided the initial idea for the questionnaire.

References

Andersen, T. (1987). The reflecting team: dialogue and metadialogue in clinical work. *Family Process, 26*: 415–428.
Anderson, H. (2007). Comment made at the European Family Therapy Association/Association for Family Therapy and Systemic Practice in the UK Conference, Glasgow.
Anderson, H., & Goolishian, H. (1992). Therapeutic process as social construction. In: S. McNamee & K. Gergen (Eds.), *Therapy as Social Construction* (pp. 25–39). London: Sage.

Anderson, H., & Roberts, H. (1993). Collaborative practice within a child protection agency system. *Supervision Bulletin, 7*(1): 6–8.

Ayo, Y. (2010). Addressing issues of race and culture in supervision. In: C. Burck & G. Daniel (Eds.), *Mirrors and Reflections: Processes of Systemic Supervision* (pp. 225–248). London: Karnac.

Bateson, G. (1979). *Mind and Nature*. London: Wildwood.

Bertrando, P. (2007). *The Dialogical Therapist: Dialogue in Systemic Practice*. London: Karnac.

Bertrando, P., & Arcelloni, T. (2006). Hypotheses are dialogues: sharing hypotheses with clients. *Journal of Family Therapy, 28*(4): 370–387.

Bond, S. (2010). Putting a face to institutionalised racism: the challenge of introducing a live supervised training programme for black social workers in a predominantly white institution. In: C. Burck & G. Daniel (Eds.), *Mirrors and Reflections: Processes of Systemic Supervision* (pp. 249–266). London: Karnac.

Boston, P. (2010). The three faces of supervision: individual learning, group learning, and supervisor accountability. In: C. Burck & G. Daniel (Eds.), *Mirrors and Reflections: Processes of Systemic Supervision* (pp. 27–48). London: Karnac.

Boyd, E. (2010). "Voice entitlement" narratives in supervision. Cultural and gendered influences on speaking and dilemmas in practice. In: C. Burck & G. Daniel (Eds.), *Mirrors and Reflections: Processes of Systemic Supervision* (pp. 203–224). London: Karnac.

Brecelj-Kobe, M., & Trampuz, D. (2010). The power of delegated authority and how to deal with it. In: C. Burck & G. Daniel (Eds.), *Mirrors and Reflections: Processes of Systemic Supervision* (pp. 267–285). London: Karnac.

Burck, C., & Campbell, D. (2002). Training systemic supervisors: multi-layered learning. In: D. Campbell & B. Mason (Eds.), *Perspectives on Supervision* (pp. 59–80). London: Karnac.

Burnham, J. (2010). Creating reflexive relationships between practices of systemic supervision and theories of learning and education. In: C. Burck & G. Daniel (Eds.), *Mirrors and Reflections: Processes of Systemic Supervision* (pp. 49–78). London: Karnac.

Burnham, J., Alvis-Palma, D., & Whitehouse, L. (2008). Learning as a context for differences and differences as a context for learning. *Journal of Family Therapy, 30*(4): 529–542.

Burns, L., & Kemps, C. (2002). Risky business: the rewards and demands of cross-cultural working with colleagues. In: B. Mason & A. Sawyerr (Eds.), *Exploring the Unsaid: Creativity, Risks and Dilemmas in Working Cross-Culturally* (pp. 148–162). London: Karnac.

Cade, B. W. (1992). I am an unashamed expert. *Context: A News Magazine of Family Therapy, 11*: 30–31.

Campbell, D., & Draper, R. (1985). *Applications of Systemic Family Therapy: The Milan Approach*. London: Grune and Stratton.

Campbell, D., & Grønbæk, M. (2006). *Taking Positions in the Organization*. London: Karnac.

Campbell, D., Caldicott, T., & Kinsella, K. (1994). *Systemic Work With Organizations*. London: Karnac.

Campbell, D., Draper, R., & Huffington, C. (1988). *Teaching Systemic Thinking*. London: DC Publishing.

Campbell, D., Draper, R., & Huffington, C. (1989). *A Systemic Approach to Consultation*. London: DC Publishing.

Fine, M., & Turner, J. (1997). Collaborative supervision: minding the power. In: T. Todd & C. Storm (Eds.), *The Complete Systemic Supervisor* (pp. 229–240). Boston: Allyn and Bacon.

Freedman, J., & Combs, G. (1996). *Narrative Therapy*. New York: Norton.

Guilfoyle, M. (2003). Dialogue and power: a critical analysis of power in dialogical therapy. *Family Process, 42*: 331–343.

Kraemer, S., & Schlicht, J. (2005). From system to psyche. In: C. Flaskas, B. Mason, & A. Perlesz (Eds.), *The Space Between: Experience, Context and Process in the Therapeutic Relationship* (pp. 19–31). London. Karnac.

Langenhove, L. V., & Harré, R. (1999). Introducing positioning theory. In: R. Harré & L. V. Langenhove (Eds.), *Positioning Theory* (pp. 14–31). Oxford: Blackwell.

Larner, G. (2000). Toward a common ground in psychoanalysis and family therapy: on knowing not to know. *Journal of Family Therapy, 22*(1): 61–82.

Mason, B. (1993). Towards positions of safe uncertainty. *Human Systems, 4*: 189–200.

Mason, B. (2002). A reflective recording format for supervisors and trainees. In: D. Campbell & B. Mason (Eds.), *Perspectives on Supervision*. London: Karnac.

Mason, B. (2005). Relational risk-taking and the therapeutic relationship. In: C. Flaskas, B. Mason, & A. Perlesz (Eds.), *The Space Between: Experience, Context and Process in the Therapeutic Relationship*. London: Karnac.

Mason, B. (2010). Some ideas about the nature of therapy: a professional history re-visited. In: T. B. Huat & C. Lim (Eds.), *Journeys in Systemic Psychotherapy: Theory, Practice and Research* (pp. 67–85). Singapore: Armour.

Mason, B. (2011). Supervision and the training context: some thoughts and ideas about the ownership of knowledge in practice. *Context, 116*: 2–3.

Rober, P. (1999). The therapist's inner conversation in family therapy practice: some ideas about the self of the therapist, therapeutic impasse and the process of reflection. *Family Process, 38*(2): 209–228.

Rober, P. (2005). The therapist's self in dialogical family therapy: some ideas about not-knowing and the therapist's inner conversation. *Family Process, 44*: 477–495.

Stewart, K., Valentine, L., & Amundsen, J. (1991). The battle for definition: the problem with (the problem). *Journal of Strategic and Systemic Therapies, 10*: 21–31.

Wiener, N. (1948). *Cybernetics: Or Control and Communication in the Animal and the Machine*. Paris: Hermann and Cie.

Wilson, J. (2007). *The Performance of Practice*. London: Karnac.

Young, J., Saunders, F., Prentice, G., Macri-Riseley, D., Fitch, R., & Pati-Tasca, C. (1997). Three journeys toward the reflecting team. *Australian and New Zealand Journal of Family Therapy, 18*: 27–37.

PART III
RESEARCH

Systemic research and research supervision: David Campbell in interview with Charlotte Burck

Edited by Sara Barratt

CB: Can we talk about research? How have your clinical and organisational ideas fed into your research work?

DC: The research began in the late 1970s when John Byng-Hall and Rosemary Whiffen got a grant to do some research into family therapy and they asked me to be the convener. This meant getting a research team together; we were looking at sessions that had been recorded, pulling out certain themes and coding the material. It was then that I discovered that I was never going to be a researcher because I'm just not patient enough, and I take my hat off to the people who have the patience and the attention to detail.

CB: But you have gone on to do all kinds of other research, haven't you?

DC: Yes, and it helped me to be careful about getting bogged down in too much detail, too much coding, because it takes you away from the process of the therapy itself. Since then I've done a few pieces of research about talking to families about their experiences of family therapy. Because I was aware of my impatience, I was looking around for something that was already administered and then Izzy Kolvin and Judith Trowell developed the childhood depression study (Campbell, 2011; Trowell et al., 2007) and needed somebody to lead the family therapy component at the Tavistock, which was perfect for me. I could develop research thinking around childhood depression, which was a very interesting topic and I really enjoyed that. I was very grateful to Judith and Izzy. It was very interesting because they produced enough data for us to begin to look at the patterns that emerged and apply them to the family sessions.

CB: The interesting thing about that project was that because you taped all the family therapy sessions, you could then do some process research. Outcome studies are very good at a policy level, but you've also looked at questions about the significant processes, haven't you?

DC: Yes, I would see myself as a clinician–researcher rather than a pure researcher, so my primary interest would always be in the clinical process and how to avoid getting too far removed from it. So trying to identify key moments for families and therapists was a fairly accessible research model that wasn't going to be too much detail and draw you away from the experience of therapy (Campbell et al., 2003).

CB: Do you think that looking at significant moments has had an effect on your own clinical work?

DC: Over the years, I've developed a pretty good nose for just staying focused on what people are really trying to say; they can talk for a few minutes and I'm thinking, wait a minute, that's not what they really want to say, and then finally something will click and I'll think, that's what they want me to hear amidst all the other words. So I'm just staying focused on that as significant and I just keep waiting and then I'll say, that's really interesting, let's talk about that. So doing research kind of sharpens your critical thinking.

CB: You've also been involved in supervising research projects on our doctoral programme. How does that experience fit with the rest of your work?

DC: I would say supervising doctorate dissertations is about twenty-five per cent research and seventy-five per cent consulting to a researcher; how do you convey certain ideas to a researcher in a way that is inspiring and encouraging and also a bit of a kick? It's about being a consultant, supervisor, a bit of a therapist, and a bit of a coach all thrown in. You need research skills, but I was surprised at how challenging this is because, when I started out, I'd say, here's the method, here's the data, here are the conclusions, write those up and that would be it. There are so many nuances about how people respond to the research, so it's more difficult than it looks.

CB: How important do you think being interested in what you can learn from the people that you're training is for a teacher?

DC: I'm a much better teacher if I am learning something during the day. I couldn't just deliver a lecture that I delivered a week before and I think that it's being interested in feedback and part of something that is evolving. I try to get a feedback loop going as soon as I can rather than going on and on. I don't like the sound of my own voice, actually. I'd rather stop and say "let's get some feedback", or get people to talk to each other about what they've heard and come up with a third idea.

References

Campbell, D. (2011). Co-morbidity: childhood depression and anxiety in family therapy. In: J. Trowell & G. Miles (Eds.), *Childhood Depression: A Place for Psychotherapy* (pp. 168–200). London: Karnac.

Campbell, D., Bianco, V., Dowling, E., Goldberg, H., McNab, S., & Pentecost, D. (2003). Family therapy for childhood depression: researching significant moments. *Journal of Family Therapy*, 25(4): 417–435.

Trowell, J., Joffe, I., Campbell, J., Clemente, C., Almqvist, F., Soininen, M., Koskenranta-Aalto, U., Weintraub, S., Kolaitis, G., Tomaras, V., Anastasopoulos, D., Grayson, K., Barnes, J., & Tsiantis, J. (2007). Childhood depression: a place for psychotherapy. An outcome study comparing individual psychodynamic psychotherapy and family therapy. *European Child and Adolescent Psychiatry*, 16(3): 157–167.

CHAPTER SEVEN

Learning from research processes and dilemmas: young people's experience of parental mental illness

Yoko Totsuka

Introduction

Research supervision was one of the major areas of David's contribution to the field of family therapy. I was fortunate to have him as my research supervisor on the Doctorate in Systemic Psychotherapy course at Tavistock Clinic. When I thought about David's influence, I recalled key moments in tutorials when he helped me to get "unstuck". Many of these conversations were about issues of research processes and dilemmas and it was these "messy" aspects of research that I learnt from most. In this chapter, I hope to share this experience as I present a few ideas from my qualitative study about young people's experience of parental mental illness.

Background

In the past few decades, the effects of parental mental illness on children have been extensively studied. Much of the literature is about adverse effects of parental mental illness on children. A number of studies investigated the association between parental illness and presence of problems in children using quantitative methods. In recent years, there has been increasing interest in families' experience of parental mental illness from their own perspectives, including children's, which had been particularly under-represented (e.g., Aldridge & Becker, 2003; Armstrong, 2002; Cogan, Riddell, & Mayes, 2005; Riebschleger, 2004; Stallard, Norman, Huline-Dickens, & Cribb, 2004). A recent issue of *Context* (Totsuka & Colmer, 2010), devoted to this topic, included research studies on families' experiences conducted by systemic therapists. My paper (Totsuka, 2010) focused on young people's experience of parents' hospital admission. Colmer (2010) interviewed children, parents and professionals. Wagstaff (2010) interviewed mothers who suffered from depression and explored the impact on their parental role.

Method

Aiming to conduct an exploratory study on young people's experience of parental mental illness, I interviewed nine participants (seven females and two males) of the adolescent and early adulthood age group whose parents experienced at least one hospital admission due to mental illness. They were attending, or used to attend, a child and adolescent mental health service (CAMHS) in Newham, London. Their age ranged from thirteen to twenty, with the average age of 16.6 years. I decided on the wide age range, hoping to explore developmental issues and changes over time. One participant was purposefully sought to explore the experience of being in care. The participants' ethnic background reflected the diversity of the local population. Four participants were of Asian background, three were white UK or European, and two were black Caribbean and African/British. The semi-structured interviews were audio-recorded, transcribed, and analysed using grounded theory method (Glaser & Strauss, 1967).

Finding my own position

One of the most memorable conversations with David was about finding my position in relation to data. I spent a long time analysing the interview transcripts, trying to stay close to the data, and being cautious about developing interpretations. However, I began to feel as if I was drowning in the details and felt tentative and uncertain about my ideas as I took numerous memos. I remember talking about this anxiety to David, who acknowledged that this was indeed a challenging, but at the same time exciting, phase that required a bit of courage! As I verbalised my thoughts with his encouragement, ideas started to form, but I also had to ask myself where these ideas were coming from. Does the data back it up, and in what way? I was reminded that, as a researcher, I cannot be neutral and value-free. During tutorials, there was always a clear emphasis on self-reflexivity, and David had a natural and fluent way of encouraging me to be explicit about the roles of my values and beliefs. For example, when I was analysing the participants' description of parents' symptoms and behaviour, the initial codes were named in almost diagnostic terms, such as "manic behaviour" and "depression". As the interviews progressed, I realised that the young people's descriptions were much broader and did not always fit with them. I wrote the following memo to explore this.

> I was trying to be "objective" and clinical towards the data. . . . Young people do not see their parents' illness like clinicians do. Their experience is more immediate and sometimes even personal—e.g. their parents can be verbally and physically abusive towards them. The analysis became even more complex when I interviewed two young people whose parents suffered from chronic illness. They had little sense of normality in their experience of their parents. From their accounts, I could not tell "objectively" what part of the parents' behaviour was arising from the illness itself. I initially grouped the codes related to observations such as "angry", "emotional", "not responsive" separately from "symptoms and behaviour", but these were often described as part of the illness experience. From the young people's point of view, whether or not these behaviours were arising from mental illness *per se* did not seem to be as important as how they affected them.

Need for information

David's intervention as a research supervisor seemed to push me towards clarity on the one hand, but he also seemed to promote space for puzzling contradictions on the other. The development of the idea about "the need for information" was one example. In the literature, the importance of giving children and young people information is much emphasised, but previous studies on children's experience showed mixed results. In some studies, children and young people were reported to want more information (e.g., Fudge & Mason, 2004; Garley, Gallop, Johnston, & Pipitone, 1997), but, in other studies, their wish was not as clear. Armstrong (2002) found that while young people were told by their parents little about their illness, most of them did not want to know any more than they had to. Colmer's (2005) study offers insight into ambivalence in both parents and children.

In my study, young people's accounts indicated that they want and try to understand their parents' illness and there were some common themes. For example, they try to make sense of the presentations of illness, such as parents' behaviour and why they do what they do. Many of them wanted to know what helps and what does not, what they and professionals can do to help. Some wanted to know what will happen to their parents and themselves. However, I was puzzled by the fact that the amount and accuracy of information the young people had did not always seem to reflect their satisfaction. For example, some participants had limited or inaccurate information, but had no wish to know any further. The procedure of "constant comparison" of the grounded theory method (Glaser & Strauss, 1967) was helpful in analysing these contradictions by comparing different participants and different experiences reported by the same participant. Gemma, whose mother had a sudden onset of psychotic illness, knew little about the illness but was satisfied with what she knew.

Researcher: Was the information too much, too little, or about right?

Gemma (seventeen years):   I think it was just about right. I knew what was going on. I didn't know why, I don't know what happened to my mum in the past to make her like that, I didn't really need to know. And I knew what was going on.

The most important information for Gemma was "what was going on", which she knew because her father stepped in and provided stability. Gemma never had to be involved in her mother's admission or subsequent treatment.

Kim's mother had had recurrent episodes of bi-polar disorder since she was eleven. Kim's father took all the responsibilities, arranging the mother's admission, looking after the children, and protecting them from witnessing her "strange" behaviour. In this context, Kim never felt the need for information, but her needs changed when her mother started to be treated in the community.

> Kim (twenty years):   When I was sixteen, the way her behaviour changed, her being ill changed, because she was in day hospital so we'd see her. She would come home every day so we would see her, whereas before she was in hospital, she stayed there for twenty-four hours, so her behaviour was completely odd to us. I've never seen anything like it. So I think, if someone had said to me, not this is what's gonna happen, but this is the behaviour that can happen, mum might get really excited and . . . and how to handle it. Because there was no help, there was no one there to tell me.

This analysis led to the idea that young people's need for information is influenced by the contextual issues and changes over time, as seen in Figure 1. The diagram shows how their understanding develops over time in multiple layers of contexts. Their developmental stages might affect the amount and type of information they need and can make sense of. Their curiosity, the wish to know or not to know, might also change over time. The meanings young people attach to their parents' symptoms or behaviour might also influence their need for information. For example, if they blame themselves, information might help to alleviate it.

> Anisha (eighteen years):   It would have been helpful if they could explain to me more about how she got it, and what they knew, and you know, it wasn't my fault in any way, that it just happened.

Young people's need for information could be influenced by external factors, such as their care-taking role and the availability of support. The participants who had to deal with their parents' illness more directly, without support, expressed a more pressing need for information on what to expect, what to watch out for, who to contact, and what they can do to help. Some of the participants from single-parent families were the first and only person to pick up on the signs of illness. One of them, Mary (sixteen), had to take on a caring role, for example, reminding her mother to take medication. She was the only participant who met adult mental health professionals and reported positive experience of them.

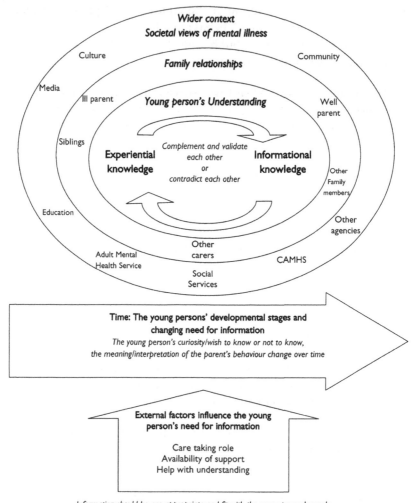

Figure 1. Multiple layers of contexts comprise young people's understanding of a parent's mental illness. The top part of the figure (multiple circles that represent contexts of relationships) was adapted from Schuff & Asen (1996)'s figure: "the person within the network of systems" (p. 136) and used here with kind permission of the authors.

Mary (seventeen years): When we had that meeting, they had already explained it to her (mother) but 'cause I was there they explained it to me and I understood.

Other participants did not have the same level of support. Gemma (seventeen) remembers doctors and nurses walking by when she was visiting her mother in hospital but no one talked to them. Kim's mother has been ill for ten years, but Kim has never met adult mental health professionals.

> Kim (twenty years): I've never met anyone who's looking after my mum. There is this doctor she goes to see quite regularly now, kind of for assessment, and . . . I don't know if it's a man, it could be a man or a woman [laughter]. They'll probably see me, but they probably don't have time to sit down with each family and say this is what's going on.

Most of the participants described in detail how they developed the knowledge of their parents' illness through experience and observations, but the extent to which they were shared with and validated by their parents or professionals seemed to vary. In some cases, their knowledge gained from experience (experiential knowledge) and from information provided by others (informational knowledge) seemed to complement and validate each other. For example, Mary, who was able to ask professionals questions about her mother's diagnosis and treatment, and was also invited to give her views, seemed to feel validated by both professionals and her mother, who allowed her to attend the meeting and gave her permission to contact professionals if necessary. In other cases, their experiential knowledge and informational knowledge contradicted, causing discomfort. For example, some young people commented on negative portrayals of mental illness in the media, which did not fit with their own experience.

I found the grounded theory method (Glaser & Strauss, 1967) helpful in building my theory about the young people's need for information. By making the theory-building process explicit, I felt more confident about my ideas and being "persuasive", one of the qualities David emphasised. It is interesting to note that not all the qualitative studies on families' experiences specify the method of data analysis.

Self-reflexivity

"Which agenda are we prepared to have challenged? What if the young people say parental mental health problems didn't have any effects on their life?"

This question, which David asked when we discussed emerging ideas, helped me to challenge my own hypotheses and assumptions. Why am I researching this topic? What agenda do I have? Am I trying to prove something: if so, what? My interest in the topic grew out of my clinical work in CAMHS contexts, but I also have family of origin stories about mental illness, which were characterised by secrecy and lack of clarity. My grandmother's history of illness was only vaguely talked about and I knew little about my uncle's illness. When he died, leaving young children behind, my parents were initially told he died in a car accident and later found out that in fact he committed suicide. I heard that his wife was never informed of his illness before they got married, which I imagine was out of good intentions not to damage his prospects for marriage, but must have had serious consequences for them. This experience made me curious about how mental illness is talked about and understood, but I also had an assumption that things need to be talked about, which might have motivated me to seek training in therapy and was probably reinforced by the training. It was, therefore, interesting to find that the participants had varied needs for information and views about talking. Although I was not directly affected, mental illness in my extended family had significant meanings in my adolescence. My difficulties in adolescent years were often interpreted as a potential sign of "mental illness", and I was, in fact, seen by a therapist at one point. This made me curious about the age group I chose and the meaning of being seen in CAMHS.

Working in the CAMHS context also meant that I was more likely to see young people who were going through some kind of difficulties themselves, which might or might not be related to their parents' illness, but I was less likely to see young people who were coping well. While some young people reported major impact on their lives, others did not, and this was a helpful reminder that I should not make assumptions about how they experience parents' illness and its impact. One of the participants had little to say about his father's illness, which was probably due to the fact that he was well protected by his mother. For this young person, the interview questions did not seem to fit well, since the illness seemed to represent only a small part of his life. Some young people talked about how individual therapy helped them cope when there seemed to be little prospect of change in their parents' functioning. I shared my thoughts with David that this challenged my tendency as a family therapist to privilege changes in contexts and relationships.

Risk and resilience: need for a "both . . . and" position

The participants' views about the impact of their parents' illness ranged from short- and long-term serious consequences to little impact. Some of them experienced little disruption or emotional impact, largely due to an alternative carer stepping in to provide care and protection. On the other hand, some participants spoke of dramatic changes in family life and some experienced neglect, parents' abusive behaviour, and their own serious mental health problems. Two experienced hospital admission, which they saw as a consequence of the effects of their parents' illness. Some of the young people could have been seen as "at risk" at different times in their lives, and three went into care at some point. Mary, one of the participants who experienced hospital admission, was doing well at the time of the interview and came across as one of the most resilient young people in my sample group. However, I was also aware from my discussion with the allocated clinician that this was a result the family's hard work and my colleagues' effort to keep the adult mental health service involved.

These accounts of variable experiences led to one of my conclusions: that parental mental illness *can* have serious impact on young people, but their vulnerability and resilience should be understood in multiple contexts, for example, experience of parental illness, availability of alternative carers, and supportive relationships within and outside the family. Some of the accounts indicated the participants' internal resources, for example, curiosity and ability to reflect. Anisha was one of the young people who were most affected by neglect and the lack of support within the family and from professionals, but gave the following account about reaching out for support.

> Anisha (eighteen years):   When I was younger, I used to do stupid things like, I used to phone people. I used to phone anyone I could, any phone number, I had to call it. And I think it was because I was lonely and wanted to talk to people. I had so many conversations, and this was supposed to be when I was like nine . . . And I used to read. I think that stopped me from feeling I was lonely.

Anisha was doing very well in education with support from her thera-pist, but described long-lasting emotional problems such as depres-sion, insecurity, and low self-esteem.

Grounded theory (Glaser & Strauss, 1967) encourages researchers to return to the literature as they analyse data. Revisiting the literature after I developed some of my own ideas was like seeing it through a different lens. Some seemed to fit my findings better than others, and I began to notice that the lack of fit was often felt when I came across what I perceived to be split discourses about children's vulner-ability and resilience. Some literature seemed to emphasise the risk by describing the adverse impact, whereas others seemed to empha-sise resilience and positive experiences. For example, Aldridge and Becker's (2003) study on young carers and their parents' experience seems to highlight their resilience: for example, the young people's positive relationships with their parents and positive views of their caring role. In this study, the families expressed negative views about children going into care and resulting separation, and the experience of social care interventions was categorised as discriminatory. This seemed to contrast with some of the accounts I heard; for example, some of the participants felt that their families should have received more support from Social Services. Two participants expressed a view that they should have been taken into care.

> Anisha (eighteen years):   They should have put us in foster care. Would have been horrible, I know. I was really scared when I was younger that they would do that. It is really scary to think for any young person. But now I look back on it and it might have been the best thing for me. I mean, two months, no, like one month of having someone, who actually made me feel safe and secure, just for one month, and I felt so good. Not having to take care of someone who is ill, not having to pick up the pieces, when my mum starts to break down.

While I acknowledge that professional interventions can be expe-rienced by families as discriminatory, some participants of my study described instances where their practical, emotional, social, and educational needs were not sufficiently met. My experience as a ther-apist and an expert witness for court is likely to have influenced my beliefs about the need for interventions when there is little possibility of change in the parents' capacity. One participant, who remains in care, chose to be interviewed with her mother being present. The young person expressed negative views towards social workers who placed her in care, and talked about missing out on the mother–daughter relationship. She assumed that she was in care against her mother's wishes as well as her own, and was surprised to hear her mother explain that she was in care voluntarily with her agreement. Despite her negative view of social care interventions, her therapist felt that she has been thriving in care. She has established a huge circle of friends whom she sees as a source of support. This account is an example of the complexity and dilemmas faced by young people when their parents cannot meet their needs and their wishes and their interest might conflict, while they continue to have concerns for, and strong loyalty to, their parents.

Cowling (1999) was one of the papers that I read at this stage and resonated with my ideas. In a case study from Australia, a parent was helped to work with the social welfare system and professionals to meet the child's needs and foster care was framed as a resource to the parent, rather than a punitive consequence for her failure to look after her child. Hetherington and Baistow (2001) compared professionals' perspectives in European countries and noted that one of the English group's weaknesses was the emphasis on crisis, acute mental illness, and child rescue, rather than prevention, early intervention, and family support. It might be that the service that reacts to crisis is more likely to be experienced as intrusive, unhelpful, and punitive and there is a need for more preventative and supportive services, which could be more acceptable to families.

Young people's accounts in my study indicate that risk and resilience are both relevant and important aspects of their experience. This points to the need for a "both . . . and" position, which allows us to think about a potential for both resilience and vulnerability of these children and families in different areas of their lives and at different times in highly complex contexts. Taking account of resilience and possible positive experience of caring is important, but I believe that it should not obscure the children's needs and potential for vulnerability in their complex circumstances. Gladstone, Boydell, and McKeever (2006) argue that the literature on children of mentally ill parents views them either as being at risk of developing a mental illness, or those who are not affected as being extraordinarily resilient or invulnerable. They argue that categorising children as either at risk or resilient in dichotomising terms is based on a social discourse that views them as passive beings, as "objects" and "victims" rather than as individuals actively participating in social life. They state that

> Research practices based on risk and resilience may have contributed to children's invisibility and silence on issues that affect them. In turn children's knowledge and experiences of difficult life circumstances may be hidden from the adults who, in an effort to protect them, end up not seeing how their lives are affected and how they in turn, respond. (Gladstone, Boydell, & McKeever, 2006, p. 2547)

Thinking about vulnerability and resilience contextually fits with Rutter's (1999) concept of resilience in a family context, where a child's resilience is understood in a context of family and other social systems. This model does not exclude factors that might also impact on individuals, such as genetic makeup and temperament. It was beyond the scope of this study to consider young people's individual disposition, but it is interesting to note that two of the above factors, family circumstances and the availability of support systems, featured more in the young people's accounts. Only one participant made a comment about her own disposition, "I never really worried about anything."

Learning from dilemmas

Ethical issues about interviewing young people

One of the ethical considerations was the possibility that the interview could cause distress to the participants due to a potentially difficult topic. The participants recruited through CAMHS might be experiencing ongoing mental health issues and difficulties in their lives. Prior to the interviews, efforts were made to protect participants: for example, liaison with their clinicians to discuss appropriateness of the interview, an informed consent, and a possibility of a follow-up meeting. One of the most challenging moments in research was when a participant became emotional and upset during an interview. Although I was used to clients' distress as a therapist, I felt inexperienced in dealing with the situation as a researcher. I tried to respond in an empathic and respectful manner, for example, by acknowledging her distress and asking her if she wanted to stop. She decided to continue and gave positive feedback on the interview at the end. However, the fact remained that the conversation initiated by me as a researcher caused her distress, and this experience left me wondering if it was ethical at all to interview young people about such a sensitive subject. Before I took this issue to a tutorial, I even imagined that David would be horrified to hear this and tell me to give up this research! As I told David that this experience left me feeling quite shaken, he was calm, curious (and smiling!), and asked questions, as he often did when I brought up dilemmas. He asked "How do people talk about emotional things to a researcher?", "Is it good for a researcher to be inhibited or not?", and "What support is needed for a researcher?" He encouraged me to write down my response to each interview. At David's suggestion, I asked all the participants for feedback about the interview at the end, and this was crucial in this interview. The young person commented that she was pleased she talked to me and that this kind of study was being done. A few other participants reported finding some of the questions uncomfortable, but overall, they were welcoming of the fact that I was trying to hear their views in order to improve clinicians' understanding and services.

David's questions made me curious about ethical issues of research interviews and gave me a focus to look for more literature. Banister, Burman, Parker, Taylor, and Tindall (1994) states that "we must recognise that taking part in research may be disturbing, it may trigger some level of disruption" (p. 155). They suggest ways to protect participants, for example, ensuring they know that they are in charge of their own degree of disclosure, that they do not have to answer all questions, or continue talking about an issue that becomes uncomfortable for them, and the interview could be halted for a while or the tape could be switched off. Although I mentioned in the information sheet potential difficulty the participants might experience during the interview and spoke briefly about this as part of the introduction, more detailed and specific discussion like this would have been helpful.

Issues of power

Another dilemma about the above situation was the fact that I was the researcher seeking information from potentially vulnerable young people, which puts me in a position of power. Yow (1994) states that

"Power in the interviewing situation is most often on the side of the interviewer" (p. 111). This is likely to be compounded by other factors, such as the age difference and my position as a professional at the clinic. There might be other differences between the participants and the researcher in terms of Social GRRAAACCEEESS (gender, race, religion, age, ability, appearance, class, culture, ethnicity, education, employment, sexuality, and spirituality, e.g., Burnham, Alvis Palma, & Whitehouse, 2008), leading to power difference, such as education and socio-economic status. Although efforts were made to conduct the interview in a respectful and empathic manner, I accept that the participants' responses could be influenced by such power imbalance. Eder and Fingerson (2001) propose that researchers should think about "reciprocity" to address power inequality in interviews with children and adolescents.

> The researcher's desire to gain information from child participants without giving something in return reflects an underlying sense of the adult researcher's privilege. However, by giving something in return for receiving this information, researchers can reduce the potential power inequality. (Eder & Fingerson, 2001, p. 185)

They propose that reciprocity might be achieved in the interview itself, where participants could receive a sense of empowerment, or greater understanding, or giving something back to the community. "Researchers can treat respondents in such a way that they receive something from participating in the study, whether it be a greater sense of empowerment, a greater understanding of their own life experiences, or both" (Eder & Fingerson, 2001, p. 185). Some young people were curious to know how the study might help. I explained that this study might contribute to the community by raising awareness of the needs of families affected by parental mental illness and informing service development. Some participants requested a copy of the subsequent publications. Some expressed a feeling that it was good to talk and some found questions interesting and facilitative. Others were more neutral about the benefit to themselves, but felt that this study, or an opportunity to talk, would be helpful for others. Some participants had a view that things should change so that their experience is not repeated, and expressed a sense of purpose. Some of my responses during the interviews might have been an attempt to be reciprocal. I felt that my reaction as a researcher was sometimes different from what I imagined as my reaction as a therapist. For example, when a participant asked if I knew someone with mental illness, I told them that I had a few extended family members who had mental illness. Some young people were curious about how my research is related to a wider context, and I explained about services and the literature. Mason states that the interviewer can "be more responsive in the interview interaction than a structure format allows, for example, answering questions the interviewee may ask, giving information, opinions, support" (Mason, 2002, p. 66).

Barriers to talking

Initially, I tried to recruit participants who were not under CAMHS through adult mental health services, but this was unsuccessful due to the lack of links between the services. Some researchers reported difficulty in recruiting participants through adult services. Stallard, Norman, Huline-Dickens, and Cribb (2004) speculate that there might be barriers on many levels, including professionals, parents, and children. Parental barriers might arise from their preoccupation with their own problems, lack of acknowledgement that children might be affected by their illness, a sense of shame, guilt, and blame, and protectiveness towards their children. In my study, one young person who was keen to participate decided not to, as her mother did not want her to talk about her illness, even though she did not require parental consent. Young people's accounts suggest that some parents are more willing or able to discuss their illness with their children. Parents' ambivalence about talking and children's reluctance to know could be recursive. It might be that the less information the parents provide, the more anxious and inhibited the young people feel about asking. They could believe that talking about the illness is upsetting to their parents and might not wish to talk out of protectiveness and loyalty. One participant commented that her mother does not remember anything about her own behaviour prior to hospital admission. The young person does not talk to her mother about her illness as it might upset her, and, as a result, is unable to seek information which she desperately wants and is left with anxiety and uncertainty about the future possibility of a relapse.

Implications for practice

Young people are active participants in the process of developing understanding, and their own experiential knowledge has an important role in this process. This means that one-directional information-giving is unlikely to be sufficient. They need age-appropriate information that fits with their needs, and this might need to be negotiated with them and their families. Professionals might invite young people to express their views as to what they need to know, and the parents think about how their children's talking and gaining more information might affect them. In some cases, adult mental health professionals might be best placed to facilitate such discussion, but, as the literature and the findings of the present study suggest, such input is not always forthcoming. Parental mental health services designed to offer preventative work might be helpful (e.g., Bailey, 2010; Britten & Cardwell, 2002; Daniel, 2010) but might not always be available.

None of the nine participants talked about their fear (or lack of it) of inheriting their parents' illness until asked explicitly. This was surprising, as some literature reports this to be a common concern. In the research context, I thought a lot about the ethics of asking sensitive questions, but not so much about the ethics of not asking questions, which often has to be considered in clinical work. This experience led to me asking questions explicitly. For example, when I was supervising a usually skilled trainee who seemed hesitant in an interview with a young person whose father has mental illness, I suggested a question about whether he worries about inheriting the illness, which opened up a conversation about his experience of his father's illness and the similarities and differences between them. This is an example of research experience having an impact on my clinical practice.

One of my hypotheses was that a referral to CAMHS might be seen as stigmatising owing to the existing adult mental health issues in the family, and I wanted to explore young people's views about connections between child and adult mental health issues and the meanings of CAMHS attendance. In my sample group, whereas some young people felt that CAMHS input helped them cope with the impact of parents' illness and some had family therapy to talk as a family about experience of parental illness, others saw no connection between their own issues or CAMHS attendance and their parents' illness. One participant said coming to CAMHS was about her behaviour at school and it was a "separate thing" from her mother's illness. Most of the young people were unconcerned about the CAMHS referral. However, for one participant, the referral meant that 'Like I'm going mad as well. I'm not normal. Like another crazy person," although she eventually found the service helpful.

Concluding remarks: David's influence

One of the things that came across in tutorials was David's conviction not only about the importance of developing a research base in the field of systemic therapy to inform our practice, but also about how our systemic skills can contribute to research. When I look back on the whole process of research, I learnt most from dilemmas and difficulties that I experienced. I owe this learning to David, who had what I can only describe as the art of tutorial. Any difficulties or dilemmas that I brought were transformed into an opportunity for learning. When I struggled to recruit participants for one reason or another, he encouraged me to write down my experience and thoughts, which led to the ideas about potential barriers to talking about parental mental illness within the family and the professional systems. A challenging experience in interviews provided an opportunity to think about ethical issues in research. When I talked about my dilemmas, David used to say, calmly and reassuringly, "OK, let's think about it", and asked questions which often surprised me and made me curious. Many ideas that came out of these conversations found their way into the discussion section. I would like to express my gratitude to David, whose warmth, kindness, encouragement, and patience helped me to carry on and stay with the young people's voice.

Acknowledgements

I would like to thank the young people who participated in this study and gave me an opportunity to hear about their experience, and their parents, who gave permission for their children to be interviewed. I thank my colleagues at Newham Child and Family Consultation Service for their support.

References

Aldridge, J., & Becker, S. (2003). *Children Caring for Parents with Mental Illness: Perspectives of Young Carers, Parents and Professionals*. Bristol: Policy Press.

Armstrong, C. (2002). Behind closed doors: living with a parent's mental illness. *Young Minds Magazine, 61*: 28–30.

Bailey, D. (2010). If we value our children, we must cherish their parents. *Context, 108*: 53–56.

Banister, P., Burman, E., Parker, I., Taylor, M., & Tindall, C. (Eds.) (1994). *Qualitative Methods in Psychology: A Research Guide*. Buckingham: Open University Press.

Britten, C., & Cardwell, A. (2002). 'Whose baby is it anyway?' Developing a joined-up service involving child and adult teams working in a mental health trust. *Adoption and Fostering, 26*(4): 76–83.

Burnham, J., Alvis Palma, D., & Whitehouse, L. (2008). Learning as a context for differences, and differences as a context for learning. *Journal of Family Therapy, 30*: 529–542.

Cogan, N., Riddell, S., & Mayes, G. (2005). The understanding and experiences of children affected by parental mental health problems: a qualitative study. *Qualitative Research in Psychology, 2*(1): 47–66.

Colmer, E. (2005). Parents, parenting and mental health: exploring parents' concerns about their children. Unpublished doctoral thesis. Tavistock & Portman NHD Foundation Trust and University of East London.

Colmer, E. (2010). Addressing mental health legacies: learning from research. *Context, 108*: 9–13.

Cowling, V. (1999). Finding answers, making changes: research and community project approaches. In: V. Cowling (Ed.), *Children of Parents with Mental Illness: Written by Children, Parents and Service Providers* (pp. 37–59). Melbourne, Victoria: Australian Council for Educational Research.

Daniel, K. (2010). The dance of attempting to break down barriers: working with children and families where a parent is experiencing mental health difficulties. *Context, 108*: 56–59.

Eder, D., & Fingerson, L. (2001). Interviewing children and adolescents. In: J. F. Gubrium & J. A. Holstein (Eds.), *Handbook of Interview Research: Context and Method* (pp. 181–201). Thousand Oaks, CA: Sage.

Fudge, E., & Mason, P. (2004). Consulting with young people about service guidelines relating to parental mental illness. *Australian e-Journal for the Advancement of Mental Health, 3*(2): 1–9.

Garley, D., Gallop, R., Johnston, N., & Pipitone, J. (1997). Children of the mentally ill: a qualitative focus group approach. *Journal of Psychiatric and Mental Health Nursing*, 4(2): 97–103.

Gladstone, B. M., Boydell, K. M., & McKeever, P. (2006). Recasting research into children's experiences of parental mental illness: beyond risk and resilience. *Social Science and Medicine*, 62(10): 2540–2550.

Glaser, B. G., & Strauss, A. L. (1967). *The Discovery of Grounded Theory: Strategies for Qualitative Research*. London: Weidenfeld and Nicolson.

Hetherington, K., & Baistow, R. (2001). Supporting families with a mentally ill parent: European perspectives on interagency cooperation. *Child Abuse and Review*, 10: 351–365.

Mason, J. (2002). *Qualitative Researching* (2nd edn). London: Sage.

Riebschleger, J. (2004). Good days and bad days: the experiences of children of a parent with a psychiatric disability. *Psychiatric Rehabilitation Journal*, 28(1): 25–31.

Rutter, M. (1999). Resilience concepts and findings: implications for family therapy. *Journal of Family Therapy*, 21(2): 119–144.

Schuff, G. H., & Asen, K. E. (1996). The disturbed parent and the disturbed family. In: M. Göpfert, J. Webster, & M. V. Seeman (Eds.), *Parental Psychiatric Disorder: Distressed Parents and their Families* (pp. 135–151). Cambridge: Cambridge University Press.

Stallard, P., Norman, P., Huline-Dickens, S., & Cribb, J. (2004). The effects of parental mental illness upon children: a descriptive study of the views of parents and children. *Clinical Child Psychology and Psychiatry*, 9(1): 39–52.

Totsuka, Y. (2010). 'Then Mum got taken into hospital': young people's experience of parents' admission to psychiatric hospital. *Context*, 108: 6–8.

Totsuka, Y., & Colmer, E. (Eds.) (2010). "Think family": Parental mental health in action. *Context*, 108.

Wagstaff, S. (2010). Depressed women talking about mothering. *Context*, 108: 3–5.

Yow, V. R. (1994). *Recording Oral History: A Practical Guide for Social Scientists*. Thousand Oaks, CA: Sage. Cited by Wengraf.

CHAPTER EIGHT

Semantic polarities:
two interpretations for one concept

Valeria Ugazio

From clinical concept to research

I have often been surprised, during family therapy, about the differences between members of the same family. In Dostoevsky's *The Brothers Karamazov* (1880), Mitja, like his father Fedor Pavlovic, is sensual, full of frenetic *joie de vivre*. Alesa, on the contrary, is a saint. Ivan, the enigmatic protagonist of Dostoevsky's masterpiece, stands in between: he has a noble heart, is concerned about suffering in the world, but is capable of behaving very badly. He needs to find something to believe in, but cannot. His pride and arrogance lead him into the abyss of nihilism until he becomes morally responsible for patricide.

The families I meet in my clinical practice often present differences as radical as those of the Karamazovs. One child is sensitive and cultured while the parents are sporting and practical. One woman is active and dynamic while her husband is contemplative and gloomy. Not to mention siblings, who are often opposites.

I have also found myself reflecting upon the differences *between* families. Even though many families I meet in my clinical practice belong to the same culture, they are so profoundly different from each other; a matter over which one family destroys itself, or rejoices, or suffers, is a matter of total indifference to another.

At the end of the 1980s, after having worked for more than a decade with families who have children with eating disorders, most of whom were devastated by power conflicts, I began to see couples and families with phobic clients. I was astonished: it was another world of meanings. What mattered here was who depended on the others and who, on the other hand, was able to manage alone and was free. Later on, curious about the profound differences I had found between families where one member had a phobic disorder and families who had an anorexic or bulimic daughter, I encouraged referrals of obsessive clients. Once again I found stories that were completely new to me. In recent years, clients with mood disorders and their families had opened up a world of meanings that I had not previously encountered (Ugazio, 2010).

The tendency in family therapy, from its earliest beginnings, to favour holistic concepts, such as those of family myth or paradigm (Ferreira, 1963; Reiss, 1981) had been a source of disappointment for me because of these differences which I had found within and among families. These concepts produce a monolithic vision of the family. They are capable of justifying similarities between the various members of the family—similarities which certainly exist—but they ignore the differences in families, which are perhaps greater, as studies on siblings have shown for some time (Reiss & Plomin, 1994; Towers, Spotts, & Reiss, 2003).

Thanks to the model of semantic polarities, which I developed during the 1990s, I finally succeeded in explaining, first of all to myself, the differences I had begun to reflect on in my clinical practice. In *Semantic Polarities and Psychopathologies: Permitted and Forbidden Stories* (Ugazio, 2013, in press; originally published in Italian as *Storie permesse, storie proibite*, 1998 (1st edition); 2012 (2nd edition)), I set out the model and analysed the processes (which are, of course, reciprocal) through which each person, while contributing towards constructing meanings in their own family, defines their own positioning and those of other members of their group. I focused on the specific semantics of families with phobic, obsessive, and eating disorders, and on the dilemmas of the particular positioning of the symptomatic member of the family.

I do not know whether David Campbell, who was influenced by this model, was particularly interested in the differences between those who take part in the same conversation. He was certainly intrigued by the possibilities offered by the concept of family semantic polarities for allowing dialogue between differences that were irreconcilable. I will return to this point, but first I would like to describe how David came to find out about a model of which there is (in English) only a single review in the *New York Review of Books* (Parks, 1999).

After the publication of the first edition of this book (Ugazio, 2013, in press), my doctoral students offered to empirically verify some of the ideas set out in it. At a time when the scientific community was increasingly sceptical about theoretical formulations unsupported by documented empirical corroboration, the project seemed to me not only meaningful, but also necessary. But what operational definition could be given to family semantic polarities and to the configurations of polarity that I had found in families with phobic, obsessive, depression, and eating disorders? How could a clinical model be transformed into empirically testable constructs?

David Campbell was the right person to help us with this task. He was not just a clinician; his background as a researcher was excellent and he was also rigorously systemic. For him, as for me, the experience of the Milan approach, in which we were involved from the beginning, had left an indelible mark in terms of a productive and fertile way of thinking. Furthermore, he had been holding seminars in Milan at the European Institute of Systemic–Relational Therapies (EIST), which I had just founded.

David enthusiastically accepted the proposal. He gave us invaluable suggestions for developing "The family semantics grid" (Ugazio, Negri, Fellin, & Di Pasquale, 2009). This instrument was created to verify whether the therapeutic conversations with people with phobic, obsessive, depressive, and eating disorders and their families are, in effect, dominated by the semantics which I had suggested in *Semantic Polarities and Psychopathologies: Permitted and Forbidden Stories*. Clinical intuition is important, but the "facts" also matter. Thanks to the family semantics grid (FSG), and David's contribution to it, we were able to confirm and clarify the clinical hypotheses that I had developed in the 1990s. Only now are we harvesting the fruits of this labour. The results of this research have been published (Ugazio, Negri, & Fellin, 2011), and also appear in a new edition of *Semantic Polarities and Psychopathologies: Permitted and Forbidden Stories* (Ugazio, 2013, in press).

David Campbell, unfortunately, is no longer with us to discuss these developments. I still recall the meetings in Milan over recent years, always extremely intense, with discussions around the table continuing until midnight, during which the model of the semantic polarities gradually became central, obscuring all the other shared interests. I could see that David was interested and gave him a rough translation of *Semantic Polarities and Psychopathologies: Permitted and Forbidden Stories*. But I had not imagined that, through this concept, David would identify interesting developments for his study and intervention in organisations, one of his favourite fields of interest (Campbell, 2000; Campbell, Caldicott, & Kinsella, 1994; Campbell, Draper, & Huffington, 1991). David Campbell's proposal to jointly write a book on organisations using that concept among its guiding ideas was a welcome surprise. However, I knew too little about organisations to be his partner in this undertaking. Since my participation in the 1980s in a group on the systemic approach to organisations, led by Mara Selvini-Palazzoli (Selvini-Palazzoli et al., 1986), I was no longer occupied in this field, but I was very pleased that a concept on which I had worked for so long had become a source of inspiration for him.

The most interesting discovery came from reading *Taking Positions in the Organization* (Campbell & Grønbæk, 2006). I realised that David was attracted to that model for different reasons than those that had led me to develop it. He, together with Marianne Grønbæk, had, therefore, applied it in a new way. And it was extraordinary how the implications that we had taken from the same model reflected our different characters and backgrounds. To enable the reader to understand these differences, I will briefly introduce the basic idea of the model of family semantic polarities.

Family semantic polarities: a conversational concept

To put it briefly, the model of semantic polarities, as developed in *Semantic Polarities and Psychopathologies: Permitted and Forbidden Stories* (Ugazio, 2013, in press), suggests that conversation in the family, as in every other group with a history, is organised through polarities of opposing meaning, such as fair/unfair, good/bad, outgoing/withdrawn, attractive/ugly. It applies a constructionist approach to the old idea that meaning is constructed through opposing polarities. As a result, "the polarities are considered as something inside the mind of each individual, but as a *discursive phenomenon*, identifiable with certain properties of the conversation" (Ugazio, 2013, in press). The most important of these are summarised in the sections that follow.

A shared plot of semantic polarities

Each member of the family constructs conversation within certain specific semantic polarities made prevalent by the discursive practices of that family. Those polarities form a kind of shared plot that generates specific narratives and storylines. (. . .)

A family is a family inasmuch as those belonging to it have a shared plot, formed by a certain number of semantic polarities and by the narratives that these polarities feed. The similarity between members of the family is limited to this sharing of a plot of semantic polarities which is derived from the conversational history of the family. This plot circumscribes the repertory of narratives and storylines within which the episodes will be constructed. (Ugazio, 2013, in press)

Inevitable positioning

All members of a family, as in the case of any other group with a history, must necessarily take a position inside the relevant polarities within their group. (. . .) For example, I will be able to feel and behave as someone who is 'full of energy' only if the polarity 'full/lack of energy' is relevant to the context in which I am (or have been) a part; otherwise I will experience other emotions and sensations. Even if my conduct might resemble that of someone who is full of energy, I will feel 'curious' or 'lively' in a situation where, as well as those who are similar to me, there are others who are 'apathetic' or 'sad'. (ibid.)

In short,

positioning does not occur within impredicable meanings. On the contrary, this process takes place within a repertory of meanings that is pre-defined, though flexible and changeable. Conversational partners position themselves and are positioned within the semantic polarities that appear relevant in a given moment in a specific context, as a result of the discursive practices of their own families and other groups to which they belong or have belonged. (ibid.)

Naturally, the relevance that the conversation assigns to each semantic polarity is continually negotiated through processes that are generally implicit. In the same way, the possibility of the conversation developing new meanings is always open.

Semantic polarities and the interdependence of multiple selves

> Conversational partners, positioning themselves with the other partners into the plot of semantic polarities relevant to their own intersubjective contexts, anchor their own identity to those of the other members of those groups. Shared subjectivities are consequently assured by the polar structure of meaning. Moreover, in all families (as in all other conversational contexts) more than one polarity is relevant, so that the number of selves become as many as the positions generated by polarity. (Ugazio, 2013, in press)

This property ensures that

> the organisation of meaning according to opposing polarities creates an interdependence between the identities of the members of the family. (. . .) Individuals, 'co-positioning' themselves into the relevant semantic polarities of the social groups to which they belong, assume a specific position within the shared narrative plot: they can position themselves as 'just', 'loyal', 'reserved' but, in order to occupy these positions, others will have to position themselves as 'unjust', 'untrustworthy', 'theatrical'. The identity of each partner thus crucially depends upon how many people, occupying different positions, allow the existence and continuity of discursive practices that generate the meanings on which his or her identity is built. That is why, when someone in therapy tells me: 'I am a good person', I immediately ask: 'Who is the bad one in your family?' (. . .)

> If, for example, the polarity 'intelligent/dim-witted' is relevant in a family—in other words, if it constitutes a semantic dimension around which conversation is organised—the members of this family will position themselves with people who are intelligent or very intelligent but will also be surrounded by people of limited intelligence or actually dim-witted. They will marry people who are intelligent, bright, stupid or painfully clueless. They will strive to become intellectually brilliant or will help those who are unfortunately less bright to become brighter. They will fight and compete to ensure that their intellectual abilities are recognised, they will end marriages and friendships when

intellectual problems arise. Some members of the family will be intellectually brilliant, or regarded as such, while others will prove to be intellectually lacking. One thing is certain: everyone in this family will have to 'position themselves' into the polar dimension in question and each member, in order to maintain their own identity, will have need of those positioned at other points in this semantic dimension.

In other families, though belonging to the same cultural background, the semantic dimension 'intelligent/dim-witted' will be irrelevant (. . .) and different polarities are relevant, and all families have more than one relevant polarity. For this reason, the organisation of meaning into opposing polarities, besides making identities interdependent, guarantees the multiplicity of the self. (Ugazio, 2013, in press)

As these properties clearly show, the model of semantic polarities envisages the family as a "co-position" of differences, or, rather, as a "co-position" of individuals united by their differences. Furthermore, the idea at the heart of the third property that the organisation of meaning into opposing semantic polarities establishes the "intersubjectivity", explains why profound differences and conflicts existing within the family (as in every other group with a history) do not necessarily cause its destruction. As the following example shows, the conflict, however severe, does not necessarily lead to the break-up of a group if it lies within the same narrative plot.

In many Italian working-class families during the first half of the twentieth century, central importance was placed upon the semantic dimension of "good/bad", expressed in terms of bigoted religiosity and a repressive attitude to sex. In some of these families with large numbers of children, where it was common for a couple of children to enter into religious orders, there was always one who was described as a "libertine". This expression was not used to mean a free-thinking follower of Enlightenment philosophy, but, rather, a member of the family, generally a brother, whose life was dissolute, or at least regarded as being so. The coexistence within the same family of opposite ways of behaving can be no surprise.

We can imagine one of these family encounters. As soon as the brothers and sisters meet together there will be a fast flow of communication. In response to the lowered eyes and disdainful glances which the religious brothers cannot fail to direct towards him, the libertine will respond with sneers and comments of doubtful taste,

inciting the clerics to step up the game by adopting indignant, sancti-
monious attitudes. The conversation will bounce backwards and
forwards. They all speak the same language, though from different
positions. But if we look closely, the libertine's idea of sex must not
have been all that different from that held by his prudish brothers and
sisters. For all of them, sex will have been something sordid, and it is
for this reason that the libertine indulged himself while the others
abstained. Even the identities of the siblings will be strengthened by
the encounter. The libertine's vulgarity and corruption will inevitably
have confirmed the clerics in their choice of the path of abstinence, just
as the evident attitude of mortification emanating from the brothers
who had chosen the path of the priesthood will have further
convinced the libertine that his enjoyment of the pleasures of life, even
though he risks the flames of hell, has been well worthwhile.

As this example shows, the concept of family semantic polarities
regards polar opposition as a matrix for the construction of individual
identities.

> The duality is in the matrix, not necessarily in the individual identi-
> ties. (. . .) The interdependence of opposites that this concept entails
> has to do with conversation which, according to Vygotskij (1934), is
> more primitive than thought both phylogenetically and ontogeneti-
> cally point of view. (Ugazio, 2013, in press)

Semantic polarities call into being opposite positionings in the conversation, thus helping to orientate mental representations of the subjects;
but they themselves are not representations as Kelly's (1955) personal
constructs are.

The polarities, the position of each person within them, and the
identities connected to the positioning are, of course, continually
changing during the family conversation and the other conversations
in which the person takes part. Above all, there is a change in the relevance assumed by each polarity during the different periods of the
family's life. When children are born, they have to "co-position" themselves within a pre-existing shared plot of family semantics that
reflects the history of their family and the emotions that mark it out.
Think of a baby who stretches her hand out to her mother. Her gesture
is ambiguous, like most of the actions of babies. It is, therefore, open
to a variety of semantic interpretations. One mother will say, "Look
how sweet you are; do you want to stroke me?" Another will joke,

"Well then, what do you want? Are you going to scratch your mummy because she won't pick you up? Look how pushy you are!" Yet another will turn round to look at the poster behind her saying, "How clever you are . . . you already want to know what that big animal is called? Yes, that's a lion . . . it has a mane and people call it the king of the jungle", or she will turn to her husband and say, "Look how she's flirting . . . she wants you . . . she's already trying to seduce you" (Ugazio, 2013, in press).

All of these mothers are attributing a meaning to the behaviour of their child by "co-positioning" themselves with her according to various patterns that reflect specific semantic dimensions. But they are also behaving as if their babies had assumed a well-defined position within a specific semantic polarity. The fact that a mother "co-positions" herself with her daughter, frequently interpreting the child's behaviour as "aggressive", and responding to the child in a way consistent with this interpretation, does not mean that the daughter constructs her own position in these terms. Instead, it indicates that the semantic polarity of "aggressiveness/gentleness" will be relevant for the child, together, of course, with other polarities. Her positioning in the group as "gentle", or, alternatively, as "aggressive", will depend instead upon the alliances and the more complex configuration of relations within the family.

Over the course of time, the centrality of this polarity could (and is, in fact, likely to) alter. As the child grows up, she will contribute more and more actively in constructing the plot of meanings within which she defines herself. This plot might (and, in fact, it will) be modified in unpredictable directions, which will depend upon the positioning that the child gradually assumes also in contexts outside the family.

The birth of a child into a family and into a culture, as well as the previous history of "co-positioning", certainly circumscribes the possible positions with which each individual can "co-position" him or herself with others. For the model of semantic polarities, the "I" is a position in the conversation. This does not mean, as suggested by MacIntyre (1981), that the "I" can be regarded as resembling no more than a "peg" upon which to hang the clothing of the infinite positions that it can assume, to use Goffman's metaphor (1959, p. 253). As clinical, as well as personal, experience has shown, it is not easy to change position.

Median positions and median personalities

David was interested in the relationships between semantic polarities, positioning, and identity. But what most intrigued him about the model of polarities was the possibility it seemed to offer him of giving everyone a position of value. It was no longer necessary for anyone to feel superfluous or out of place in the situations in which they were a part, because everyone inevitably found themselves taking a position in relation to the relevant semantic polarities of their particular group. Everyone is, therefore, equally important "in the sense that everyone can be constructed to occupy a position within the same discourse" (Campbell & Grønbæk, 2006, p. 5). And each position is equally essential for the construction of the meanings which the discourse creates. It is the recognition that each person makes an essential contribution to the construction of meaning which assures a basis, according to David and Marianne, from which to begin to discuss and negotiate new positions. Where there was a conflict in an organisation, David's objective was to polarise it: he presented it as a dilemma where, at the two extremes of a semantic polarity, two equally legitimate values came into conflict. If, for example, someone in an organisation was pushing for a change whose results were uncertain, though promising, while others opposed the change, the conflict was polarised by David as a dilemma between those who wanted innovation and those who wanted to safeguard security. David was careful, of course, not to present the conflict as a clash between courage and fear, which would have cast those at one of the two extremes in a negative light. Precisely because a positive value was attributed to both of the extremes, each person could, therefore, attach themselves to the polarity identified, clarifying (both to themselves and to others) their own position within the polarity and identifying connections between their own position and those in opposition. The opening of dialogue, achieved by polarising, valuing, and anchoring everybody's positions, made it possible, according to David and Marianne, to negotiate new positions for everyone and, as a result, to overcome fruitless conflicts.

One of the concepts that most intrigued David about the model of semantic polarities is the median position and the related idea that this position has its own specific characteristics because it is generated by conversational processes different from those which fuel the two opposing polar positions. He told me this on several occasions, and its implications can be seen in *Taking Positions in the Organization* (Campbell & Grønbæk, 2006).

It was meeting people with obsessive disorders that led me to think about the median position. Working with them, I realised how different their positioning was from those with whom I had been involved until then. Even though they were composed within very different family semantics, people with eating, phobic disorders and depression all had a positioning at one of the extremes of the semantic polarities directly connected with their disorder. This was not the case with obsessives. Therefore, I realised that there was a third, median position, which, of course, related as much to normality as to those with psychopathological disorders.

> Those positioning themselves at the extremes define themselves in relation to the others in terms of difference or likeness. (. . .) Precisely because their attention is focused on the others, they acquire increasingly specific individual characteristics: there is no "I" without a "Thou" as Buber (1923) put it. (Ugazio, 2013, in press)

When schismogenic processes intervene, there is what Bateson defined as an "excellence". As a consequence of the process which I have called exteriorisation, and of any symmetrical and complementary schismogenesis, people at the extremes have a stronger feeling of their own individuality and a personality which, to paraphrase Bateson (1936), we can describe as "specialist"; in other words, characterised by the maximisation of few traits. On the other hand, those who take a median position set up processes of centralisation.

> Their attention is directed primarily towards maintaining equilibrium in relation to the two extremes. Precisely because there is a prevailing interest for their *personal* position in relation to the polar positions, these individuals acquire a less specific individual character but their personality might be multi-dimensional and polyphonic. (. . .) Both the positions at the extremes and the median positions present advantages and risks for the individual. Excellence and harmony are resources, but can drive individuals into areas of difficulty. Excellence is risky by reason of its one-sidedness. It is inevitably accompanied by some deficiency. (. . .) Harmony also contains within itself equally disturbing risks. To be perfectly balanced in relation to a relevant semantic dimension means withdrawing from the conversation: the individual, to the limited extent of that semantic game, is no longer a conversational partner. (Ugazio, 2013, in press)

Of course, nothing of the kind generally happens. People in a median position actively participate in the conversation as much as those at the extremes, so that they continue to move towards one or other pole of the salient polarities in their own relational contexts. These movements do not generally produce any difficulties for that individual. However, for people suffering from obsessive disorders, movements towards one of the extremes of the good/bad polarity (prevailing in their family) causes intense suffering. For this reason, their bad behaviour is often egodystonic. Persons with obsessive disorders want to be good, but cannot. In fact, they place themselves in a median position in relation to those in their family who are wicked, addicted to vice, or selfish and those, on the contrary, who are pure, unblemished, capable of sacrifice.

Median personalities, whether untroubled, or tormented (as obsessives generally are), need not "co-position" themselves in all important relationships with people positioned at the extremes. In my clinical practice, I have met couples whose marriage works well (such as Costanza and Guglielmo, described below), where both partners are positioned in the median position, at least for the polarities most directly connected to the problem for which the therapy was requested. There have, of course, been plenty of happily married couples where both partners are positioned at one of the extremes. To understand the dynamics of a family where both spouses are at one extreme, it might be sufficient to widen the field of observation to those who occupy the other extreme. The same cannot be done when both spouses occupy a median position. The three poles of the relevant polarities in the family have to become the subject of the therapeutic conversation, as in this example.

"I want at least five children!" Costanza had told Guglielmo when they first started going out together. For Guglielmo, it hardly seemed true: he had found the woman of his dreams. Unlike other people of his age, he, too, could not wait to have a large family. For this reason, they got married immediately, at the age of twenty. The fact that they were both university students was not going to stand in their way. When Guglielmo was eighteen, he had received a large inheritance from an uncle and Costanza also came from a well-to-do family. The birth of Alessandro, a year and a half after their wedding, therefore brought great joy to both of them. And yet I had great difficulty in getting them to remember this happy beginning. They sat there humiliated and disillusioned as if to ask me: "Can you help us to understand how we could have produced such a child?" One thing was clear, even though they lacked the courage to admit it even to themselves: they both dearly wished they could turn their backs on this child, Alessandro, who had destroyed their dream. The idea of a large family had been forgotten and Guglielmo and Costanza were no longer considering even a second child. What disturbed Alessandro's parents was his aggressive and demanding behaviour. It was visibly apparent that he was a difficult child: he stood erect, with the direct and imperious glare of a little tyrant. He wandered around the therapy room, every now and then pushing a book or a piece of paper across the floor so that I, too, would understand who I was dealing with. His parents told me that the teachers at the nursery school had complained that Alessandro wanted to control the other children, would hit them if they failed to do what he wanted, got his way through violence, and was even aggressive towards the little girls. The contrast with his parents could not have been clearer. Costanza and Guglielmo were affectionate and gentle with each other. They had the appearance of mild, thoughtful, rather dreamy children. Alessandro and his parents did not seem to have anything in common. Costanza and Guglielmo were doubly upset because they had taken personal care over Alessandro's education. They told me immediately that they had not left him with grandparents or babysitters, but looked after him personally, sharing responsibilities on an entirely equal basis.

Working with them, I quickly became aware that it was useless looking for conflicts between the couple: they had never had any arguments because they shared the same ideas, the same interests, and, most importantly of all, they explained, neither of them enjoyed *commanding or obeying*. Perhaps it was for this shared characteristic that they chose each other; certainly, according to what they told me, this was the secret of their relationship. And it was also the reason why Alessandro's behaviour left them so helpless and impotent.

It was precisely this similarity in the couple that gave us an insight into how to understand and deal with the problems they were experiencing with Alessandro. For Costanza and Guglielmo, "command/ obey", "dominate/submit", "impose/succumb", were polarities that had played, and continued to play, a central role in the construction of their subjective position and an important part in their identity. No one describes themselves as people who *neither command nor obey* unless they have lived in a context in which someone dominated and someone else submitted. Who commanded and who obeyed in the families from which Costanza and Guglielmo came?

From the answers, much suffering and pain emerged. Even Alessandro stopped his provocation and took part in the session, giving me a drawing that showed, as he explained, an enormous grandpa lion and a tiny grandma mouse. Both Costanza and Guglielmo had a family history in which one of the parents was aggressive while the other submitted. There were commanders and subordinates, at least in their accounts of the stories. On these matters, there had been serious conflict and drama in their families, and their plans for the future had been developed precisely because of what had happened to their parents.

They had imagined themselves as parents with a large family in which *no one commanded and no one obeyed*. But their plan for a large family did not relate to the future, but to the past: to show their parents how they should have behaved towards their children. At first, they had constructed a family like the one they had dreamed about. For the first two years, Alessandro had caused no difficulty, and the young couple had behaved with their son in the same way that they wished their own parents had behaved with them when they were children. Whenever they interacted with him, they were speaking at the same time to their own parents, even though their parents were not physically present. Alessandro was therefore the apparent receiver of their communications. To paraphrase T. S. Eliot (*The Waste Land*, 1922), Alessandro might have asked his parents "Who is the third who walks always beside me?" Even if no one seemed to realise it, the parent–child field of inference always included the grandparents as well. Was Alessandro, through his behaviour, now expressing all his anger because his parents were not actually talking to him? Was he challenging their "median identities", forcing them to adopt assertive forms of behaviour which their conflict with their own parents prevented them from assuming? By placing them in difficulty as parents, was he requiring them to deal with their unresolved problems as children? In order to help Costanza and Guglielmo, we certainly had to construct new meanings that would transform the command/obey and impose/succumb polarities and their positionings within them. (For a detailed analysis of this clinical example, see Ugazio, 2013, in press.)

Personal histories and fields of application in a clinical concept

But let us return to David. He considered himself, in my view rightly, to be a median personality. He was multi-faceted and versatile, as his professional history demonstrates. David was a therapist, but also a researcher and a business consultant. He studied family interactions and the therapeutic process, but also focused his interests on large organisations. It is difficult to identify a hierarchy of interests in his intellectual biography or his professional positioning. I think that he had found in that concept a way of reconsidering some of his own personal resources.

The median position certainly plays a central role in the action model in organisations elaborated by David, together with Marinane Grønbæk (2006). This position is that which characterises the consultant and relates to a higher level of meaning, in so far as it can be compared with "an elevated platform from which an observer can look down and see the pattern of relationship between A and B", the two polar positions (see Grønbæk, this volume). And it is the position that the consultant, through dialogic conversation, seeks to enable members of the organisation to assume. When the members of an organisation are able to put themselves into a median position, it becomes possible to overcome conflict and to negotiate change.

> When we, as consultants, get to this stage, we begin to feel that we are closing one chapter in our work—not that we have necessarily completed the consultation, but that we have resolved one impasse, raised awareness of positions, and offered opportunities for people to create new meaning through dialogue. (Campbell & Grønbæk, 2006, p. 40)

The various implications that we have drawn from the model of polarities are certainly derived from our own personal history. David, in his introduction to *Taking Positions in the Organization* (2006), connects his interest in the model of polarities with his personal story. As the second child, five years younger than his brother, during his childhood and adolescence he had developed the feeling "of having arrived into a ready-made family preceded by a brother who seemed to already occupy an important place in family life" (Campbell, 2006, p. 5). Other places at the valued extreme of the family semantics did not seem to be available and "it did seem like this was an 'occupied position'—position not vacant, applicants need not to apply" (Campbell, 2006, p. 5). The model of polarities enabled him to appreciate his position in his original family: being at the extreme is no more advantageous than finding yourself in the middle. Both positions have limitations and resources. The limitations and resources are simply different. Much depends, of course, on the ability of each person to use their own resources. And, by being a consultant, David had made the best use of the abilities he probably derived from his median position.

I, too, had a brother who was five years older than me, who took up a large and significant position in the family: all of my parents' attention focused on him. I think it would have been difficult to try to occupy a similar position. I found myself thinking about this while my brother and I were dividing up the photographs of our childhood, after the recent deaths of our parents. There were far more of him than of me. I did not, in fact, even try to put myself in a similar position. At the age of six, I cut off my pigtails, which my mother used to plait hurriedly for me each morning, and made the first important decision of my life: from that day on, I would go to school by myself. And so it was that every morning, from my first year at primary school, carrying my school-bag, I overtook my class-mates, apparently pleased with my independence, while my brother, who was five years older, was being accompanied to school by my mother. In this, as in almost all the important semantic polarities, we were at opposite poles. We still are today. Likewise, our parents were also different from each other, and also from me and my brother. In developing the model of semantic polarities, I was not only looking for tools for my clinical activity with clients who had eating, phobic, obsessive, and mood disorders. I also wanted to answer certain enigmas in my own family story, and, most of all: why were we so different? Why did the sometimes fierce conflicts, caused by the differences between us, never cause us to break apart?

The interpretations that David and I have given to semantic polarities reflect, of course, our different fields of application. For David, this concept was an instrument that helped him to intervene in large organisations. For me, it is a guideline for therapy with families with phobic, eating, obsessive, and depressive disorders, with whom I carry out much of my clinical activity. In *Semantic Polarities and Psychopathologies: Permitted and Forbidden Stories* (2013, in press), I have reconstructed the semantics of these families, and the particular position of the client and the other members of the family, drawing from it certain general implications in terms of therapy. At present, I am working to identify the most appropriate therapeutic approach for families with different semantics. The hypothesis that I have is that the dominant semantics in the family developed allows certain therapeutic strategies to be pursued, while precluding others.

References

Bateson, G. (1936). *Naven*. Cambridge: Cambridge University Press.

Buber, M. (1923). *I and Thou*. Edinburgh: Clark, 1937.

Campbell, D. (2000). *The Socially Constructed Organization*. London: Karnac.

Campbell, D., & Grønbæk, M. (2006). *Taking Positions in the Organization*. London: Karnac.

Campbell, D., Caldicott, T., & Kinsella, K. (1994). *Systemic Work with Organizations*. London: Karnac.

Campbell, D., Draper, R., & Huffington, C. (1991). *A Systemic Approach to Consultation*. London: Karnac.

Dostoevsky, F. (1880). *The Brothers Karamazov*. New York: Bantam Books, 1970.

Eliot, T. S. (1922). *The Waste Land*. New York: Boni and Liveright.

Ferreira, A. (1963). Family myth and homeostasis. *Archives of General Psychiatry*, 9(5): 457–463.

Goffman, E. (1959). *The Presentation of Self in Everyday Life*. New York: Doubleday.

Kelly, G. A. (1955). *The Psychology of Personal Constructs*. New York: Norton.

MacIntyre, A. (1981). *After Virtue. A Study in Moral Theory*. Notre Dame, IN: University of Notre Dame Press.

Parks, T. (1999). Unlocking the Mind's Manacles. *The New York Review of Books*, XLVI(15): 43–48.

Reiss, D. (1981). *The Family's Construction of Reality*. Cambridge, MA: Harvard University Press.

Reiss, D., & Plomin, R. (Eds.) (1994). *Separate Social Worlds of Siblings*. Hillsdale, NJ: Lawrence Erlbaum.

Selvini-Palazzoli, M., Anolli, L., Di Blasio, P., Giossi, L., Pisano, I., Ricci, C., Sacchi, M., & Ugazio, V. (1986). *The Hidden Games of Organizations*. New York: Pantheon Books.

Towers, H., Spotts, E., & Reiss, D. (2003). Unraveling the complexity of genetic and environmental influences on family relationships. In: F. Walsh (Ed.), *Normal Family Processes* (3rd edn) (pp. 608–631). New York: Guilford Press.

Ugazio, V. (2010). L'appartenenza negata. Il contesto intersoggettivo delle organizzazioni depressive. *Terapia Familiare, 94*(3): 41–59.

Ugazio, V. (2013). *Semantic Polarities and Psychopathologies: Permitted and Forbidden Stories,* R. Dixon (Trans.) (2nd edn, extended, revised, and updated). New York: Routledge (in press) [originally published in Italian (1998, 1st edn; 2012, 2nd edn) as *Storie Permesse, Storie Proibite.* Turin: Bollati Boringhieri].

Ugazio, V., Negri, A., & Fellin, L. (2011). Significato e psicopatologia. La semantica dei distrurbi fobici, ossessivi, alimentari e depressivi. *Quaderni di psicologia clinica, 2:* 45–59.

Ugazio, V., Negri, A., Fellin, L., & Di Pasquale, R. (2009). The family semantics grid (FSG). The narrated polarities. A manual for the semantic analysis of therapeutic conversation and self-narratives. *TPM. Testing, Psychometrics and Methodology in Applied Psychology, 16*(4): 165–192.

Vygotskij, L. S. (1962)[1934]. *Thought and Language,* E. Haufmann & G. Vakar (Eds.). Cambridge, MA: MIT Press [originally published as *Myslenie i rec'. Psichologičeskie issledovanija.* Moscow-Leningrad: Gosudarstvennoe Social'no-Ekonomiceskoe Izdatel'stvo].

PART IV
CONSULTATION

Evolving applications of systemic ideas. Towards positioning and polarities: David Campbell in interview with Charlotte Burck

Edited by Sara Barratt

D avid discusses the development of his ideas that led to his application and use of the ideas of semantic polarities and positioning, and reflects on his consultative work.

CB: You were very well known for your writing about the Milan method. How did you decide to move on from that idea and develop something new?

DC: There are different strands to that. One is the clinical strand; I gradually began to feel that there was too much emphasis on the technique of interviewing and people fell in love with the idea of circular questions, and gossiping in the presence of, and so on, and after a while, it was being done in a way that was losing touch with some family members. You'd see puzzled looks in terms of: "What are you talking about?" and I thought we needed to revisit the question of what is family therapy and what does it mean to conduct an interview. So I tried to develop a model that was more responsive to feeling and tone in the room, but at the same time using some of the questioning techniques. I'm also interested in how family therapy takes its place in relation to other types of therapy, and how we train people to be working in the NHS or other settings. I began to think that the ideas were getting little bit stale and was looking for something that would take the Milan model forward, so Ros Draper and I wrote a book about applications of the Milan model (Campbell & Draper, 1985) which opened the door for me to apply the ideas to organisational systems. Another strand to this question is that I'm intellectually restless and I would feel kind of bored with repeating myself, so if I'm doing some training event or seminar on a topic I've done before, I will always do it differently, because I think it communicates much more intensively to people if you're fresh about your own thinking.

CB: And your book *Applications of Systemic Family Therapy: The Milan Approach* (Campbell & Draper, 1985) was applying it in many different settings. What effect do you think the feedback from the book had on the field and on you?

DC: I think it was a very important book because it gave the Milan model a profile and developed systemic thinking beyond the world of therapy. It said, we can apply these ideas to how organisations change and develop. I was pleased to bring so many authors into the book and I got interested in doing a series through pushing the authors to articulate what they were doing in their own setting.

CB: Can you say how the transition from Milan to post-Milan and the connection with other postmodern ideas influenced your work with organisations?

DC: I make the association between post-Milan and second-order cybernetics. I got very excited about the work of von Foerster (1974, 2002) and others who put the therapist in the centre of the process. I thought this was a real leap and go back to Lynne Hoffman's (1985) phrase/idea that we used to think that the family had a problem and now we think that the problem has a family, or the problem has a system around it. That was a seminal idea that represented turning a corner into post-Milan work. In relation to organisational work, I think organisations are purer systems than families because they have to accomplish something. The system has to work together to produce a widget or a service and you can judge the effectiveness on the basis of what they've produced and whether they have come in under budget. So it lends itself to a systems model in the purist, theoretical sense. I've always been interested in organisations and teams, and how people work. To have a team working together to produce something is exciting, intellectually and emotionally. I like the idea of having to produce something, so when I started here at the Tavistock, there were lots of seminars and writings on how the organisation had to fit together to maintain a primary task. Then I moved away from psycho-analytic thinking to work more on the application of systemic ideas to organisations.

CB: And then you wrote some influential books about the applica-tion of social constructionist thinking to organisations; can you say a little bit about how you developed those ideas?

DC: With families, you're intervening as a therapist, in organisa-tional life, you're intervening as a consultant, so I got interested in the interventions that can help an organisation and these ideas seemed to fit. As a family member, you've got to fit in with the family group to feel you belong, and similarly, with an organisation, you've got to feel you belong or you begin to drift away and think more about yourself. If you don't feel a part of the system, the system begins to break down, because it's a group of individuals rather than an organisation pulling together. That central idea helped me move into the organisational work from a conceptual point of view. Organisations don't like the reflective spaces that clinicians are used to, so you have to find a way to intervene that's more active, suggesting certain types of structures or meetings. For example, I may suggest that they end their meetings with five minutes to discuss the question about how we did as a group today, which I've passed on to lots of organisations. You've got to present systemic thinking in a different way as a consultant; they want more expertise and direction, so a lot of the time is spent defining your role in a way that fits into that environment.

CB: So you are paying attention to the kind of language that would fit best for the kind of organisation you're working with?

DC: Yes. They often say, "Are we going to increase our profits if we hire you?" If people are prepared to take an indirect answer, that in the long run, profits will improve if people are more aware of the process they're in, then yes. If they want, they want to see profits shift within the next few months, you're probably not the right person; they probably need a more traditional management consultant.

CB: What do you think distinguishes your approach to consultation to organisations from, for example, the Tavistock Consultancy Service, which has a psychoanalytic approach?

DC: The biggest difference is that I'm not particularly interested in the interpretative style or in trying to understand why things are the way they are in organisations. I'm not looking for causes. My approach is based in the present and leaning into the future, so I would be more interested in thinking of what structures can be set up, what kind of conversations can you have within your organisation that will help you dis-solve these problems rather than making interpretations about the history and why things have got the way they are. Organisations are more complicated than families, and if you're spending a lot of time pursuing that line of thinking I don't know how productive it is. I'm not a psychoanalyst, so I'm not trying to transfer psychoanalytic concepts from the consulting room into the organisation. I don't think that they work that well. Maybe if you're doing one-to-one coaching, or working with a small team and certain rivalries and Oedipal feelings are getting stirred up, maybe that would be helpful. But in terms of organisational process, I think it's more helpful to work with a model of helping people listen and talk about differences and difficult things that are getting swept under the carpet. They need structures to be able to do that, rather than just somebody telling them what's going on.

CB: In that book, *The Social Construction of Organisations* (2000) the first chapter pulls out ideas from quite a number of thinkers from outside the systemic field. How did you get drawn to their ideas?

DC: I'm curious to pick up ideas from related fields. So I gathered bits and pieces over a few years and didn't know how they all fitted together, but thought there must be a way of bringing these ideas together. So I set myself a little project one summer and read original texts in more detail, putting together a framework that was more social constructionist than Milan, and that was the basis of doing more organisational work and having a model that I could fall back on. I believe that the attempt to maintain a power structures stops people listening to one another. The idea that you needed to have words in order to have thoughts and feelings was a revelation; it sounds so obvious, but I had trained with a psychoanalytic framework and the assumption that feelings emanated from internal states, so the idea that you can only have certain thoughts if you have the words to express them was an exciting part of the linguistic turn for me.

CB: How did the work that you then developed in consultation with organisations affect you as a clinician?

DC: I always felt that the work with families is satisfactory at an emotional level in a way that work with organisations isn't, and the work with organisations is more challenging at an intellectual level. So I like to do both. When you're doing organisational work, it's harder to get close to people's emotions and maybe it's not appropriate anyway, so I think it's a privilege when families allow us to come into their lives and to be vulnerable. I'm probably needing to move back and forth on that polarity, because I do see them doing different things for me.

CB: I wonder whether we should go into those ideas you developed about polarities, which, I think, came about for their use in organisations rather than clinical work?

DC: If I follow a social constructionist model as a therapist, I would just keep asking "how can we help people construct meanings together?" Then I began to study how dialogue works, because it's a vast field and if you can help people listen to each other, you're nintey per cent of the way there. So I saw family therapy differently, that it's not so much about the formulation that you make, it's whether or not people can strip away some of their biases, their anger and preconceptions, and let themselves hear something new. The Public Conversations project (Becker, Chasin, Chasin, Herzig, & Roth, 1995) was a big influence on me as they've got rules which people have to follow in order to have dialogue. That got me interested in what needs to happen for dialogue to work. I was looking for a more intellectual model, which led me toward positioning theory in that if you can appreciate the positions people are coming from and use that as the basis of a dialogue, you've got some tools that you can use as a therapist or as a consultant. I was in Italy doing some work with Valeria Ugazio, and she had been looking at semantic polarities in clinical families with a member with anorexia or depression or OCD, and she had identified semantic polarities in these families, such as winning and losing, and she would work with these and other polarities that families use to explain the world [see Ugazio, this volume]. If you have to be a winner in this family, then everybody else is a loser, if you have to be in control, then you're seeing the world as being out of control, and that, for me, was the kind of thing I was looking for because it linked positioning with clinical work and therapeutic process, so I spent some time with her and started writing it up and pulling those bits together in the semantic polarities book. Subsequently, I was doing a seminar in Denmark and trying to present these ideas about semantic polarities when Marianne Grønbæk came up to me and said, "I'm very interested in this idea about polarities and maybe we could work together." So I went to Denmark a few times to work on this model and do some more training and consulting. She was an organisational consultant, mainly in schools and social services, so we tried to clarify some of the concepts and the way they held together so that we could link dialogue, positioning theory, and semantic polarities into one framework [see Grønbæk, this volume]. I liked working with her because she's very creative and it's nice when you work with somebody who's picking it up and running with it in the same way that you are.

CB: And then you can develop things in conversation as well. I remember early on in your work you always asked the question: "What if you think the opposite?", so I think it's quite interesting that you are now using this in a different way under this term "semantic polarities".

DC: I always thought that was a good clinical technique to always ask yourself and your families about the opposite to create space for other ways of thinking. But I suppose positioning theory gave it a philosophical or theoretical basis and of course if you talk to anybody who's a philosopher, they'll say, this is about 3,000 years old and the Greeks were talking about this on Mount Olympus and all kinds of people have used this dichotomy. I've been interested in dilemmas since I started working as a therapist, I've always wanted to bear in mind the point at which you feel you're pulled in different directions, what's the issue, the feeling you get and how can we study it and get interested in it, because the more I use this model, the more I think if you just get to that point and just step back and support people with it, they'll find their way through the dilemma, you don't have to do anything.

CB: To take a slightly different tack, you once gave a lecture here called "The ideas that divide the Tavistock" and people were very interested in that topic, and I wonder whether your ideas have changed about that since then?

DC: I'm interested in the fault-lines in organisations, the things that are not able to be said, and as I'm in this organisation, I'm feeling the power differentials and the fault-lines, so there's also a personal way to kind of get something off my chest, get something into the discourse. I think I missed some opportunities to go more deeply into the differences and really challenge people conceptually and in terms of organizational oppressions and boundaries. I sometimes regret that I didn't push it further, but it felt a bit risky. I thought maybe I should tone it down so they're not actually going to stop speaking to me in the corridors, and I did tone it down a little bit, and then I wondered afterwards whether I probably could have pushed it a bit more, maybe I would have ruffled a few more feathers, but I would be interested to go a little bit further and push some of these issues, you know, in a stronger way.

CB: How do you think you would use those ideas now in relation to the work you've developed around semantic polarities?

DC: Yes, we could organise another one, which is part two. It would be interesting to identify three or four of the polarities that are really important and that would help diffuse, because the power of the polarities model is that it's respectful and it's egalitarian. We're all here together, we're all taking positions, and it's just a position, it's not the truth, these are not tablets of stone, and people relax and listen differently when you put it to them that way. I suppose an important polarity would be: "We must preserve the purity of our way of think-ing" as one strong position that's held here, and the other would be, "We must preserve the ability to co-create new ways of thinking with strange people and strange ideas"; those could be really interesting polarities and then you could have the discussion across the polari-ties, that would be interesting for people. But they'd have to commit themselves to wanting to be interested in the polarisation process first, so you'd need a preliminary one which is about "Why did you come into the room today"? and, "Do you really want to be here?", "Is it more helpful to stay in your office or is it more helpful to come up here and be a part of a lecture/seminar that is talking about the inter-face between ideas?" That's where you may need to start.

CB: Can you think of other semantic polarities that are central to this institution?

DC: Possibly maintaining positions of power, which everybody's interested in in different ways, or "We've had the power, we want to hold on to it", and "We haven't had the power and we want more of it"—I wonder what that would be like? Power is expressed in many different ways here in terms of courses and budgets and the models of thinking, and I'm interested in how people preserve power by ignoring certain questions, or getting confused, or being unclear, or all these techniques for preserving things and at the other end, to start off with clarity and understanding and openness and as though that would give us more power, that would be interesting. Transparency would be a good polarity line. It's very important and it's something we should aspire to.

CB: We haven't talked very much about the term "discourse", which is another concept that's been really important .

DC: I think British psychology is well known for being the leader in developing discourse in psychology and critical realism that are very much models of the way realities are presented and conveyed in society. That was an interesting development, because it combined the political and the personal very neatly, and some of those early papers by Potter and Wetherell (1987) describing the oppressiveness of certain discourses were very challenging and new. I'm probably more interested in the micro-level of creating dialogues between people, because I think I can do more with that as a therapist and as a consultant. I've always liked models that combined theory and practice and that's what I liked about the Milan models, and I think that this polarities model is similar in that I've used it, mainly with organisations and, to some extent, with family groupings, and it has a profound effect on people because it can be a dramatic demonstration of the way people are connected when they don't think they are connected, and it also has a way of easing people off their own stance and their own position, which is done by being able to say, it's just a position. If you do it in a respectful way, they will let go of some of the power of their position and begin to look around and consider themselves as being connected to other positions. The other thing that I've been struck by is the visual component, which I hadn't appreciated before I started using it, but there is something about getting a flip-chart and putting people's marks on a line that has a big impact on them, because they can see themselves being connected and somehow it's different than if you just say it. The challenge is to get people in the room in the first place. That's why I was interested in the Public Conversations project, but they had to be self-selected in the sense that they wanted to take part, so they must have been open-minded enough to take part.

CB: My understanding of the way they worked is that they spent a lot of time meeting with people individually to prepare them

DC: I presume, then, some people were deselected in that process. The challenge is to get people to take the first step to want to take part in a project to see the relationship to other people they don't agree with. In order to get to that point, sometimes you have to do preliminary work like individual meetings or polarities work with people that don't want to be there and let them talk about why it's important for them not to take part in the study and other people why it is important to take part in the study. I would give them a little talk about how we as individuals grow and develop by seeing differences and getting a distance from differences so that we feel safe, but can also be curious about how other ideas, other people, other views, could be helpful for us. I make it very much centred around the self, rather than you're going to be holding hands and going off into the horizon together. So that's the kind of thing I would probably need to do to get people involved in taking an interest in these other positions.

CB: But how does that work, David, because giving people pep talks doesn't always work? I imagine you must use other methods to get people engaged in the process.

DC: Yeah, well, I would, I would use it with people that I had some kind of contract to work with and probably offer it to them as a different way of working, different way of talking. You could say, "I have a technique or a method here that we could use; it's called dialogical conversation, would you like to try it? It requires a particular way of working, it's got some ground rules we can think about and then if you like, we'll try it, and if not fine, we'll carry on with the work we're doing." So I would probably make it a separate activity that they could pick or choose. Then, if there's enough interest, you're halfway there because the question is to try to learn why it's so important for those people to take the other position. I want to come back to the point you raised earlier, that in using this model the thing that is the most difficult is to find the polarity line that everybody wants to join, and I keep digging and thinking until I find one that people voluntarily want. I work with organisations and they'll say, let's have a meeting and we'll have a polarity line about open management or open dialogue, and some people don't want it so they're not going to want to explore positions on that theme, so you find another theme that they do want to explore, which might be, how can I avoid being influenced by other people, or something like that. It might be a theme, if they all want to be independent and autonomous, that's probably what they want to talk about and all of the different ways or the different positions in that theme.

CB: But what's the process of finding a theme that's going to be significant for most of the people?

DC: Well, I just keep asking that question until something clicks and it takes a while and when you've got there you feel, oh yes, that would work. If I don't get that I need to go back and start with something very basic, like how to win, how to become the most prominent member of this team without upsetting my colleagues, you know, something that's a bit closer to the bone, maybe a bit cheeky, and you just have to kind of gauge at what level of honesty and openness and realism they want to present themselves.

CB: Can you give an example of using polarities that you feel has worked well?

DC: There was a multi-professional service of about ten professionals who had some bitter experiences of going to a tribunal because of complaints within the team of one person harassing another . This split the team apart, with people taking sides. I was asked to work with them and felt they were really stuck. It occurred to me that a polarity might help. I went to the flip-chart and made a polarity in which at one end I wrote, "This is wrong", and at the other end, I wrote, "This is understandable", and I said that as their consultant I would help them move back and forth on this continuum and assume that people would take different position at different times. But it was up there on the flip-chart and I asked them each to mark "where are you now", and most people were clustered down at the "this is wrong" end and were furious, and I said, "Fine, I want to hear how you feel about it and, if you're furious, please share it and we'll stay with that as long as we need to, but remember that you're on a continuum and you're taking a position, and if and when you're ready, there are other positions available to you." That's all I needed to say and then they felt safer about being angry because they knew it was part of a bigger process; we would come to some kind of resolution, but neither was I pushing them away and saying "I don't want to hear about your anger", which would have been also a mistake. But it's putting in front of them that possibility of being connected to this process that empowered them. I said, "It's up to you, I'm a facilitator and I'll help you identify where you want to go and what position you want to take, but my lead always comes from you."

CB: It strikes me that part of the process is that it validates people in the position that they're in at the time and it leaves something open to be different, doesn't it?

DC: I think that visual presentation is important. They can be talking away for five minutes and, just out of the corner of their eye, they look up and think that's me and I'm in that position and there are other positions down there and it just begins to kind of be part of their consciousness. It wasn't articulated.

CB: So it's as if you gave them a new possibility of a different place to be . . .?

DC: Yes, and the final bit of the application of this model is to make it possible for people to have dialogue, so it would eventually be helpful for the people who think this is wrong to want to talk to those who say this is understandable. If they have a dialogue and appreciate the others' positions, then they'll broaden the base for their position, so that each will have a little more understanding of the other and start to fill the blank void of anger.

CB: And do you have a structure?

DC: I've got a handout with rules saying why it's important to another person to try to let go of your own ideas and just listen and try to be respectful. Sometimes, I say other things, like, how can you talk to each other and make it a little bit more possible for people to disagree with you, or to present a different point of view, but that's actually when we're in the preliminary stages in order to get people to respect positions.

CB: Do you think there are some situations in which you wouldn't be able to use semantic polarities, or do you think it's something that, as long as you're able to identify a semantic polarity, everybody could get connected to, that it could be applied to almost any situation?

DC: I can't think of one where it wouldn't apply when you're in a situation where people don't agree. The only caveat might be about language and whether everybody understands what the word position means. It's a little bit of a jargon term, and you might have to use "point of view", or something else. It might vary in terms of whether you get to a dialogical process with people talking to each other in a room, or whether you just raise it with kind of a flip-chart map and let people get on with it. That would depend on the organisation, what they want, and what their experiences have been with you. I'm pretty active, it's more of a facilitating a process than just stepping back and letting it happen. I really steer it.

CB: What do you think Rom Harré would make of the developments?

DC: He wrote the foreword for the book (Harré, 2006) and talked about appreciating the clinical application because he's not a clinician. I haven't met him since the book came out, but I think he'd probably be quite pleased with the way it's been used. I don't go as far into the conceptual framework as he does; he's into the morality of positioning, and I'm just not going there because it makes it more complicated than I need. This is a very good tool to get people to slow down and listen and it builds in a lot of mutual respect.

References

Becker, C., Chasin, L., Chasin, R., Herzig, M., & Roth, S. (1995). From stuck debate to new conversation on controversial issues. A report from the Public Conversations Project.

Campbell, D. (2000). *The Social Construction of Organisations*. London: Karnac.

Campbell, D., & Draper, R. (Eds.) (1985). *Applications of Systemic Family Therapy: The Milan Approach*. London: Grune & Stratton.

Campbell, D., & Grønbæk, M. (2006). *Taking Positions in the Organization*. London: Karnac.

Harré, R. (2006). Foreword. In: D. Campbell & M. Grønbæk (2006). *Taking Positions in the Organization*. London: Karnac.

Hoffman, L. (1985). Beyond power and control: toward a "second order" family systems therapy. *Family Systems Medicine, 3*: 381–396.

Potter, J., & Wetherell, M. (1987). *Discourse and Social Psychology. Beyond Attitudes and Behaviour*. London: Sage.

Von Foerster, H. (1974). *Cybernetics of Cybernetics*. Urbana, IL: University of Illinois Press.

Von Foerster, H. (2002). *Understanding Understanding. Essays on Cybernetics and Cognition*. New York: Springer.

CHAPTER NINE

Dialogue: keeping in touch

Marianne Grønbæk

D avid Campbell often said that the most important thing in a dialogue is for the individuals involved to "keep in touch" with each other and with each other's understanding. To be able to do this, it is necessary to become interested in what the other person is saying and thinking, and why they are talking and thinking in that way. In a passionate conversation, when you are convinced that you are right, it can be very hard to give up your own opinions. In David's view, it is important to understand that, in such situations, it takes courage to let go of your own opinion in order to listen to the other person's ideas.

In my consultancy work with people and organisations who want help with problems or with their development, "keeping in touch" is an important issue for those I work with as well as for myself. With David's absence, this seems even more important, as his work and his skill in "being in touch" was proof of how significant this is.

This chapter is about taking positions and *keeping in touch* in a variety of conversations when there are disagreements. We call these *positioning conversations with semantic polarities* (Campbell & Grønbæk, 2006; Campbell & Huffington, 2008; Grønbæk, 2008). This chapter invites you to comment, contribute, and explore these ideas further, to continue to develop the thinking about semantic polarities.

Once upon a time . . .

In 1998, like many others in Denmark and other countries, I became fascinated by "appreciative inquiry" (AI). I was introduced to this approach by Peter Lang from Kensington Consultation Centre (KCC), London and could see how appreciative thinking brought a new perspective to relationships between people *in* conversations. People felt more relaxed, happier, and found it easier to have conversations together.

From 2000 I worked with appreciative inquiry and began to learn that there was more to it than people had described. However, I started to discover, when I began using the approach, that I was conveying that there was a "right" way and a "wrong" way. The "wrong" way created difficulty and involved the things that we felt we should not discuss. It disturbed conversations when those who felt the need to express "negative" themes were perceived to be "wrong". I began to question how I could work with appreciative enquiry in conversations when some people are "right" and others are "wrong", and we did not want to stay in conversation with those who are "wrong". In such situations, the discussion often split into "the insiders" and "the outsiders". How was that to be understood as appreciation?

In my consulting work with organisations or groups, many people were very interested in learning about appreciative inquiry as a model, but it also seemed difficult for them to apply it to their organisation and their relationships. Managers and leaders found it difficult to apply to their leadership and their relationships with each other and their staff, and staff found it a challenge to apply to their relationships with each other and their clients and customers. At every level, individuals wanted to use the AI model but found it difficult to put into practice.

As teachers of AI, we were very eager to tell people what AI was and what it was not. On one occasion while I was teaching AI, one of the group commented that he was born negative; hardly a statement about feeling appreciated. However, because I found it so easy to be appreciative, I did not see the problem. Being the consultant, I could manage to stay appreciative, but some of those I taught were unable to make it to work in their conversations. There had to be more to it, and there had to be someone with whom to discuss this.

Then, in 2002, David Campbell, a very appreciative person himself, introduced the "semantic polarity conversation" in Denmark as a conflict-solving conversation model based on positioning theory. Through learning, exploring, and developing the semantic polarity model, I was able to look back at Peter Lang's work and recognise that he was always interested in the "outsider position" and in the "opposite position", which is very appreciative. I had to be in a different position to be able to see this. From my present position, developing semantic polarity ideas, I can see that its underpinning is AI. The use of semantic polarities makes a space in which appreciation can become part of the conversation.

When David introduced me to the "semantic polarity conflict-solving model", I learnt from my own experience that there is not one right answer to the question "What did you hear?", but many different answers, which depend on what position you take and offer in the conversation. Using the semantic polarity model, the question "What did you hear?" becomes "From which position did this comment come?", and "In which position did you hear it?" We always think and talk from one position to another—this is our definition of a relationship. The relationship can be visualised as between these two questions:

What did you hear?
(a) From which position did it come?   →   The relation between
(b) In which position did you hear it?   the two positions.

Taking part in this relationship means constantly developing your own and the other person's positions and even changing your position.

What was crucial, as David emphasised, was that both ends of a polarity line need to be understood in a positive way. There is not one truth about what is positive or what is negative, which is to be appreciated in the best meaning of the word. This became key to my work. Each time we work with an individual or a group, both ends of any polarity line have to be understood as positive. The conversation about developing an understanding of both ends as positive can be the most important and interesting one that you have as a consultant with a group. Instead of feeling they are in the "wrong", through using a semantic polarity people experience their own thinking as understandable.

In developing any model or theory, there seem to be times when you think that you know very little and times when you experience that you know a great deal. Let us assume that those are just "positions". Therefore, when exploring and developing a theory and practice, this encompasses moving back and forth between the two positions:

Knowing a lot _____ Knowing very little

I often use this semantic polarity in my consultation work. When starting work with an individual or group in an organisation, it can be very helpful to know a lot about the organisation and it can be helpful to know very little. Whatever position you take as a consultant is revealed in the questions you ask from that position. Questions asked from the "knowing a lot" position seem to take the conversation into a direction of a "we both know" relationship. Questions asked from the "knowing very little" position takes the conversation into a direction of a "we are exploring together" relationship. But it also takes the conversation into a more uncertain, insecure relationship and in the direction of a "do I trust that you know enough" relationship. This direction is often most present at the beginning of a relationship between a consultant and the client. These conversations can be successful if the consultant can take a 50–50 position: both the "knowing a lot" and the "knowing a little" positions in the first conversation with the organisation. In this way, the consultant can show that it would be safe to take both positions, and all the positions in between these two positions.

Based on other people's work with positioning theory, we developed the semantic polarity model to be used as a conflict-solving model. We then began to consider it as a way of "thinking". This was important for me, because I connect a "model" with a "description" to be used as described. Doing it as described is doing it "right", which includes the idea that there are many ways it can be done "wrong."

Right _____ Wrong

If both ends of the polarity line are to be understood as positive, what is positive about the "wrong" position? What can be learnt in taking that position? And what can be learnt taking the "right" position?

When a colleague and I were teaching AI to a large group of academics, one of the participants (A) was very insistent in saying that she did not understand AI and that she could not see how it could be used in her work. She was so insistent that the other participants started to avoid her in the exercises we asked them to do. To begin with, my co-teacher and I thought that perhaps she should not take this course. Then I thought that maybe we should see her reaction as a position. My co-teacher said that as I was the one who worked with positions, it would make sense if I was the one who would help her, and, with a smile, she said that she would take care of the rest of the group.

I then said to A that understanding and not understanding could be understood as just two positions. I drew a polarity line and explained that she was very much taking the "not understanding" position. I then asked her if she could try to take the "understanding" position and tell me what she understood. Her response was that I should not try to play these educative games with her. A day and a half later, during which she continued to hold the "not understanding" position, she suddenly said, "Now I think I do understand something!" By this time, I just wanted to go to lunch and have a break, but here she was, finally taking the position that I had continually been asking her to take. So I asked her what she now understood. She answered, "Isn't it the case that talking about the problem is talking about the behaviour we want to leave behind?" I had never heard AI described in such a short and clear sentence! And that gave me the opportunity to make the opposite statement: *talking about the success is talking about the behaviour and competences we want more of.* And we were able to continue the conversation about how important it is to appreciate the "not understanding" position (the "wrong" position), and that both sentences could be understood as a semantic polarity where both ends should be recognised in a positive way and be appreciated.

This participant taught us something important about AI, about taking positions and their influence on relationships, and the use and meaning of semantic polarity in conversations and teaching.

Teaching a "model" can construct the relationship between the students and the teacher as two positions: the students take the "asking questions" position, and the teacher then has to take the "having all the answers" position. This is one of my prejudices. However, a semantic polarity allows me and those I work with to take positions along the whole line between

Giving answers _____ Asking questions.

Therefore, in Denmark, we call semantic polarity a way of "thinking"; a way of "thinking" which we define as always on the move, to be improved, developed, retold, to be understood within the relationships of the individuals in the present conversation and in the process.

A lot of David and my "working together" involved David working in England and me in Denmark. I worked with my clients and organisations and developed semantic polarity thinking in those contexts. After two years, I telephoned David and said that my clients and I were ready for a "check up" in this way of thinking, but David replied that there was not a way of thinking. What became apparent were the differences in our ways of developing and working with polarities, which itself could be illustrated by semantic polarities.

Through complexity _____ Through simplicity

Through "certainty" _____ Through "experimenting"

Through theory _____ Through practice

Through working with _____ Through working with
SP all the time   SP some of the time

If you construct a semantic polarity like those above, you visualise that you are disagreeing, but are still in the conversation, you are secure in your own position because it is "acknowledged", and you can also see the other's position. You are able to answer questions addressed to your position and can get interested in the other's position by asking questions of that position and the conversation about the difference can continue. You are able to feel free to take a new position and have a new conversation about those differences and the different ways to look at things.

Let us take one semantic polarity that we used in our co-work. David would often take a theoretical position to look at a conversation. He often focused on thoughts *about* people, behaviours, and relationships in his teaching and writing. I would often take the position of a practitioner, from my work *with* people. At times, we would shift positions, where David talked about his work with people and I would take a theoretical position and place his practice into semantic polarity thinking. Every time we explored our work, we took different or opposite positions. Every position you take will have an impact on the conversation. Having that in mind, you can take a different position in a conversation when you think it needs a change of direction.

A theoretical perspective _____ A practical perspective

Some people develop mainly by looking at things from a theoretical perspective and others mainly from a practical perspective. But these are just positions. In conversations, it is often very helpful to visualise these positions. So take your own position.

There is an understanding connected to both of these positions and to all the positions. Taking the polarity line above, a question to ask of the two different positions is: What is the most simple thing to do? What is the most complex thing to do? This use of semantic polarities enabled us to constantly discuss and get interested in the other person's position(s), and enabled us to develop semantic polarity thinking in our work with organisations and people. And the people and organisations we worked with, in turn, enabled this development.

So, if it is all just a position, every time a person takes a position there will be at least the "opposite" position. And if that person becomes interested in that "opposite" position, the conditions for a dialogical conversation are present. If there is no "right" or "wrong" in this, you have to take your own position and work from there. So, is this semantic polarity thinking complex or simple? Take your own position:

Complex _____ Simple

In conversations, there seem to be three positions that people take:

- I am right—therefore I am not listening, because I do not need your thoughts.
- This is complex and I need to help you understand this better. I know this better than you.
- This is on the whole interesting. I need to learn more about your thoughts.

Position three will invite you into a semantic polarity conversation.

A famous Danish artist, Bjørn Nørgaard, said in connection with a recent exhibition at the Modern Museum of Art in Copenhagen, that

> You cannot see a sculpture without seeing it in relation to yourself as a person. You walk around it, you take its measure in relation to your own size; it can be hard, it can be smooth, it can be rough . . . for we do not only think with our brain, we think with our entire body. (Nørgaard, 2010)

A conversation is like seeing a sculpture; you are *in* the conversation. Using semantic polarities makes it easier to be in disagreeing conversations, where disagreeing is not a matter of convincing the other. It is a matter of becoming interested in the other person's view and thoughts, in the other person's position. If both individuals are asking questions of each other's positions, they are having a semantic polarity conversation or a dialogical dialogue. Appreciative inquiry cannot be more appreciative than if people appreciate each other's positions.

The use of semantic polarities started as a conflict-solving model.

A school manager contacted me because two teachers had such a serious conflict that both teachers were talking about leaving the school. The chair of the school board, the manager, and the trade union representative all thought there was an urgent need to solve the conflict. The conflict had spread to the whole group of teachers and everybody was taking sides. The two teachers concerned, a man (A) and a woman (B), did not feel the same need. They were afraid that it would be too hard. So, at our first session, I explained to both teachers how I would handle the conflict-solving conversation. I talked about the semantic polarity model. Both teachers were relieved and we set a time to meet with the two teachers, the school manager, and a witness chosen by the woman.

In the conflict-solving session, I made a semantic polarity with each teacher's statement at either end:

A's statement _____ B's statement

I described how, in all conversations, we take and give positions, and in that way we are connected in the conversation. In this case, there was a conflict. And when we are in conversations we think we understand the other person, whereas in conflict we think we do not. But this is still a conversation where each position should be appreciated by the other person. Therefore, I would take the position of managing the conversation during which both individuals would tell their view of the situation that led to the conflict and would be asked to comment on the other person's comment. First, I asked A to talk about his position, his side of the story, and then I asked B to talk about her position, her side of the story. Then I asked A to say three to five things he liked in what B had said. A looked at me and said very quietly that he had not heard a word of what B had said, because he had been very much into his own thoughts. I said that that was very natural, and that, indeed, that is often what creates conflict—that we stop listening to the other person. So I asked B to say more about her position. And A listened! And then A was able to say five things he liked in what B had said.

Then I asked B to say three to five things she liked in what A had said. And she smiled and admitted that she was in the same situation as A had been. She had not heard a thing of what A had said. We all smiled, and I repeated that that is just natural and then asked A to say more from his position. This time, B was listening and came up with five things she liked in what A had said.

Then I asked each of them to take their position (2) on the same semantic polarity line as before:

A's statement _____ B's statement
     A2   B2

I asked both A and B to talk about their new positions. A said that it was the things that B had said and that A had never thought about the situation and B like that before. B said the same about her new position. Then B said that she was impressed by A taking such a large step. He said he was impressed himself, but that it was the things B had said that made him take the new position. They both said that they had had a good conversation. It had not been too difficult. A said that it was like magic. I said that it was a result of their taking positions to listen to each other and to talk clearly from each of their positions, and that it was they themselves who had taken new positions.

The manager said that he was pleased that both teachers would now consider staying at the school. And the witness said that she would let the other colleagues know that there was no longer any conflict. We thought that the manager should be the one to tell all the teachers that the conflict was resolved and that it was time to move on.

To be able to get interested in the other person's thoughts and thinking, is that easy or complicated?

One thinks it is complex, another that it is simple. That is also just a position.

The consultant position

By getting interested in the other person's thoughts and stories, your own stories come to life. As a consultant, I often find myself in this situation, when I connect to stories both about my professional and my private life. Instead of trying to change that, we use the semantic polarity model. And we take a position, not on the line, but underneath the line: the position C.

A's position _____ B's position
C

The C-position is *not* to take a position on the polarity line. If you are the conductor of the process with two individuals, for example, you have to keep asking questions of the two positions. Is it possible not to "get into the conversation" with your own stories and take a position on the line? I do, at times, find myself taking a position on the polarity line as a leader of the process, and it is at those points that it is crucial to continue to ask questions of the two positions, in order to get back to the C-position.

Working with semantic polarities has opened up "dialogical dialogues". David was a master at this and was able to stay "in conversation" longer than I could imagine was possible. To stay "in conversation", to support the dialogue by asking questions of the individuals' positions and not to take over the talk, is a challenge for many professionals. If you want to work with your own position in this matter, this semantic polarity line below might be helpful.

I am involved with _____ I like people
professional conversations   I work with to
because I like to be effective   be effective

Take your position in any of the professional conversations you are having. Both ends of the polarity line are fine. It is a semantic polarity that helps us to stay interested in the other person's positions. A story might be helpful.

An organisation in Denmark was, as many other organisations, going through a lot of changes. The leaders contacted me and we discussed their problems. They wanted to work with the two most acute problems. Because two departments in the organisation were merging, many people who had never met before had to work together, and there were mainly negative stories about the necessary changes. I constructed the following semantic polarities and wrote them on the whiteboard.

Playing with position:
"Change"

It is inspiring to get _____ I like it the way
new colleagues   things are

It's a piece of cake _____ It's a difficult challenge

All the staff members in the department were asked to take a position, and then discuss why they had taken that position. This created a conversation where everybody was able to be recognised in his or her position, could speak from it, and could be heard in it. We then had a dialogue about how each of them pictured their organisation, and this created an idea of responsibility for the whole department by taking and being seen in a position. We talked about how positions are "just positions", that it was possible for everyone to take new positions in this situation, and how they felt at that particular moment. They agreed to use the phrase "It is just a position" in order to be able to stay in these difficult dialogues, and, instead of talking about someone, they could use it to talk with the other person.

The leader of the department was then asked to take her positions. Now the staff and the leader could be in dialogue about being the leader and how important it was that everybody took clear positions.

The consultant story

All through this process, I needed to work to stay in the C-position because the change they had asked me to help them with as consultant was a major change of the whole public system in Denmark. And I had my own values, meanings, and thoughts of what was "right" and "wrong". The manager was very helpful to me in relation to this, by describing a previous consultant whose intervention they had not found so helpful. When I asked what had not been helpful, she told me that the consultant had said that the change to the whole public system was not a good one. The manager said that the staff had agreed with the consultant. She, as the manager, had had a tougher job afterwards convincing the leaders and the staff that these changes were not to be discussed. This conversation led to my next question: "What can be discussed and what cannot be discussed?"

I explained the semantic polarity thinking to the manager and clarified how I would work first with the group of leaders (five) and then with staff group (eighty). I explained that because of the story she had told me, I would suggest that the group of leaders needed to take positions about the changes, and that in her giving them this opportunity, she also had to ask them to manage the changes. That meant that she needed to trust the leaders in taking their positions as leaders in the change process. That would give her the opportunity to take the C-position in the whole process. She looked a little puzzled, and I said I would provide some literature and she could observe me working with the group of leaders from the C-position and also take the C-position in this first process. She seemed very relieved after this first part of the consulting process. We agreed on two sessions with the group of leaders. There would be a period of time between the two sessions, where the leaders could practise their new positions and then I could help them discuss what they had accomplished and what they still needed to address. Between the two sessions, and more generally, she was to take the C-position.

At the end of the second session with the group of leaders, the manager and I described the next step, the session with all the staff. They were to take the same position as they did in their daily work, as leaders of the processes, where the staff were working in groups with tasks. This seemed natural to them following their own changes. We looked at their differences and different positions as leaders in these changing processes.

At the beginning of the session with the staff, the group of leaders agreed to take a position on the "change" polarity line we had worked with when we began. The group of leaders stood up and each took their position on the imagined line on the floor.

The new changes are exciting   The new changes are challenging

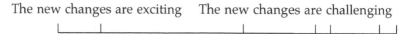

Then I asked them to take their position where they each thought they were now after having worked with the changes for some weeks. And again each individual discussed why they had taken this position.

The new changes are exciting   The new changes are challenging

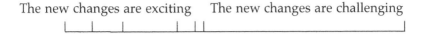

When the staff saw their leaders take their positions they said that they were not surprised about the leaders' positions on the first line. They were surprised by some of the leaders' second positions, but, in reflecting on this, they had seen the changes in positions but had not recognised it until now when they saw the leaders standing in their position.

In the consulting process with the leaders, I used another conversation model I have developed from the semantic polarity thinking called the "growth model". The growth model is a conversation model which is made visual, based on an appreciative mindset and clear positioning, and is both process and action orientated, focused on defined tasks which are developed in positive constructive directions to create new thinking and practice. It provides an agenda for handling challenging conversations in a safe context. Disagreements are a part of the context and all challenges can be heard in future-orientated language (Grønbæk & Pors, 2009; Grønbæk, Pors, & Campbell, 2011).

The manager and the leaders agreed to use this model throughout the whole process, and later they agreed that the model would be one of two models that the organisation would use and be known for. At the end of the day's session with the group of staff, I gave the staff and the leaders this polarity line to take positions on and to discuss from:

Using the growth model _____ Using the growth model
a lot   a little

Coming back six months later for another session with the whole organisation, I wanted to check up on their use of the growth model, because I thought that was a good way of getting the whole group to think about what had been discussed at the last session. Therefore, I talked with the manager about setting up the same polarity line as last time, and she said no. So I asked her to construct a better polarity and she said that it should be:

Using the growth model _____ Using the growth model
a lot   very, very much

She explained that the first polarity was no longer useful because they had decided on using the growth model and she expected them all to be using it a lot, and this was the case.

Complexity and simplicity as positions

In practising and teaching the semantic polarity thinking since 2002, I realise that the ideas of "complexity" and "simplicity" are dynamic and change constantly. As a practitioner, the most difficult aspect was to find ways of constructing the semantic polarities. I was very focused on finding the *right* polarity line. However, the more I practised and worked with the thinking, the easier it was for me to work to construct these to fit with others. I moved from finding it complex to finding it simpler. After working further with semantic polarities, David and I realised that semantic polarity thinking was about more than "just" solving conflicts. We began to look for other applications. In Denmark, I developed the model to be used in many different types of conversations and constructed another semantic polarity:

The model can be used _____ The model can only be used
in all conversations   in certain conversations

By keeping both ends of the polarity line active and in the dialogue about the model, we gave each other and ourselves space to develop the thinking further. Then we started to teach and write about the thinking as a model, and the whole process came into action again. This time, we often took the opposite positions from the beginning. Teaching the "hard" part of constructing the "right" semantic polarities has been a process during which the more I felt free to make semantic polarities, the easier it was for the students. I find that the more I can stay in the "C" position, the easier the model and the thinking becomes for my students and my clients. We are in the relationship together. When I am exploring new things, it can be experienced as complex and difficult. But what if that is just a position? And if that position is not appreciated and looked at as interesting, we might not get to a new and interesting development.

Because I have been able to make it so straightforward for myself and those I teach, people are beginning to question the model because it is so "simple". Maybe that is because the "thinking" is considered to be a "model". There are, however, many more ways in which semantic polarities can be explored.

Future conversations about semantic polarity

In our attempt to understand the thinking we were developing, we started to visualise the polarity lines. We thought this would help the people we worked with to understand and go along with us in the process. We have learnt that it has a huge impact on the conversations, but remain uncertain about how and why. This is an important discussion to be had, and to explore from all the positions: consultant, client, observers, and others.

When David and I had finished writing the book, *Taking Positions in the Organization*, we were very pleased. I told David that the best thing for me had been our working together taking different positions: he having the theory, and I having a lot of practice. David smiled even more and said, "The thing is that I didn't have the theory." And then I said, "Then it is good that you are telling me that now and not before we started the writing!" We laughed, and then honoured all those who had helped us with their ideas about positioning and positioning theories. We celebrated the richness of this way of thinking and felt inspired about its potential further developments. We felt we had the courage to let "our work" go and to meet the challenge in discussions with others.

Words have their own lives in the special context of the present. In David's last year, the sentence "It does take courage to let go" changed its meaning. He had always been a brave individual, and in talking with him about death I remembered an inscription I had seen. *Those who live in the hearts of those who love them cannot die.*

References

Campbell, D., & Grønbæk, M. (2006). *Taking Positions in the Organization.* London: Karnac.

Campbell, D., & Huffington, C. (Eds.) (2008). *Organizations Connected.* London: Karnac.

Grønbæk, M. (2008). The power of keeping it simple. In: D. Campbell & C. Huffington (Eds.), *Organizations Connected* (pp. 99–126). London: Karnac.

Grønbæk, M., & Pors, H. (2009). *VækstModellen – Vejen til den gode samtale* (*The Growth Model – Developing Dialogues*). Copenhagen: Dafolo.

Grønbæk, M., Pors, H., & Campbell, D. (2011). *VækstModellen – Vejen til dialogbaseret Ledelse* (*The Growth Model – Developing Dialogical Leadership*). Copenhagen: Dafolo.

Nørgaard, B. (2010). *From A to Z. Re-modelling the World.* Exhibition at the National Gallery of Denmark, 16 April–24 October 2010.

CHAPTER TEN

Uncoding landscapes:
systemic shapes, maps, and territories

Marie Murray

D avid Campbell's influence extended internationally in shaping thinking and the working practices of many psychologists, clinicians, psychotherapists, and consultants.

The tyranny of language

My introduction to David's work preceded my meeting him in person. Having practised as a clinical psychologist in the 1970s, I embarked on an MPsychSc in systemic family psychotherapy in the 1980s in Dublin, at a time when systemic metaphors were at their most linguistically extravagant. This was the theoretical time when first order cybernetics (Selvini-Palazzoli, Boscolo, Cecchin, & Prata, 1978; Wiener, 1948), was transmogrifying into "cybernetics of cybernetics", or "second order cybernetics", a time when "information was news of a difference" (Bateson, 1972), a time of mechanistic metaphors with steam engines, "servomechanisms and governors", "thermostats", and "error-activated equilibrium", "feedback loops", "entropy and negentropy", "morphostasis", "morphogenesis" (Bateson, 1972; Hoffman, 1981), and "homeostasis" (Jackson, 1957). It was a time of "circularity", "positive connotation" (Selvini-Palazzoli, Boscolo, Cecchin, & Prata, 1978, p. 56), "undifferentiated ego mass", and "enmeshed", and "too richly cross-joined systems" (Minuchin, 1974); a time of "triangulation", "symmetrical and complementary relationships", and that wonderful Batesonian (1972) concept, "schismogenesis", a "deviation amplifying mutual causal process" which represented the breaking point for a system, as it did for systemic students, especially those from the tidy, monocausal, meticulous, deductive, certitude of psychology prior to its own "interpretative turn" (Bruner, 1990).

Armed with this alien nomenclature, students of systemic psychotherapy attempted to interpret the psychotherapeutic world while cognisant of the pitfalls of "epistemological error", and the seduction of "linear causality", the dangers of "secret coalitions", the potential for "pseudomutuality" under "the tyranny of linguistic conditioning" (Selvini-Palazzoli, Boscolo, Cecchin, & Prata, 1978, p. 51). Appropriating the Milan guidelines (Selvini-Palazzoli, Boscolo, Cecchin, & Prata, 1980), we moved from mechanistic metaphors into biological models, and the new lexiphanic territory of "invented reality" (Watzlawick, 1984), "objectivity in parenthesis", "autopoiesis", "structural determinism" and "structural coupling" (Maturana & Varela, 1980, 1987), and then from biological models to linguistic models (Anderson & Goolishian, 1988). We began "languaging", we confronted "hermeneutics" (Ricoeur, 1985), and were especially adept in the "not-knowing approach" (Anderson & Goolishian, 1992), while still wondering whether or not the map was or was not the territory (Korzybski, 1931, in Bateson, 1972), or if there was any reality, any map, or any territory at all that one could know. We were systems that were deeply perturbed.

Into this morass of impenetrability, instability, opacity, incomprehensibility, verbosity, and sheer "unpronounceability" came Campbell and Draper (1985) and Campbell, Draper, & Huffington (1988) with readable work, in comprehensible language, from recognisable clinical contexts, asking and answering relevant intelligible questions that provided information on theoretical and practical recursivity in the systemic field.. They asked "twenty questions" (Campbell, Draper, & Huffington, 1988) that answered questions we never knew we had and decoded that landscape of systemic thinking for all of us at that time.

Uncoding landscapes

The title of this chapter, "Uncoding landscapes: systemic shapes, maps, and territories", was selected for a number of reasons. First, because the idea of "uncoding" landscapes derives from a poem entitled "The Peninsula" by beloved Irish Poet Seamus Heaney (1990) and contains concepts and images that resonate with the conduct of therapy as I construe it, especially the positioning of the therapist and use of self in therapy.

"Uncoding" differs from decoding. Decoding implies that there is a reality to be deciphered, a code to crack, rather than signs and symbols to be excavated for meaning and possibility. Speaking to the activities of therapist in therapy, "uncoding" suggests a process through which meaning unfolds gently and aesthetically in therapeutic endeavour.

Second, the poem has a special connection with David Campbell's work in Ireland and the manner in which he conducted consultations in what might be termed the "too richly cross-joined system" of the Irish systemic psychotherapy domain. There is an inevitable initial enmeshment among therapists and training courses in a developing discipline in a relatively small population. The smaller the society, the greater the susceptibility for dominant discourses to emerge— external consultation dilutes that propensity. According to Campbell self-diagnosis by organisations "is always made within the context of relationships and is therefore a political process", one that is naturally intensified in smaller contexts (2000, p. 44).

Third, the poem was chosen because of David Campbell's own systemic positioning in relation to poetry, which he described as "an attempt to deconstruct a small part of the world we know" (2000, p. 12) He said that "a poet deliberately challenges accepted interpretations, challenges understanding and sets the reader on another course" (2000, p. 12). The applicability of this statement in systemic terms is that no assumptions are made about systems, each is "read" from an innovative prospective. In this way the distinction between literal meaning and metaphorical meaning is not in terms of "two sorts of meaning but as a distinction between the familiar and the unfamiliar" (Campbell, 2000, p. 13).

Fitting into what is familiar confines people to "certain meanings that have been agreed upon, whereas metaphor may be used to introduce a difference to the conventional meaning of the words being used" (Campbell, 2000, p. 14), providing a liberating experience for therapist and client. For example, the writings of James Joyce and Samuel Beckett "break up the habitual paradigms of narrative order, in order to leave the ordering task of creation to the reader" (Kearney, 1988, p. 22), in the same way that therapy involves a reordering with clients of their stories and opening up of possibilities for new stories. "To repeat our story, to retell our history is to recollect our horizon of possibilities" (Ricoeur, cited in Kearney, 1984, p. 21) and poetry has a place in that.

> Discourse analysts (like poets) often find that marginal and abnormal uses of language are highly significant because they reveal, in a way that more normal linguistic usages do not, the extremes of which a system is capable. (Fiske, 1994, p. 196)

Finally, the poem mirrors an approach that David Campbell described in his own consultation work. Taking one instance of organisational consultation for example, he abandoned his prepared lectures and planned course for a group during consultation and "ventured with them into unknown territory" (Campbell, 2000, p. 45). To do so is to absorb oneself in the landscape of client's lives, rather than adhering to one unalterable map of systemic territory.

The Peninsula

When you have nothing more to say, just drive
For a day all round the peninsula.
The sky is tall as over a runway,
The land without marks so you will not arrive

But pass through, though always skirting landfall.
At dusk, horizons drink down sea and hill
The ploughed field swallows the whitewashed gable
And you're in the dark again. Now recall

The glazed foreshore and silhouetted log,
The rock where breakers shredded into rags,
The leggy birds stilted on their own legs
Islands riding themselves out into the fog

And drive back home, still with nothing to say
Except that now you will uncode all landscapes
By this: things founded, clean on their own shapes
Water and ground in their extremity.

This poem reminds us that by listening one learns more than by saying, when we are engaged with clients: the investment of time and reflection that being a therapist requires in order to see the shapes and contours of what is relevant in the client's world. There is an Irish proverb: "a silent mouth is sweet to hear". The Milan approach always distinguished itself by listening; by the circularity of its questioning and by its attention to the perspectives of all family members with intense curiosity (Cecchin, 1987) to understand the system. And dialogical communication is defined as "that which emphasizes the ability to listen carefully to the experiences of the 'other', the ability to be reflexive about one's participation in the conversation and the capacity to change one's ideas through conversation" (Campbell & Grønbaek, 2006, p. 153). The poem suggests taking a panoramic meta-position to observe the topography of clients' worlds before returning to the detail of what is happening in the therapy room. It means not progressing in a perfunctory, formulaic manner with predetermined "marks" or immutable stages in the conduct of therapy, or with beliefs, assumptions, suppositions, and superior "knowing" driving the therapist towards a preconceived outcome (Cecchin, Lane, & Ray, 1992). Instead, it requires engagement in a more aesthetically leisurely process where the destination is indeterminate and the images revealed by the process are attended to as they appear, one where therapists recognise when they are "in the dark", uncertain how to progress in new territory not previously encountered.

Peninsular maps follow contours. There is fluidity in following them that is denied if heading resolutely towards specified places. In terms of map and territory, the difference between places on a map identifying destinations, and peninsular outlines that delineate the shape of a country is that the former are fixed, while the latter are tentative. "Uncoding" recognises the exploratory nature of each therapeutic encounter, the manner in which we position ourselves as therapists in the landscape of our clients' lives, and operate according to the paradigms that facilitate our doing so: paradigms which themselves change as therapists explore new epistemological terrain that they articulate in practice, which, in turn, reinforces epistemology in an ever-evolving process. It is this recursivity that has facilitated the therapist's journey over the past four decades, in its repositioning of the therapist's stance from that of fixed, all-knowing, detached, expert "observer" to relational "participant" in what was observed; to "constructivist", "non-instructive interaction" in the pursuit and generation of meaning with clients; to "socially constructed" within prevailing discourses about therapy itself. The evolving narrative of "self" or therapist's identity within systemic therapy has also shifted from "singular" to "relational" to "multiple" to "integrated" "selves", to a position of ethical subjective complexity that is "both relational and autonomous" (Larner, 2008, p. 355) and that recognises the therapist's "self-as-emergent-narrative" (Boston, 2000, p. 452).

As the lens through which therapists have viewed the therapeutic world has altered (Mellor, Storer, & Firth, 2000), therapists have concurrently adjusted their perception of themselves in therapy in a way that brings new ethical imperatives for self-reflexivity, particularly with regard to issues of power (Campbell, 2000). The critique of systemic therapy has challenged therapists to attend to their power within the therapeutic relationship and the manner in which therapy has, in its time, supported societal abuse of power (Foucault, 1980; Shotter, 1989; Shotter & Gergen, 1989). Therapy shifts from a focus on technique designed to bring about desired outcomes, as constructed by therapists, and from powerful prevailing dominant discourses, to self-reflexive (Cecchin, Lane, & Ray, 1992, p. 9) intersubjective engagement which validates emotion (Richardson, 1992; Stocker & Hedgeman, 1996) and brings new ethical imperatives to therapists in a "constant process of evolution and self-questioning" (Jones, 1993, p. 19) and understanding of the confluence of the different theories and discourses within the psychotherapy world.

Therapists might hubristically construe their interactions with clients as seminal landmarks in clients' lives, but the therapist merely "passes through" the domains inhabited by clients, skirting the landfall of their experiences through circular questioning and silence in a process of uncoding, shifting from light to darkness and from silhouettes to the clean shapes of the lived reality of client's lives. In summary, each instance of therapy involves entry through unknown territory, attempting to make sense of maps, of systemic terrain, exploring new possibilities; the peninsular, never-ending, unbounded routes of the work we choose to do for others and for ourselves.

Consultation: therapists in academic contexts

Appropriating the metaphors above, my work has been most influenced by consultation with David Campbell when I have encountered difficulty finding my way through organisational complexities, when I have been uncertain about how to position myself in new situations, the contours and shapes of a project being undertaken, the map that would guide, and the psychological terrain into which I was entering. This is when the challenge has been to negotiate unfamiliar territory by "saying less and seeing more", by not seeking answers, but simply being silent in the landscape and allowing it to unfold and uncode itself in the process.

University of Limerick

The first examplar was a decade ago, when David explicated a new consultative approach to the role of university extern and guided the delivery of a new Masters in Systemic Psychotherapy in the University of Limerick, for which I was course director. This was an innovative tripartite agreement between the then Mid-Western Health Board, the University of Limerick, and St Vincent's Psychiatric Hospital in Fairview in Dublin, where I was Director of Psychology at the time this venture began (Murray, 2003).

The powerful tranquillity of David's approach extended systemic thinking and practice into new territory, while disentangling the complex tripartite organisational intricacies and convolutions such a venture required. What was crucial was the identification of the constructions being brought by each party to this venture, in which each stakeholder held depths of "taken for granted knowledge" (Cecchin, Lane, & Ray, 1992) in their own domain: St Vincent's Hospital about clinical practice, family therapy, and supervision; University of Limerick about academic programmes, structures, standards, and grading formats; the Mid-Western Health Board about their clientele and service requirements. "It is at the moment when the therapist begins to reflect upon the effect of his own attitude and presumptions that he acquires a position that is both ethical and therapeutic" (Cecchin, Lane, & Ray, 1992, p. 9). David Campbell's dialogic organisational consultation style created the course context in a way that I believe was a special collaborative shedding of power.

"Listening" and acute attention to positioning involved examining the system and asking questions that would allow a position to be taken within it. Such questions included the following: Who is seeking this programme at this time? Who is not? Who has most to gain? Who has most to lose? What is the meaning of this (for the different tripartite contexts)? What is the meaning for other systemic family therapy programmes and degrees already available in other institutes and universities? To what extent, if any, does it alter relationships in any of these contexts or between them or in the systemic field in Ireland? In what ways might it do so? In summary, the constraints and affordances at every level of the potential project were considered and there were questions posed that explored a continuum of semantic polarities.

University College Dublin

The second consultation with David Campbell involved a personal and professional shift when I returned to my alma mater, University College Dublin, as Director of the Student Counselling Service, after more than thirty years working primarily in clinical contexts. This was a place familiar and unfamiliar, engaged in its own adaptations and transitions. According to Campbell, the socially constructed organisation is being constructed continuously and is constantly changing or reinventing itself through interactions going on within it, so much so "that it would be helpful if agencies placed a sign above their entrance-way which read 'under construction'" (Campbell, 2000, p. 28). Therefore, how one positions oneself is crucial in entering evolving organisational systems. Campbell's approach cautioned: remember, you are trying to bridge two very different worlds between education and counselling so you have to develop a keen interest in the "other" position by asking the question: *Why should educationalists be interested in counselling?* And be able to argue the case 50–50 (Campbell & Grønbaek, 2006).

This intervention was, for me, a catalyst in understating the system, an outline of the new territory into which I was entering, a shape, a map, a landscape "uncoded", an exemplar of how change happens, by the question asked. This question halted what otherwise might have been an invasion into a new context. It enabled a less intrusive return, aware of the importance of understanding systems "clean on their own shapes", of the necessity to balance issues of stability and change, to employ organisational thinking as much as enthusiasm, and to ask self-reflexively about the meaning of my return to this place with systemic questions such as the following:

How has this University altered? How is it the same? How have I altered? How am I the same? How am I construed in this context? What is familiar/unfamiliar? What affective resonances of a former self does experiencing what is familiar and unfamiliar evoke? How do I position/reposition myself in what is old and new? What within the clinical world has relevance for this context? How does location in an educational academy alter clinical endeavour? In what way? What expectations will there be of this new post? Why should my clinical voice be heard in this academic setting? If this new post is to be useful, what are the steps and processes towards that positioning, who will define what that means: university, colleagues, students, and how will I know when that is being achieved?

I continue to use circular questioning: questions about differences in relationships, difference in degree, now/then differences, and hypothetical and future questions as a standard means of establishing my own positioning in interacting with systems (Boscolo, Cecchin, Hoffman, & Penn, 1987; Penn, 1982, 1985; Tomm, 1988).

Narrative in therapy

Narrative therapy (White & Epston, 1990) has particular compatibility with the Celtic tradition of storytelling, in which narratives of the past are woven with myth and fantasy, conjuring up imaginary locals of eternal youth, characters of absolute wisdom, heroes and anti-heroes, and multi-dimensional perspectives on life. The significance of this oral tradition continues in the artistry of day-to-day conversation and in the stories clients provide to elucidate their situations and their lives. The stories told in therapy are often metaphorical or allegorical narratives, which invite therapists into their weave. Campbell's positioning was an engagement with stories *as stories*, which he believed were "not to be judged for their veracity", but to ask why particular stories emerge and "what is the meaning for us in taking particular positions within or outside these narratives?" (Campbell, 2003).

Therapist as an evolving narrative

As I position myself as therapist today, I retain the capacity to evoke, as contextually appropriate, positions that derive from former paradigms, while doing so through the lens of current thinking in addition to understanding the transience of certainty and the durability of uncertainty in all that I do as therapist today. Systemic therapy has storied itself in many different ways. "Different voices are required in different contexts and it is these voices that are the basis of our sense of self" (Campbell, 2000, p. 9). I appreciate and interweave psychology and psychotherapy, aesthetics and pragmatics, clinical exactitude and necessary "irreverence" (Cecchin, Lane, & Ray, 1992), expertise and acknowledgement of uncertain territory. I invoke fact, fiction, and film in therapeutic endeavour (Murray, 1997) (specifically the use of film in adolescent narrative identity, which I have researched clinically for twenty years). Whether writing or speaking or being silent, I am aware that we cannot separate "dancer and dance" (Yeats, 1926), neither can "self" and "therapist" be separated. Therapy is not something that we "do". Therapists exist in language, in intersubjective dialogue with others, constructed by clients in each encounter with them. Therefore, the ontology of therapist is not independent of client. We are brought into being as therapists by clients.

Being systemic, therefore, is something that we are and that is afforded us by others. It is how we position ourselves in each encounter we have, how we speak to and about others and to each other, and about those who consult with us. It is about our biases and prejudices recognised and unconscious. It is about our use of words, embracing them, selecting them, scrutinising them, weighing them, considering and choosing them carefully, knowingly, reflectively, and ethically. It is putting ethics first, foremost, central, last, ever and always in all that we do and all that we are.

Just as the poet often articulates for us that which we might otherwise be unable to say, so we as therapists also use words as a primary tool in our own work with others every day. Therefore, a poet who reminds us, as therapists, about our use of words conjoins two creative professions in a special way, which is encapsulated in the following poem about words.

Make words work: make them tell the tale you want to tell.
Let them show who you are and how you feel: use words well.

Move words around: make them step out, march, advance,
Feel the pulse of them, the sway, the spring: make words dance.

Make words sound: hear them loud and clear, listen to their ring
Hear them hum to each other, catch their tunes: make words sing.

Dig with words: turn up meanings, rake over, hoe,
Uncover buried stories, incantations: make words grow.

Polish words now: make them glint and glimmer, cast a spell.
Ready? Take hold then and dazzle us: wear words well.

(Jack Ousbey, 2003)

A precious legacy of David Campbell was the interface between his life and work: in professional integrity, in personal disposition, in therapeutic positioning, in the possession and shedding of power, in manner of questioning, in reflecting and imagining, acknowledging polarities, questioning at the extremes, monitoring systems, and in determining what was fair, 50–50, with utter respect for all.

Note

David Campbell visited or consulted in many places, in many contexts in the Irish systemic landscape, to show what he believed: that you absorb yourself in the landscapes of your clients' lives. He knew and understood the contours of our culture, our thinking and imagination, who we were, where we came from, the "sites" of our lives. Ní bheidh a leithéid ann arís (We shall not see his like again).

References

Anderson, H., & Goolishian, H. A. (1988). Human systems as linguistic systems: preliminary and evolving ideas about the implications for clinical theory. *Family Process*, 27(4): 371–395.

Anderson, H., & Goolishian, H. A. (1992). The client is the expert: a not knowing approach to therapy. In: S. McNamee & K. J. Gergen (Eds.), *Therapy as Social Construction* (pp. 25–39). London: Sage.

Bateson, G. (1972). *Steps to an Ecology of Mind.* New York: Ballantine Books.

Boscolo, L., Cecchin, G., Hoffman, L., & Penn, P. (1987). *Milan Systemic Family Therapy: Conversations in Theory and Practice.* New York: Basic Books.

Boston, P. (2000). Systemic family therapy and the influence of post-modernism. *Advances in Psychiatric Treatment, 6:* 450–457.

Bruner, J. (1990). *Acts of Meaning.* Cambridge, MA: Harvard University Press.

Campbell, D. (2000). *The Socially Constructed Organization.* London: Karnac.

Campbell, D. (2003). The Christmas story. Scientific Lecture, December 2003, Tavistock & Portman NHS Foundation Trust.

Campbell, D., & Draper, R. (Eds.) (1985). *Applications of Systemic Family Therapy: The Milan Method.* London: Grune and Stratton.

Campbell, D., & Grønbaek, M. (2006). *Taking Positions in the Organization.* London: Karnac.

Campbell, D., Draper, R., & Huffington, C. (1988). *Working with the Milan Method: Twenty Questions.* London: Institute of Family Therapy.

Cecchin, G. (1987). Hypothesizing, circularity, and neutrality revisited: an invitation to curiosity. *Family Process, 26*(4): 405–413.

Cecchin, G., Lane, G., & Ray, W. A. (1992). *Irreverence: A Strategy for Therapists' Survival.* London: Karnac.

Fiske, J. (1994). Audiencing: cultural practice and cultural studies. In: N. K. Denzin & Y. S. Lincoln (Eds.), *Handbook of Qualitative Research* (pp. 189–198). London: Sage.

Foucault, M. (1980). *Power/Knowledge Selected Interviews and Other Writings 1972–1977.* New York: Knopf Doubleday.

Heaney, S. (1990). The Peninsula. In: *Seamus Heaney: New Selected Poems 1966–1987.* London: Faber and Faber.

Hoffman, L. (1981). *Foundations of Family Therapy.* New York: Basic Books.

Jackson, D. (1957). The question of family homeostasis. *Psychiatric Quarterly Supplement, 31*(1): 79–90.

Jones, E. (1993). *Family Systems Therapy: Developments in the Milan Systemic Therapy.* Chichester: Wiley.

Kearney, R. (1984). *Dialogues with Contemporary Continental Thinkers.* Manchester: Manchester University Press.

Kearney, R. (1988). *The Wake of Imagination.* London: Hutchinson.

Larner, G. (2008). Exploring Levinas: the ethical self in family therapy. *Journal of Family Therapy, 30*(4): 351–361.

Maturana, H. R., & Varela, F. J. (1980). *Autopoiesis and Cognition: The Realization of the Living.* Dordrecht: Reidel.

Maturana, H. R., & Varela, F. J. (1987). *The Tree of Knowledge; The Biological Roots of Human Understanding*. Boston, MA: Shambala Press.

Mellor, D., Storer, S., & Firth, L. (2000). Family therapy into the 21st century: can we work our way out of the epistemological maze? *Australian and New Zealand Journal of Family Therapy*, 21(3): 151–154.

Minuchin, S. (1974). *Families and Family Therapy*. London: Tavistock, Social Science Paperbacks.

Murray, M. (1997). Dancing on the edge with adolescents: the co-construction of identity using the film medium in adolescent therapy. *Proceedings from the Fifth European Congress of Psychology, 'Dancing on The Edge'*, July 1997, Dublin, Ireland.

Murray, M. (2003). Reaching out or outreach. University of Limerick Masters in Systemic Family Therapy. *Feedback*, 9(3): 12–18.

Ousbey, J. (2003). Taking hold. In: J. Foster (Ed.), *One Hundred and One Favourite Poems*. London: HarperCollins Children's Books.

Penn, P. (1982). Circular questioning. *Family Process*, 21(3): 267–280.

Penn, P. (1985). Feed forward: future questions, future maps. *Family Process*, 24: 299–311.

Richardson, L. (1992). The consequences of poetic representation: writing the other, rewriting the self. In: C. Ellis & M. G. Flaherty (Eds.), *Investigating Subjectivity: Research on Lived Experience* (pp. 125–140). London: Sage.

Ricoeur, P. (1985). *Time and Narrative, Vol. 2*. Chicago, IL: University of Chicago Press [first published as *Temps et Recit, Vol. 2*. Paris: Editions du Seuil, 1984].

Selvini-Palazzoli, M., Boscolo, M., Cecchin, G., & Prata, G. (1978). *Paradox and Counter-paradox*. New York: Jason Aronson.

Selvini-Palazzoli, M., Boscolo, L., Cecchin, G., & Prata, G. (1980). Hypothesizing, circularity, neutrality: three guidelines for the conductor of the session. *Family Process*, 19: 3–12.

Shotter, J. (1989). Social accountability and the social construction of 'you'. In: J. Shotter & K. J. Gergen (Eds.), *Texts of Identity* (pp. 133–151). London: Sage.

Shotter, J. & Gergen, K. J. (Eds.) (1989). *Texts of Identity*. London: Sage.

Stocker, M., & Hegeman, E. (1996). *Valuing Emotions*. Cambridge: Cambridge University Press.

Tomm, K. (1985). Circular interviewing: a multifaceted clinical tool. In: D. Campbell & R. Draper (Eds.), *Applications of Systemic Family Therapy: The Milan Approach* (pp. 33–35). London: Grune & Stratton.

Watzlawick, P. (Ed.) (1984). *Invented Reality*. New York: Norton.

White, M., & Epston, D. (1990). *Narrative Means to Therapeutic Ends*. London: Norton.

Wiener, N. (1948). *Cybernetics: Or Control and Communication in the Animal and the Machine*. Cambridge, MA: MIT Press.

Yeats, W. B. (1926). "Among School Children". In: W. B. Yeats, *Collected Poems*. London: Macmillan Publishers, 1982.

CHAPTER ELEVEN

The ultimate ethical position is to keep talking: dealing with difference in teams, in supervision, and in therapy

Angela Abela, Roberta Zahra De Domenico, Ruth Formosa Ventura, and Jenny Zammit

T his chapter was inspired by David Campbell's work with us, which started in the late 1990s. We want to demonstrate how his systemic thinking about therapy, supervision, and organisations influenced the growth of family therapy and systemic practice in Malta. His fascination with difference and his creative ways of bringing about change were the aspects of his work that have made the most impact on us as a Maltese group of systemic psychotherapists.

The construction of difference in our cultural context

Differences become dysfunctional when they create an impasse, "cause psychological and/or physical injury, decrease interpersonal trust and fail to generate constructive changes" (Abela, 1998, p. 21). David believed that differences can be expressed without fear when it feels safe to talk. It is perhaps not coincidental that we would connect particularly to the notion of difference. As he points out: "broad societal and organisational discourses offer specific positions from which we construct, through dialogue, the day-to-day realities that govern our behaviour" (Campbell & Draper, 2006, p. vii).

Malta has a long history of dualism, which can be traced to traditional village culture, where feasts often pit rival band clubs against each other (Boissevain, 1993). The dualism between church and state has also been very strong (Friggieri, 2008), and there has always been keen rivalry between the two major political parties, who seem to want to make us believe that issues of national importance can only be painted in black or white.

The rapid social changes that have marked these past two decades, including the accelerating increase in secular beliefs, the reshifting of gender roles, and the influence of the European Union on our practices have increasingly rendered this polarisation untenable. Over time, many villages have done away with having two rival band clubs. The change in the intensity of political polarisation is reflected in the relatively recent floating voters and cross-voting phenomena (Grech, 2009). This points towards a shift in people's conventional political beliefs, which were traditionally characterised by entrenched intergenerational affiliations. On a political level, the "either . . . or" position typically held by Malta's two main political parties on a number of hotly contested issues is also shifting. The recent political debate about the introduction of a divorce law in Malta is one such example. The traditional position of the Nationalist Party (which upholds Christian Democratic values) against such legislation has now been broken, with some members expressing themselves in favour. On the other hand, the Labour party, which, in the past, spoke in favour of the legislation, has within its ranks members who have spoken against such a law.

Nevertheless, the dominant discourses in politics are, more often than not, characterised by categorical statements. This is not surprising, given that it is convenient for political argument to tap into the tendency of the human mind to evaluate important issues from two diametrically opposite standpoints. This precludes the possibility of exploring the issues in all their complexities.

At the same time, the idea of maximising different viewpoints at different levels has permeated modern organisational culture and promotes working in teams. However, scarcity of resources on the Maltese islands creates competition, fear, and mistrust (O'Reilly Mizzi, 1994), which are echoed within organisations. This is exacerbated by the prevailing norm of assigning political appointments in key government positions and other jobs meted out on the basis of one's political and social connections. Population density, which is one of the highest in the world, gives the Maltese greater awareness of the wielding of power. It also makes us extremely mindful of each other's business, which often becomes the focus in *tête-à-tête* conversations. The overall effect contributes towards a decrease in trust, hindering co-operation and collaboration in and among teams and organisations.

In this context, it is, therefore, understandable that the expert position continues to have such a hold on corporate governance, where many would find it much easier to toe the line, rather than work collaboratively. This guarded approach, while giving a sense of safety, especially to those who do not wish to burn their bridges (Sultana & Baldacchino, 1984), has the disadvantage of ensuring that change happens from a top-down position.

The setting up of business operations by global companies, as well as the accession of Malta to the EU, has, however, given some leverage to the younger generation to do things differently. Despite the fact that people in power continue to have a lot of say in how things are done, there is a growing need to give voice to different ideas at different levels of organisational structures.

In terms of professional practice, particularly in the caring professions, the expert position was still predominant in Malta in the 1990s. However, Fsadni, a Maltese anthropologist, argued that the need for a more collaborative approach could be extremely helpful:

> I am not making an anti-expert argument . . . I am simply noting that authority has flowed too much in the expert's direction. There are many stories I could cite – many people can cite – where expert opinion overrode, with horrific consequences the good sense of a family who knew its members better. (Fsadni, 2002, p. 9)

Contrary to the power dynamics present on a broad societal level, the majority of Maltese couples prefer to adopt a predominantly constructive style of conflict resolution (Abela, Frosh, & Dowling, 2005). In our clinical work, we often witness the perseverance and the resilience that couples demonstrate to continue to maintain harmonious relationships in the face of disagreement.

However, this dichotomous way of managing power in the private and the public domain is not always so clear-cut. Some families get locked into "us" and "them" positions. This is especially visible in the context of marital separation, where spouses become increasingly polarised and loyalty to the family of origin takes over. In our practice, we often witness the contradictions many experience between the stuckness of polarisation, dominance, and competition and the struggle to move towards a more collaborative way of working. These processes make us increasingly mindful of how people are moving away from a position of certainty in a quest for a more personalised way of being and relating. This shift has perhaps come along with the the advent of modernity, where, as Frosh aptly points out, "a compromise made up of openness to new influences and perceptions on the basis of a secure foundation of self . . . may be a central problem for every modern person" (Frosh, 1991, p. 7).

A collaborative approach

In 1996, the Social Work Development Programme (SWDP), the leading social work agency in Malta, wished to establish the first family therapy service, and its professionals were tasked by the chief executive to train themselves, establish a service, and set the profession in motion in the Maltese islands. David Campbell accepted an invitation, with other consultants from the Tavistock Clinic, to offer the training, eventually leading to qualifications for seven family therapists (AFT and UKCP Registered), and over 400 people had trained in systemic practice by 2004.

When David came for his first consultation visit, the issue of professional training was high on the agenda and he supported the team's position by helping them develop a training plan. Uniting us through our desire to value our professional standards, David successfully created "a safe environment, for drawing out the key issues that required discussion" (Campbell, 2000, p. 52). David's belief that in an environment where it feels safe to talk, differences can be expressed without fear that they will undermine relationships, and the idea that different perspectives need not be seen as fixed, but are simply positions on a polarity line, has been particularly important to us. Making space in therapy, supervision, and consultation for the juggling of different positions, and generating conversations that broaden the context and introduce different levels of meanings have been crucially significant in the Maltese context. In these ways, we contribute to helping clients, trainees, and professionals to negotiate and manage power differently, at those times when individuals find themselves locked into an either . . . or position informed by our traditional ways of managing power.

David's collaborative way of working was very new to Malta. Collegiality became even more important in the context of working in a team when seeing families, challenging prevalent beliefs that being observed would open us up to criticism and competitiveness. David's appreciation of everyone's contributions created a learning community in which different ideas could be valued, and this way of working continues to surprise other professionals who join in our work today. David was able to give a voice to all, whether he agreed with their ideas or not.

As we became more established as a systemic team, we began to put our new ideas into practice in a consultation with care workers in a residential home for girls. In tune with our new way of working, we engaged in conversations with all the members in the organisation, rather than responding to the manager's request to carry out training for the care workers (Abela & Sammut Scerri, 2003). This was very different from the usual practice of the organisation and challenged their view of a consultant as the expert. However, when different care workers started blaming one another, they looked to us to provide them with a way forward:

> . . . not having tackled directly issues of trust and safety in the group early on in our conversations, made it rather difficult for us at this stage of the consultation process to invite the group to share responsibility for the progress of the consultation. (Abela & Sammut Scerri, 2003, p. 48)

We learnt that collaboration needed to be negotiated in relation to all aspects of the work, and particularly issues of safety.

We also learnt that addressing issues of safety explicitly keeps a team together and helps foster trust and responsibility. In our experience, similar to blame, gossip is one of the ways in which safety is corroded in organisations. We have found that naming such a phenomenon and having a conversation about its impact on the group and on ourselves is an important reflexive exercise that can provide the catalyst for safety.

Positioning theory as a way of understanding difference

In the initial stages of a consultation, each individual is, to some extent, "protecting" himself or herself (Campbell, 2008, p. 84). This is a natural reaction and needs to be acknowledged. To reduce anxiety and enhance safety, David offered a systemic understanding of teams early in the consultation, explaining that the perspectives people hold are not about themselves, but about how they position themselves, and are, in turn, positioned on a continuum. When we have offered this explanation during consultations, we have noted members of the organisation nodding as if they have always known these dynamics.

Moving away from attributing positions to team members based on their personality is liberating. When people assess the contribution of others in the light of their character traits, their hope that the other person might change their position plummets and they stop listening and talking. Encouraging the interconnection among a range of different individuals' positions encourages people to listen to each other and liberates them from the notion of blame.

In one consultation to an organisation, the team had just experienced a reshuffle. It was useful to note the positions that old and new members took on what makes a good leader. What was previously considered acceptable behaviour was now being challenged, and members were invited to step back and reflect on how they had repositioned themselves. They came to understand how this restructuring allowed them to "determin[e] the possibilities and content of [these] repositionings" (Harré, 2006, p. xiii). Such a systemic understanding, which includes oneself, is effective in neutralising blame, generated conversations around the respective positions of the different members in a safe way, and invited them to take responsibility, both individually and collectively. This notion of tying safety to responsibility through collaborative conversations is an important principle for us.

Productive conversations include ways to regulate affect, which might involve choosing not to say things. For example, it is not so helpful to have a conversation about gossip aiming to name and shame. Regulation of affect can be difficult in couple and family therapy and organisational meetings. David's interventions helped individuals find ways to make distinctions between conversations that were productive and those that were not as yet therapeutic.

Grabbing the dilemma

An important idea in David's work was to search for and "grab" the main dilemma and to stay with its tension until something new emerged. This concept helped shift us from an "either . . . or" position so typical of a Maltese mindset (Boissevain, 1993) to that of a "both . . . and position" (Goldner, 1992), introducing space for different perspectives. It avoided the need to defend one's own position and invited deeper reflection on the issues at stake, and offered opportunities to bridge the gaps between perspectives. David was committed to putting competing views on a level playing field. This worked particularly well in the Maltese context.

When he was consulting with the very first family we had invited him to help us with, there was a lot of debate on the length of the uniform skirt that their adolescent daughter was allowed to wear to school. In attendance were the four family members, who had also extended the invitation to two other significant family members, one of whom was the mother's uncle and a priest; the other was the child's aunt. This was a very different family from the families we grew up in, and a challenge to the therapist. Even more colour was added to the session when, as soon as the family entered the therapy room, there was a sudden burst of fireworks and bells tolling, while a brass band struck up. The Floriana parish, which was only a few metres away from the clinic, was celebrating the feast of St Publius with much aplomb!

David was smiling as he took all this in and gave the family the opportunity to relax and feel at home. This gave the conversation a tinge of warmth that later developed into a passionate debate on the adolescent's request to dress like her peers. When working through this dilemma, David explained, "Some families do it this way, some families do it the other way. How do you wish to do it?" This gave space for family members to find ways to bridge the gaps between the generations. He managed to address the differences within the family as well as the differences between the family and our team.

David's idea of putting competing views on a level playing field influenced our work with a family where the adolescent girl was suffering from a severe case of trichotillomania, and the therapist often found herself having to "manage" the girl's bouts of anger towards the mother. At one point, the therapist found herself between a rock and a hard place when the girl insisted that her mother buy her an expensive wig as a birthday present. After consultation with the team behind the one-way mirror, two of them came into the consulting room and staged a debate (Sheinberg, 1985) in front of the family members, each putting forward arguments for and against the idea of buying a wig. Members of the family were thus freed to hold different positions from each other and could develop conversations that embraced their different stances (Campbell, 2000, 2008).

Bringing about change in organisations by getting people interested

David presented his ideas of working with organisations (Campbell, 2000) at a public seminar that challenged the audience, who were not familiar with social constructionist concepts. There was a view that these ideas could not be applied to the Maltese context because management was seen as having absolute power, with the workers having very limited manoeuvrability. David proposed that one way to introduce change was to get one person interested and then to move together to find another, so that change happens in very small steps through dialogue. His idea was that getting people interested mollifies defensive behaviour, allowing individuals to accept different views. This ran counter to some individuals' understanding of change in a socio-political context, where the previous generations in Malta had learnt to fight for change.

David's ideas were put into practice in a number of ways in Malta. There was a request to build a small therapeutic unit within a correctional facility on the island, which was contrary to the prevailing ethos of the facility. It was decided to try to spark interest in the project to overcome the barriers. The two professionals began to have lunch in the officers' mess to build relationships and have conversations, which eased tensions and softened resistance, and this enabled a change in the management's perception of the need for such a service.

Another request came to introduce a critical incidence stress management team, using a peer system, into a male-dominated agency in which it became evident that vulnerability was considered taboo. It had been very difficult to introduce the concept of seeking help for those experiencing stress. The trainer/consultant asked her peers to have conversations with those who showed any curiosity at all about the stress management training. This process slowly led to a request for a meeting with the team to see how the service could be useful to their colleagues. This approach might take a considerable amount of time, but change is built around a consensus as people come to understand the initiatives being proposed.

As systemic practitioners David thought we always needed to consider the "other side of the coin". When professionals insisted that it was very difficult to bring about change in organisations, he invited them to explore other possible scenarios. Some people succeed in exploiting difficult organisational set-ups to their advantage. At other times, deep unhappiness can bring issues to a head, allowing the individual to "make the 'healthy' decision to leave, rather than to struggle on in a bad working environment" (Campbell, 2000, p. 103). In a small country like Malta, however, it is not easy to move from one organisation to another. Organisational culture in the public sector is very often hierarchical and operates on a tight budget that does not invest in innovative practices. Healthcare practitioners work under their own steam and invest a lot of hard work in lobbying for change. It is important that consultations include those at the top of the hierarchy to interest people in change and better practice. However, people in key positions might not welcome a collaborative management style when they have to deliver on a very tight budget, which precludes them from putting into action proposals from the grassroots. This has become increasingly the case in the current economic climate.

It was in his consultation to us, the family therapy team, after some years of developing, when the team was finding it difficult to accept its differences, where we learnt most about David's mantra that "the ultimate ethical position is to keep talking". His consultation highlighted the team's tension between wanting to remain as it was and the desire to move on to something different. David's ability to talk about competition and the wish to challenge the hierarchy had a very liberating effect on the group. It encouraged the different members to voice their anxiety and frustration openly and, by so doing, attempt to find some resolution within the group. Taking the risk of being vulnerable with each other, and being able to talk about how each member felt, allowed for the re-establishment of safety. The ability to talk about uncomfortable situations and experiences has remained with us and has kept us together over time, as has David's emphasis that learning is also about refraining from taking a particular position and moving on in a system that keeps evolving.

Supervision practice has become an important instrument of change, and, in the past decade, has become mandatory in the helping professions. Systemic practitioners have developed supervision groups, which make use of reflecting teams where supervisees are encouraged to take responsibility for their own learning as they work through their dilemmas.

Conclusion

Besides David's systemic theoretical underpinnings and his systemic techniques, his personal attributes used to come across as an essential component of his interventions. In his work, he demonstrated a high degree of self-awareness and awareness of others, self-regulation, motivation, and expertise in managing relationships and building networks (Goleman, 2010). He provided a helpful model of how to regulate affect and passion. His calmness helped clients to stop and think. He made some of us aware that our "Mediterranean temperament" could, at times, be experienced as overwhelming for some families. He appreciated and validated our warmth, and helped us reflect on how to regulate our ways of communicating, such as letting one's eyes wander around the room to mitigate the intensity of one's gaze.

It was in taking a deep interest in the other person that David was able to create a calm and serene atmosphere in which deepest thoughts could be communicated. His professional stance resonated with his personal beliefs: "all my life I felt I should be the one to look after others . . . looking after others to make their world a safe place, where people can learn and love and make good relationships, and that's very important to me" (Campbell, B., 2010). He embodied a sense of safety, and "practiced out of his 'personhood'" (Protinsky & Coward, 2001, p. 377).

While acknowledging the enormous influence David had on our way of working, we are very conscious of the fact that he was a male foreign consultant with a lot of expertise, and that in itself gave him currency, with us as well as with others. Our own authority depends on a different set of attributes in a society that is increasingly seeking to provide a space for women where they can be recognised in their own right. As women pioneers in the systemic field, we continue to develop our ways of working from a feminist, postmodern, collaborative perspective (Abela & Sammut Scerri, 2003, 2010). This new way of doing therapy and consultation is slowly gaining ground. David's phrase "the ultimate ethical position is to keep talking", in combination with the ideas and practices we have learnt from him, are slowly contributing to changes in the wider context.

References

Abela, A. (1998). Marital conflict in Malta. Unpublished PhD thesis. Birkbeck College, University of London.

Abela, A., & Sammut Scerri, C. (2003). Collaborative enquiry versus didactic training with organisations: a case study. *Human Systems, 14*: 41–54.

Abela, A., & Sammut Scerri, C. (2010). Managing multiple relationships in supervision: dealing with the complexity. In: C. Burck & G. Daniels (Eds.), *Mirrors and Reflections: Processes of Systemic Supervision* (pp. 289–308). London: Karnac.

Abela, A., Frosh, S., & Dowling, E. (2005). Uncovering beliefs embedded in the culture and its implication for practice: the case of Maltese married couples. *Journal of Family Therapy, 27*(1): 3–23.

Boissevain, J. (1993). *Saints and Fireworks: Religion and Politics in Rural Malta* (3rd edn). Valletta, Malta: Progress Press.

Campbell, B. (2010). The dad project. Accessed at: www.brionycampbell.com/film/the-dad-project.

Campbell, D. (2000). *The Socially Constructed Organization.* London: Karnac.

Campbell, D. (2008). Locating conflict in team consultations. In: D. Campbell & C. Huffington (Eds.), *Organizations Connected: A Handbook of Systemic Consultation* (pp. 79–97). London: Karnac.

Campbell, D., & Draper, R. (2006). Series editors' foreword. In: D. Campbell & M. Grønbaek, *Taking Positions in the Organization.* London: Karnac.

Friggieri, O. (2008). *Fjuri li ma jinxfux. Tifkiriet 1955–1990.* Malta: Klabb Kotba Maltin.

Frosh, S. (1991). *Identity Crisis: Modernity, Psychoanalysis and the Self.* London: Routledge.

Fsadni, R. (2002). A Christian model of the family needs to be invented. *The Times of Malta*, 20 January, p. 9.

Goldner, V. (1992). Making room for both/and. *Family Therapy Networker*, 16(2): 55–61.

Goleman, D. (2010). What makes a leader? *Harvard Business Review*: 35–44.

Grech, H. (2009). Voting trends quirks. Accessed at: www.timesofmalta.com.

Harré, R. (2006). Foreword. In: D. Campbell & M. Grønbæk, *Taking Positions in the Organization* (pp. xi–xiv). London: Karnac.

Protinsky, H., & Coward, L. (2001). Developmental lessons of seasoned marital and family therapists: a qualitative investigation. *Journal of Marital and Family Therapy*, 27(3): 375–381.

O'Reilly Mizzi, S. (1994). Women in Senglea revisited. Paper presented to the Third Annual Conference of the Anthropology Programme, University of Malta, Mediterranean Institute, 11–12 April.

Sheinberg, M. (1985). The debate: a strategic technique. *Family Process*, 24: 259–271.

Sultana, R. G., & Baldacchino, G. (1994). Sociology and Maltese society: the field and its context. In: R. G. Sultana & G. Baldacchino (Eds.), *Maltese Society: A Sociological Inquiry* (pp. 1–21). Msida: Mireva.

CHAPTER TWELVE

Applying systemic thinking in pastoral contexts

Patrick Sweeney

A t various times over twenty-five years, David Campbell was my family therapy teacher, trainer, and my supervisor. At all stages I counted him as a trusted friend. He taught me much. In particular, he assisted me and encouraged me in transferring systemic ideas and practices into my primary working setting, which is that of a Catholic priest. This enriched my work and enabled me to navigate through very challenging situations. In this chapter, I try to describe three such situations

Setting one: preparation

It is common knowledge that recent times have been very difficult for clergy generally, and especially Roman Catholic clergy. The number of priests is falling, the workload increasing, the context within which they minister is increasingly less receptive, and the scandals demoralising. I was invited to facilitate an away week by the in-service unit of an English diocese to give clergy a context within which to talk, debate, and develop a vision for the future in the light of contemporary challenges. The clergy saw it as offering too little, too late, fearing they were being subjected to a "talking shop" that would make no difference. While they were unenthusiastic, their loyalty and respect for the leadership of their diocese demanded their presence. The leadership was very nervous lest the event diminish, rather than enhance, morale. There was also a worry that tensions between traditionalist and progressive clergy might scar the whole experience. Alongside the invitation to act as facilitator, there was also a strong suggestion that I would offer something that would up-skill attendees to help them face the challenges of the future. The event took place several months later and was deemed to be useful and effective; those present felt that they took away something that was nourishing and morale boosting.

In planning the workshop, the voice of David Campbell had been in my head; he always stressed the importance of preparation, which involved attempting to develop hypotheses about the meaning of the invitation, and the meaning of the event within the life of the organisation. His voice also reminded me that in getting to understand the context of an invitation, I should note the range of stances towards the proposal within the system and, in particular, the stance of the leadership.

Preparing: meeting the commissioner

I sought a preliminary discussion with the man who commissioned me, who had special responsibility for in-service training and the professional and personal development of clergy in that diocese. I learnt about the lack of direction in the diocese, dissatisfaction among rank and file clergy, tension between traditionalist and progressive clergy, timidity and cautiousness in the leadership, frustration at the lack of planning for the future, and disappointment with the planning processes already under way. Various parties held others responsible for their dissatisfactions. Everyone believed something should be happening, but no one could agree as to what.

David's voice reminded me that when working with organisations and groups, one must bring on board all elements, that nothing must happen to undermine the authority of the leadership, and, at the same time, the issues of the membership must not be suppressed in favour of the sensibilities of leadership.

Preparing: meeting the leadership

The next step was to seek a meeting with the bishop, any other person in authority that he wanted to invite, and the head of in-service training. I suggested that they might like to interview me closely to see if I was a person with whom they could work, and that I would like to question them similarly, and that we should enter this meeting without any sense of obligation. David always suggested that anxious persons should be allowed to take limited steps rather than having to make grand-scale commitments. I was "interviewed" closely and many of my ideas and prejudices surfaced. I received confirmation that there was a lot of unarticulated concern about the feasibility and desirability of the event. I led a discussion that eventually discussed fears openly and nudged it towards a consideration of options, without polarising and slipping into redundant patterns of interaction. I departed with the understanding that they would reflect on all that had been discussed, make a decision, and contact me if they wanted to proceed.

Later feedback indicated that this meeting was very significant. The bishop and his assistant came to respect and trust me, reassured that I would not be partisan. The in-service training officer was pleased. He was delighted that the leadership was becoming involved in the planning, that I was trusted, and that an event was likely to emerge that he could be content with.

Their reworked proposal

Some weeks later, they contacted me saying that they had redesigned the event. It would attempt to assist clergy by offering useful inputs and opportunities for discussion and exploration. It would take the form of two workshops, each for 2½ days. One would focus on developing a priestly spirituality for the contemporary situation, and the second would focus on the stresses experienced by clergy and how these might be alleviated. I was asked to lead the second workshop and to take a consultative role for the whole event.

Building support

After I agreed, the bishop again contacted me to see if I would meet the Council of the Diocese (the full leadership team), representatives of the clergy, and other personnel, so that this wider group could be included in the proposed project. I was questioned closely, and I asked questions like: "What would have to happen for the proposed event to be a disaster?" and "When the priests are going home, what do you want them to be thinking, feeling, saying, and doing?" Again, the voice of David was here. I had witnessed his ability to turn a conversation with a well-framed question, especially a future or hypothetical question.

This meeting reflected the tensions and concerns that had surfaced earlier, but there was now a leadership, and a group of significant clergy, that were involved, positive, and committed to the success of the event. Further suggestions were made: for example, that I might be available for private consultation to individuals and teams in the fringes of the main event, that there be a strong social dimension to the occasion, with opportunities for the bishop and clergy to meet in a relaxed way.

The event

The event took place several weeks later. I was pleased that I had engaged with the leadership of the diocese, and the task ahead was to engage all the attendees and create a space within which they could come to think and feel differently about their lives and work and go home open to acting differently. To facilitate the experience, I decided to attend to several matters: the language I would use, the establishing of new connections, surprise, and humour. All would be in the service of enabling us to co-construct an interaction that would be different and, above all, useful. I paid attention to my language, hypothesising that those attending would feel burdened by experiences in their lives and ministries, but would not want to be "psychologised", or patronised. I anticipated that there would be a lack of curiosity, feeling that they were in for a retravelling of well-worn ground. David would have told me to avoid flattery and unwarranted praise, to find ways of throwing a new light on well-worn experiences.

I began by naming the workshop "When stones get in your shoes", and in my introduction said that as people journey through their personal and professional lives, they regularly pick up stones in their shoes. These are often small pebbles and it is often not difficult to rid oneself of them, but if left, although small, they can become very painful. Some of us get crippled, and others stop walking. The workshop would name common stones in clergy shoes and discuss ways of dealing with them. The attendees would be invited to name additional stones and contribute ideas for solutions. This delineation of the workshop caught their imagination and fuelled curiosity.

Constructing my identity

I had a hypothesis that participants might construe me as some sort of "domesticated and tamed" clerical animal, recruited by leadership to pacify. I had to debunk this potential construction without unnerving the leadership with whom I had built a good relationship. I used the fact that I was an unknown figure and offered some information about myself, my professional trajectory, and my ministry as a priest, among which were several episodes in which I challenged leadership, sometimes winning and sometimes losing. I recounted those stories with humour, showing that these conflicts assisted me in becoming the person I have become. I was also empathetic towards the leaders with whom I had battled.

I recounted that, in 1989, my bishop asked me to take studies in family therapy at the Tavistock Clinic in London. This was a wonderful opportunity and privilege. During my two years there, I pondered on how I would be used on return to my diocese, possibly creating services for disadvantaged families, a bereavement service, and many more ideas. I arrived home proud of my MSc in Family Therapy, only to find that my new appointment was to work under a priest leader with a reputation for being very severe, difficult, and insensitive, who had worked with others, all of whom asked to be relieved of working with him. Priest friends assured me, tongue in cheek, that I had been sent to London to prepare me for work with "crazy" colleagues!! The gathering was highly amused when I told them that I returned to London two years later to undertake doctoral studies, wondering what "monster colleagues" I was being prepared for. Such stories evoked a strong response. The men I was addressing knew that I understood a lot about the seemingly irrational things that people who work in big organisations—not just the Church—have to live and cope with. When I went on to tell how my relationship with the "severe and difficult" colleague turned out to be pleasant and that we became good friends, another twist was put on the experience. By the end, I was

perceived as suitably "street wise", and I think they got the embedded message that problems and struggles are for overcoming, not a
justification for opting out, carrying lifelong grudges or dumping on
leadership. This appealed very much to the leadership.

The stones in the shoes

In the workshop, I named "stones" and discussed them. This turned
out to be very powerful. Many commented that it was the first time
certain matters were talked about publicly; some had never experienced some of the "stones" described, but they, and the bishop, felt
the naming and exploring assisted them in understanding colleagues.
The "stones" we discussed were based on the issues that occur
frequently in my work with priests: for example, the pain of trying to
minister in a culture that seems less and less receptive to the Christian
message; conflictual relationships in ministry; the experience of serious chronic illness, the trauma of the death of the second parent and
the dissolution of the family home; wear and tear arising from many
years of serving people; overwork; difficulties in exercising authority
and being subject to authority; anxiety and stress and the shame that
priests experience because colleagues have abused children and
church authorities have dealt badly with these crimes.

The next section of the workshop attempted to offer help in
ridding one's shoes of these stones. I used stories about events, some
of which happened to me, some to others, some gleaned from therapeutic literature and "folklore". They were geared to challenge beliefs
and patterns of practice to nudge participants into taking up different
ways of thinking and acting. A major "stone" for clergy is the challenge that arises from the effort to minister collaboratively. I described
an experience when the well-known Milan therapist Gianfranco
Cecchin was offering a workshop in Dublin. The organiser knew that
I was researching the work of Cecchin and invited me to join as a
commentator. I asked Cecchin how he might view my involvement.
He suggested that I join him as a co- presenter. I felt honoured and
agreed, but, as the time approached, I became highly anxious. I asked
if he could come to Dublin early so that we could prepare. When we
set about preparing, he said, "This workshop is happening in your
city, it is very important that you cut a 'bella figura' here, so you
choose what to do, do what is most comfortable for you and I will

work around you." I was taken aback, to which he commented, "If I work to make you shine and you work to make me shine, we will have a beautiful workshop, if, however, I work to make me shine and you to make you shine, it might all become very ugly."

The priests were very moved by the story, the sensitivity and generosity of a celebrity figure, and his kindness to a junior partner. I then put some questions: How are the priests helping the bishop to shine, helping colleagues to shine, or helping members of the congregations to shine? The story initially had a shock effect, turning assumptions about working together on their head. It was then possible, through questions, to get them thinking about the implications for themselves. The workshop ended on a very high and positive note and the feedback was most satisfying.

Setting two

Supporting conversations

In the year 2001, I was asked to take on responsibility for the care and support of priests in the Dublin area. It was a time of low morale among clergy, due partly to the child abuse scandals which had shamed priests deeply and profoundly, challenged the integrity of the church, and, owing to falling numbers of new trainees for the priesthood, heavier workloads for aging priests, falling church attendances, and the weakening of the voice of the churches and faith communities in society. Societal change, economic affluence (it was before the financial recession), and the advent of a postmodern culture were leaving many priests and pastoral workers disorientated and dispirited. There was concern that many priests were fragile and there was evidence of higher than usual levels of physical illnesses, which, according to conventional wisdom, was due to stress. Concern with the well-being of priests was felt keenly by the leadership, who were expending an undue amount of time and effort in supporting stressed or sick priests. Priests and their representatives were calling for greater care of priests, echoed by their families and congregations.

My appointment was to be an answer to these problems. The thinking behind it was accepted by all, except, possibly, by those who were felt to be fragile. As a priest, I would understand priests and their issues, and as a psychotherapist, I would have the therapeutic skills to help those suffering from psychological problems. My appointment would free the authorities of the demanding task of dealing with these men. They would advise those struggling with problems to see me or someone I might recommend. This initiative, a first in the church in Ireland, was received with enthusiasm both within the diocese and in wider church and secular circles.

It was decided that it need not require much of my time, predicting that I would be working with about six or seven men per annum. It was suggested that the best approach would be to set up a panel of psychologists and psychiatrists to whom I could refer, and that I could administer the scheme, thereby freeing myself for ordinary parish duties.

I might have bought into this way of working. But systemic family therapy and social constructionist ideas made me question the request; it seemed that the thinking underpinning my appointment was completely linear. There was no consideration as to how the way in which diocesan and parish life was organised contributed to the generation of problems. The solution was one that, to my mind, privileged the needs of the powerful and those considered "well". The leaders and my colleagues would be freed of burdens; I would help the people with problems to change, and there was no sense that the powerful would have to make changes. I was disturbed by the way the so-called "fragile" and "stressed" and "dysfunctional" ones were described. I worried that I was about to collude in a solution that pleased everyone except the ones it was meant to help, and that they would see me as an instrument of social control. This, in turn, might lead the supporters of the scheme to being reassured as to how resistant, fragile, and dysfunctional the "problematic ones" are. This seemed a lost opportunity to bring much needed support to men facing great challenges. By pathologising the matter, the possibility of offering real help would be jettisoned. It was difficult in church circles to discuss my worries; they just could not "get" my difficulties, but, having discussed the situation with family therapy colleagues, I decided on a plan of action.

My solution

I wrote to all 700 priests working in Dublin or retired, saying a little about my training and describing my role. I said that I could provide counselling, psychotherapy, or referral elsewhere, but that above all, I could provide something I called "supportive conversation". While the authorities might recommend men to talk to me, no one would be pressed to come. I pointed out that priests wanting to use this service should contact me directly, that the conversations would be confidential, within the norms of good practice as set out by the authorities in state and church, and that I would inform the appropriate authorities should I feel a crime had been committed.

Within forty-eight hours, I was contacted by individuals wishing to know more about "supportive conversation". I explained that I believe that anybody's journey through life requires the negotiation of many challenges, which might arise from a loss experience, a change of job, a trying relationship, ill health, faith and commitments shaken, or just wear and tear. Sometimes, challenges continue and one can embrace solutions that only amplify the difficulties. In such circumstances, it is often easier to have conversations with people who are at an emotional distance. To experience challenges and to need to talk about them is normal and part and parcel of the human condition—indeed, a gateway to growth and development. By the end of a year, over forty people had come to talk, some carrying very severe burdens. Some were already in psychiatric care, so I had to co-ordinate with their doctors. Now, ten years later, I have worked with over 200 priests in the Dublin area and priests elsewhere in Ireland and Britain who have heard of this service, have made contact, and availed themselves of it.

The issues and concerns

The men I have worked with presented a very wide range of issues and concerns. Many have been embroiled in conflicts with other priests, with parish councils, boards of governors of schools, with church workers and with authority. Many conversations have been with men suffering from serious illness, to help them come to terms with the illness. With others, the conversations are about helping them negotiate with the authorities about how they can make a contribution to church life in a way that is satisfying and manageable for someone chronically ill. Training in family therapy enables me to speak with all parties and facilitate their conversing with each other. Other conversations have been about bereavement and losses of various kinds. As Catholic priests do not marry, the death of parents, especially the death of the second parent and the dissolution of the family home, can be very upsetting, as can the death of a brother or sister with whom the priest has had a close relationship. There have been conversations about other losses such as change from one congregation to another, which occurs every eight or nine years. Conversations have taken place with men falsely accused of child sexual abuse and their families, who were, of course, shattered. In some cases, there have been supportive conversations with men rightly accused, now out of ministry and dealt with by the courts and under supervision, but needing help in trying to go on in life.

There are conversations about vocational matters. Priests, at times, feel compelled to review their decision to become priests. They might seek help to think about how to go forward, whether to leave the priesthood, and if they opt to stay, how to deal with the situations that triggered the whole review. If they go, they need to talk through the transition involved as they journey into a new life. Vocation reviews are triggered by a range of situations: sometimes by the wear and tear of a life spent in the service of others, sometimes oppressed with a sense of sacrificing much to minister to a world that does not care, sometimes the priest has fallen in love and is drawn to a life with the loved one but dreads the loss of his ministry, feeling guilty about the abandonment of a lifelong commitment. There have been conversations with ex priests now deeply regretting leaving priesthood, and wanting to attempt a return to ministry. These men seek help in negotiating their return with church authorities, and others, including their partners, have also sought conversations.

Today, this work is an established part of church life in Dublin. Feedback shows that the clergy value it, trust me, and are ready to use the service. The authorities seem very happy with how things have developed and are committed to its continuation. I am increasingly invited to facilitate teams of clergy "away days", when parish councils review their work, or are experiencing conflicts, and when church bodies want to plan for the future. I am regularly asked to offer workshops as a facilitator, or to consult to groups outside Dublin setting up services to support priests. These developments are based on the view that my work and role in Dublin has been successful.

Changes in church culture

This work has led to a change in church culture; the issue of the care of priests now has a much higher profile in our diocese. This is maintained by the fact that I am invited to join various committees and bodies within which I can try to keep the needs of priests on agendas. There is now a different understanding of what is involved in the "care of priests". Care is now seen more in terms of creating the conditions within which priests can do what they want most of all to do, minister well. This is a shift away from the idea of seeing to the wounded and a move towards seeing the priest as a valued collaborator. Priests' problems are understood in relation to their work, rather than within the personality of the individual. I think that my efforts have helped to loosen the trend to stereotype individuals as difficult, fragile, or incompetent. Above all, a culture is developing which sees it as normal for priests to have stones in their shoes.

Child sexual abuse

Since 2002, there has been a focus on the issue of priests and child sexual abuse. It was decided that this needed specialist intervention by a group, mainly lay men and women and some priests, while I concentrate on the kind of issues set out above. This is not to say that my work is not affected by the scandals. Priests generally are devastated by what has occurred. Most are resilient and are working their way through the difficulties as they arise, but some become over-burdened and this can show in diverse ways: downheartedness, depression, anger, vocational doubts, anxieties, worries about good practice regarding boundaries, worries about false accusations, and about helping parishioners work through the events. Clergy carrying such burdens often avail themselves of what I have to offer, and seek supportive conversation. Additionally, groups of priests have come together in *ad hoc* ways to discuss the events and offer each other support. I have regularly been asked to facilitate such meetings.

At these meetings, I have found it important to give space to each man to express their feelings, but it is also important to help people to get on with their day-to-day work and lives and not throw their daily programmes overboard and become incapacitated by the crises. Thus, my work occurs against a backdrop of the crisis of child sexual abuse by clergy. I do not work with perpetrators, or victims, except in tangential ways. My work is in the realm of supporting the majority to cope with the crisis, and by far the greater time and energy is spent helping clergy struggle with one or more of the issues touched on earlier. Priests used to operating in a society in which the priesthood was greatly cherished now find themselves in situations where there is palpable ambiguity. The priest has long felt himself to be part of the solution to problems in Irish society. Nowadays he is often made to feel that he is one more of the society's problems.

Setting three: consultation in Africa

The most unusual development was a request to undertake work in an African country. The Catholic Church in this country is a minority church among other churches and faiths. Around the year 2000, church life was blighted by very troubling problems. One hundred and fifty priests, all citizens of the country, but members of different tribes and ethnic groups, and all members of an international religious Order with its headquarters in Rome, became embroiled in conflict that was, at root, inter-tribal. The priests and brothers were members of eight different ethnic groups, each with their own identity, language, culture, and geographical location. The problems began as those affiliated to particular tribes were put under pressure from their kinsmen and women to get a greater share of material aid coming in from Europe and elsewhere. This led, in turn, to claims that there were unjust and unfair practices occurring in the distribution of donated resources. The conflict boiled up, and a very unhealthy and un-Christian atmosphere was developing. Soon, members of one ethnic group were refusing to live and work with members of another tribe; rumours spread rapidly, and nurtured long-standing prejudices. As the crises deepened, an atmosphere of fear and suspicion set in and pressure for different groups to disengage from one another heightened. Eventually, the situation escalated to a point where there was a fear of violence.

The Rome based authorities of the Order stepped in and took disciplinary measures; the local leadership were removed from office and replaced by a new team of non-nationals; those in charge of training were replaced by foreigners from other African and Asian countries. Over twenty men who had taken a leading role in fanning the conflict were suspended and told they could only work again as priests in different countries under strict supervision. There were deep divisions. As in many conflicts, there was a middle group who had felt helpless to prevent the things that occurred and were particularly devastated.

The international authorities, following disciplinary action, attempted to set up a programme of reconstruction and reconciliation. They sought to engage experienced facilitators who would be neutral and who would appreciate and understand church life. A member of the religious Order in question was appointed as facilitator: he had years of experience in Africa, and was a trained systemic family therapist. He was commissioned to find a partner for the work who knew church life, but was a complete outsider to the Order. I was invited to become his partner.

The work

I visited the country five times over a three-and-a-half-year period. Each visit took three weeks. We travelled all over the country, holding meetings with groups of about a dozen priests each time. Later, we met with configurations of different kinds, for example, those in leadership, those in formation, those living abroad, and, finally, there was a general assembly.

The task was complex, demanding, and, at times, confusing. In one of my earliest encounters with David Campbell, he consulted to an organisation to which I was attached, and created huge shifts by using future questions and unexpected questions. I noted the salutary effect when we spent a long time responding to David's questions about our personal and individual career hopes and dreams. I had expected him to talk about the past and present; he talked about the future. I expected him to talk about the problems; he wanted to know about assets and resources. I expected him to talk about organisational issues, but he focused upon individual aspirations and career plans.

We used the first set of meetings in Africa to introduce ourselves, to check their expectations, and to try to build trust. As both of us were Irish, we were able to draw on the good connections that have existed between Ireland and Africa, created by Ireland's relief efforts, the positive reputation of Irish missionaries in Africa, and the fact that

Ireland never had colonies in Africa or elsewhere. We connected easily; usually, when introducing ourselves, we would tell them what little we knew about their country and we would ask them what they knew of Ireland. These introductory conversations achieved a step toward the construction of us as agents of assistance rather than of control, as possible mediators, rather than imposers of some new arrangements.

We put them in small groups to discuss how they wanted their Order to be in five years' time and how each man himself wanted to be. Issues that arose included the need to recover pride and dignity. They were very troubled and, indeed, humiliated by the fact that they had proved incompetent in self-government and that now local leadership was in the hands of Italians, and the formation of their trainee priests in the hands of Asians and other African priests, who, in some cases, came from countries Christianised much later than their own. They were troubled by the fact that they might be seen as the "bad boys" of the family by the international and Roman leaderships and would be governed from abroad for the foreseeable future. They agreed that the past must not happen again, but worried as to how to avoid repeating mistakes. There were financial difficulties because the international authorities had introduced stringent controls that were biting severely. There was the matter of the "exiles" and a strong sense that peace could not come at home until the fate of the "exiles" could be resolved.

We attempted to focus on what had to happen so that the future could be brighter.

Suggestions were made as to how the Order in their country could become economically self-sufficient, rather than looking to international help. Ideas were developed for the up-skilling of the priests in the areas of spirituality, theology, and social and psychological disciplines. This came from a wish that they could conduct their dealings in a more productive way, influenced by the kind of conversations they were having under our facilitation.

The reaction to this initial round of meetings was very positive. They seemed happy with the emphasis on the future, having gone through the past so many times; they were delighted to have a way of talking differently about issues, and discussions about individual hopes, assets, and resources seemed to achieve that.

Some challenges and responses

Although the feedback from these initial conversations was positive, certain features challenged us. The young in Africa have a great respect for the elders. Young attendees would tend to repeat what the elders had said and, because there had been years of discussion about the issues in question, they knew the minds of the elders. Our future emphasis was not robust enough. The story of the main events had been re-edited in a way that the "baddies" were now the Rome based authorities and the foreigners who had been sent in as local leaders. The mantra had become "of course, the leaders had to make an intervention, but they did not have to do what they did". In our next round of meetings, we introduced two new exercises.

Exercises

The first exercise was based on the idea of bible parables. We could be sure that they were very familiar with the stories that Jesus told to promote his vision of God and of his own mission, and that they understood that a story told by Jesus could only present a partial image of God, mission, and discipleship. To get a richer vision, one had to hold the various stories in dialogue with each other, and in tension with one another. We asked each man to write a story/parable that would give insight into the crisis, how it arose, and how it might be resolved. Each had to make and present his parable to the whole group. We did not realise at the outset that they were such natural storytellers, and they took to the task with great enthusiasm. The exercise brought to the surface a much richer and nuanced account of events and solutions, exposing tensions which we could then tease out with the group, often using the images embedded in the stories.

The second exercise involved role-play. The aim was to get people "to stand in the shoes of one another" and develop an understanding of the dilemmas of the other. While the use of role-play is not singular to David Campbell, he regularly used role-plays of different types to give people a "here and now" experience. We got the men to take on different identities; one was asked to play the international leader of the Order in Rome, another the Italian who had been imposed as local leader, another the formation leader from Asia, and others the priests from the different ethnic groups. They were then asked to discuss one of the big themes that had emerged in earlier discussions. Either I or my colleague acted as facilitator of these discussions. After about forty-five minutes' discussion, they de-roled and a discussion was held as to what they had learnt from the exercise, how it affected them, and how their thinking on the issue had changed.

They liked it immensely, and a pronounced increase in empathy and softening of the attitudes to "the enemy" ensued. The aim of the parables exercise was to disrupt established discourses and thinking. I hoped the request for the parables would bring forward the need for several stories in order to understand the events under discussion and break the monopoly of the accepted version. I knew that they would be anxious to appear competent and carry out the task, but that in order to appear competent and talk in a new genre, a mould would be broken. Storytelling also facilitated the saying of things that might annoy others, but there was the fallback that it was a story. The story-telling achieved these goals.

The second exercise aimed at introducing a plurality of thinking and empathy towards others, especially those for whom there was very little positive regard. Again, it was possible to say things "in the voice of another" that could not be said in one's own voice; it under-mined self-censorship without too much exposure to risk.

Working with the leaders and the "exiles"

At this stage we began to work with the leadership. The whole crisis had been a bruising one, with which they needed help to process in order to regain curiosity about the rank and file members of the Order, who had been involved. Our conversations prepared them for a more productive engagement with these men.

Then came a big challenge. We suggested that we would like to facilitate a meeting between those who were in exile, the foreign imposed leadership now in charge, and the international leader. We suggested that a delegation of three be elected from among the many men we had worked with in Africa, who would tell the "exiles" about the state of affairs at home (there had been a vast number of rumours) and the story of our work there. Eventually, this meeting took place in a different country. All the invited parties came, except two of the exiles. We interviewed the international leader, in the presence of the others, ascertaining what would have to happen for the "exiles" to be repatriated. He spoke clearly and surprised many with his compassion and his openness to repatriation upon certain conditions.

The "exiles" worked through exercises similar to those at home, concentrating on the future and on appreciating the positions of one another. The delegation from home made a presentation that greatly moved the "exiles" and the international leadership. We then invited the "exiles" to draft a letter that would be taken back home and sent to each member of the Order there. In this letter, they greeted their brothers at home, congratulated them on what they had achieved so far, reported on their meeting with the international leader and his conditions for repatriation, which they said they accepted and would work towards fulfilling. They declared unambiguously that the past was the past, that they were now fully committed to building a new future and that they accepted the new arrangements governing the Order's life back home. This gathering ended on a very high note of joy and hope for the future. Now, five years later, a reasonable stability has set in and an indigenous leadership has taken office; most of the exiles are home.

I recently met one of the priests in London. He said that progress was being made, that there are hiccups, but that there is lots of hope. He remarked, "I come from a remote village, and some months ago I was home to visit my parents. There was trouble in my village and they asked me to intervene." I asked what he did by way of intervention. "The role-play," he said, "the one you did when we had to talk in the voice of each other." This method, he said, is very suitable for his culture, and he thought all our priests now use it in their work.

It is fascinating to think of David's exercises being practised in remote African villages. It is also fascinating the way an American psychologist, born and reared in the Calvinist tradition, living and working in London, has made a difference to the lives of Catholic priests and church workers from Ireland to Britain and Africa.

Connections with theory

Looking back over the three pieces of work and linking them with theories and ideas from the professional literature, a number of connections can be made. A fundamental connection is the link with Milan systemic therapy (Selvini-Palazzoli, Boscolo, Cecchin, & Prata, 1980). The understanding of problems, the theory of change, and the approach to the role of the therapist developed by the Milan associates, and especially by Gianfranco Cecchin, underpin everything that I have described. Hypothesising, neutrality, and curiosity (Cecchin, 1987) were cornerstones and questioning, particularly future and hypothetical questioning, a major tool. In Africa, the value of working with my colleague in the manner of a Milan team was exceptionally helpful. The ideas developed by Cecchin and Boscolo in the mid 1980s (Boscolo, Cecchin, Hoffman, & Penn, 1987), a second order cybernetic approach, and their ideas drawn from constructivism informed the work. All three pieces of work were influenced by social constructionism and the emphasis on language as creative of the worlds we experience. These theories were all espoused by David Campbell (Campbell, 2000). I have also been interested in the work of Milton Erickson, and his idea, taken up by Jay Haley (1973), that change is best achieved outside the consciousness of the one who is changing. Erickson used stories, powerful metaphors, and embedded messages to trigger change; I think my work shows considerable evidence of such practices. My interest in stories and word pictures as tools comes from the experience of preaching, which has led to my becoming practised in the art of storytelling as a means of spurring reflection and challenging thinking. Andersen's (1987) ideas about reflective teams have also been influential. I am interested in the processes of reflective practice and ideas developed in these contexts. John Byng-Hall, once my clinical supervisor at the Tavistock Clinic, introduced me to the importance of "normalising situations" and the dangers of "pathologising" (Byng-Hall, 1995).

Early on in his career, David Campbell took a special interest in how systemic ideas could be used when working with wider systems (Campbell & Draper, 1985). This was one of the points around which I connected with him. I have practised, and still practise, family therapy, but most of my work is in other contexts, where I have found systemic thinking and practice a wonderful resource. Over the years, David's help and support has been invaluable to me in this work. I do hope that I have demonstrated this influence, at least to some extent.

References

Andersen, T. (1987). The reflecting team: dialogue and metadialogue. *Family Process, 26*: 415–428.

Boscolo, L., Cecchin, G., Hoffman, L., & Penn, P. (1987). *Milan Systemic Family Therapy. Conversations in Theory and Practice*. New York: Basic Books.

Byng-Hall, J. (1995). *Re-writing Family Scripts*. New York: Guilford Press.

Campbell, D. (2000). *The Socially Constructed Organization*. London. Karnac.

Campbell, D., & Draper, R. (Eds.) (1985). *Applications of Systemic Family Therapy. The Milan Approach*. London. Grune and Stratton.

Cecchin, G. (1987). Hypothesising, circularity and neutrality revisited: an invitation to curiosity. *Family Process, 26*(4): 405–413.

Haley, J. (1973). *Uncommon Therapy. The Psychiatric Techniques of Milton H. Erickson*. New York: W. W. Norton.

Selvini-Palazzoli, M., Boscolo, L., Cecchin, G., & Prata, G. (1980). Hypothesising, circularity, and neutrality: three guidelines for the conductor of the session. *Family Process, 19*: 3–12.

INDEX